Dark Tales of Devon's Past.

@ Helen Charlesworth 2021

Cover image – Street scene of Thurlestone village near Kingsbridge. Taken from an old postcard. Private collection.

Introduction.

'Dark Tales of Devon's Past' is the fourth in a series of books covering accounts of events chronicled in newspapers from the early 1700's up until 1959. My previous books on the same subject are: 'Dark Tales of Victorian Plymouth 1850-1899' 'Grim and Gruesome Plymouth 1860-1959' and 'Plymouth Tales of a Forgotten Past'. In this volume I cover nearly two hundred years of murders and mayhem, accidents and incidents, hangings, ghosts, hauntings, and even witchcraft, which was still practiced in Devon well into in the 19th century. In many places even into the early 20th century many folks in remote parts of the county still believed in the practice. I'm sure you will have much sympathy for many of the offenders, as well as the victims in some of these stories. The crimes they commit, being done out of desperation rather than malice. There are some lighter moments in the book too, including acts of boldness and bravery, daring exploits, and a smattering of humorous stories thrown in to lighten the read. All in all, it shows how life in the county of Devon was between the years of 1740 to 1950.

During this time in history, our forefathers experienced many changes – firstly and probably most importantly the Industrial revolution which began in Britain. This was quickly followed by the introduction of the railways, which made the transportation of goods, especially perishables and heavy goods readily available to the masses. The first train line into the county was in 1844 when a rail line was introduced between Bristol and Exeter. Over the following years more and more lines were added, until eventually the whole county became accessible, when previously people rarely travelled more than a few miles from where they lived. With the age of industrialisation also came the invention of metal printing presses that could churn out hundreds of newspapers an hour. No longer was it a case of waiting for the town crier to pass by ringing his bell and calling out the latest news. Newspapers were the social media of the day. They brought with them news from across the county, the country, and the world.

You are about to read about some of the many events that occurred in and around the towns, villages, and hamlets of Devon. A Devon quite different from the one we know today, no mass tourism for a start. When poverty drove many to desperate measures and the only place left for them to go was the workhouse. Possibly you will come across an ancestor; a hero, a villain, maybe even a witness to an event? You might even come across the house in which you now live or where an ancestor once lived.

Thanks to the British Newspaper Archives and the British Library, who are gradually making copies of all available newspapers as far back as the 1700's, searchable by the public through their online archive facility, you can now join me in a journey through a very interesting time in British history. Nearly two hundred years of happenings, that took place in Devon.

This book is copyrighted. No part of it may be reproduced without permission from the author except by reviewers who wishes to quote brief passages.

1740 – 1799

Devon Assizes, August 1740.

Six people were convicted and sentenced to death at the Devon Assizes held at Exeter in August 1740 including John Mounson for setting a house on fire, Martha Allen for sacrilege and horse stealing, and John Avery, for the murder of his illegitimate child. Nine people were ordered to be transported to the colonies and one person to be whipped. John Mounson's, Martha Allen and John Avery's executions were carried out on the 29th of August. The other three were possibly commuted to penal servitude on appeal or sent to the colonies with the other nine who also received that sentence.

* The first executions at Exeter, thought to have been carried out at Northernhay, just beyond the walls of the castle, took place in late December 1285. Alphred Duport also known as Alured De Porta, the then Mayor of Exeter, was convicted for the part he played in the murder of Walter Lechlade, the Lead Chanter at Exeter Cathedral. Allured was hung along with Richard Stonying – the porter of the South Gate. Elias Poyfed and Richard Stonying were said to have carried out the murder. Thomas had planned it, and Alured was guilty of harbouring the offenders of the crime. Richard Twate was found guilty of 'allowing' the murder. The trial was presided over by Edward I and ran from Christmas Eve until the 28th of December. There were several other men also found guilty of being involved in the murder of Lechlade. Of those convicted, eleven claimed benefit of clergy and were handed over to the relevant ecclesiastical authorities for punishment.

Executed for rape, and the shooting a Constable.

Peter Vine under a strong guard was escorted to Exeter gaol in April 1743, after having been convicted of the murder of Constable Roger Ashton, near Bideford, and the rape of Elizabeth Dark in the village of Hartland.
After having committed the rape upon poor Elizabeth he then fled the village, but on his return three months later having learnt that his father had died ten days previously and left him an estate worth one thousand pounds; Constable Ashton informed him that a warrant had been issued for his apprehension. Vine responded by saying that the first man who tried to arrest him would be shot dead on the spot. Ashton went towards him to make the arrest and Vine drew his pistol and shot him dead.
Peter Vine was executed at Heavitree gallows on the 5th of October 1743.

Hung for selling counterfeit stamps.

In 1744 William Facey was capitally convicted at the Devon Assizes for forging stamps and selling them on knowing them to be counterfeit. He confessed to the crime and was executed at Heavitree near Exeter on the 1st of April that year – all fool's day. A caution was made to others who were possibly tempted to attempt to do the same and try to avoid stamp duty; the penalty of doing so would-be death.

Appledore flood.

The village of Appledore in North Devon sits at the mouth of the river Torridge. In January 1749 there was a great storm that lasted two days. The tide was so high and the sea so violent that it washed away a street of houses drowning many of the inhabitants. It twice broke the sea bounds and created damage amounting to more than three thousand pounds. Many of the poor of the village were entirely ruined.

Capital Convictions.

The March Assizes held at Exeter in March 1750, saw eleven prisoners receive the sentence of death. John Lennard was convicted of making counterfeit coins. Elizabeth Packard for poisoning her husband with arsenic. Mary Willis and Susannah Phillips, for the murder of their illegitimate children. Neal MacDaniel and William Lovell, for robberies on the highway. Elizabeth Burley for setting fire to an out-house. Robert Bale for horse stealing. Mary Woodmason for stealing seventeen guineas from a dwelling house. Edward Murphy for burglary and Mary Gregory, otherwise known as Saunders; for stealing goods and money from a dwelling house.

Of the eleven convicted, seven received a reprieve and the remaining four were condemned to the noose. In total there were upwards of fifty prisoners tried at the Assize. Eight people were ordered to be transported for seven years, four were ordered to be whipped, and two fined five shillings each and to be imprisoned for six months.

As well as Mary Willis and Susannah Phillips, there were four other women tried for the murder of their illegitimate child, but the jury [which was said to have been a very merciful one] found them not guilty.

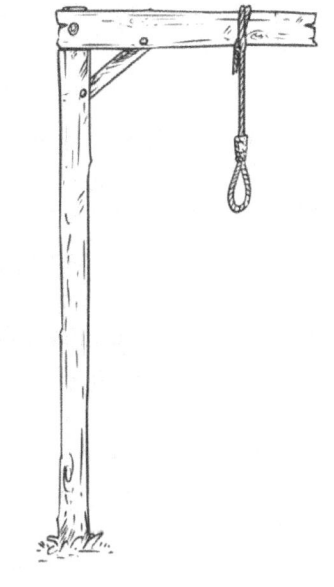

The four unlucky felons who went to the gallows at Heavitree were John Lennard, Elizabeth Packard, Edward Murphy and Susannah Phillips; their executions taking place on the 12th of April 1750. Husband poisoner Elizabeth Packard's death created the most interest as she was to be burned at the stake. This punishment was reserved solely for women; men being hung for the same crime. Legend has it that the women were usually strangled [until dead or insensible it is not known] before being put to the flame; we do not know if that was the case in this instance.

*Prior to 1795, the sentence of death in Devon meant that most hangings took place at Heavitree gallows near Exeter. A number of military crimes led to the sentences being carried out on board ships in Plymouth. From 1795 onwards, the sentence was carried out at the county goal in Exeter. The first execution at Heavitree was in 1735, the victim being a woman, Mary Warren, for the murder of her illegitimate male child. There were two executions that year, the second also being for the murder of an unwanted illegitimate birth.

William Huish – executed for parenticide.

At the Devon Assizes held at Exeter in October 1751, William Huish was charged with the murder of his mother Elizabeth, at Cheriton Fitzpane. There was very strong evidence against him of his beating, kicking, and dragging the poor woman about by the hair, and frequently declaring in other people's presence that he would kill her. Elizabeth had also told several people that the illness with which she was suffering from was brought on by the blow with a bar to her stomach by her son. William was acquitted of the charge, there not being enough evidence to show that it was his behaviour towards her that brought about his mother's death.

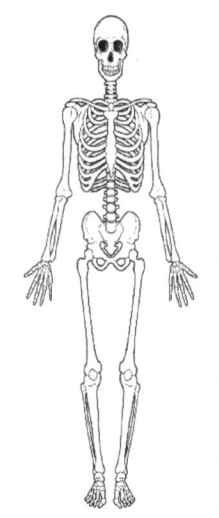

In March 1853, William Huish was again brought before the Exeter Assize, this time for the murder of his father; also called William, in December 1752 by poisoning. William was also accused of having stolen from his master to whom he had been apprenticed and then fled. He was described as appearing to be a genteel young fellow and extremely well dressed. The trial lasted several hours and the jury finding him guilty, the Judge ordered him to be executed. Had he been found not guilty of the poisoning of his father; he would have been indited for forgery. After his execution on the 31st March at Heavitree, William Huish's body was sent to the Devon and Exeter Hospital where it was dissected and his skeleton kept for many years as an anatomical aid for medical students.

The murder of John Harvey.

On April the 2nd 1759 Robert Lattimore was executed at Heavitree gallows for the murder of John Harvey on the 4th of March that year. Lattimore had served fourteen years in the Regiment of Old Buffs, though had deserted on several occasions for which he had received punishment. On the 4th of March he had gone to Mr. Harvey's shop in Plymouth market to buy a breast of mutton. Noticing Harvey take a handful of gold coins out of his pocket, Lattimore decided to lay in wait for him returning home at the end of the day. He knew in which direction Mr. Harvey would be travelling, so that evening he positioned himself in a secluded spot on the road from Plymouth and Tamerton. When he saw Harvey approach, he jumped from his hiding place and scaring the horse caused it to throw its rider to the ground. Lattimore then attacked Harvey and robbed him of seven guineas. To make sure he wouldn't be followed, he landed John Harvey several fatal blows to the head with a stick. When arrested, to protect himself he turned evidence against two young men who he said were with him when the act was committed. Both men were apprehended; one was committed to Winchester gaol and the other to Exeter. In giving evidence against the two, Lattimore betrayed himself by proving that he was the only person who could have committed the crime.

April 1759 was a busy month at Heavitree; on the 25th of the month, Charles Darras, Fleurant Tremaine, Pierre Pitiel, Louis Beudecq and Pierre Lagnol, were all hung at the gallows near Exeter, for the 'murder and mangling' of Jean Menaux, a fellow French prisoner of war on board the 'Royal Oak' man of war, which was anchored in the Hamoaze, Plymouth.

More executions at Heavitree.

March the 19th 1762, saw a number of death sentences passed at the Devon Assizes held at Exeter Castle. Robert Haynes, for the murder of a young lad near Kingsbridge, whose name remained unknown. What the motive was we shall never know. His execution was originally ordered for the following day, Saturday the 20th of March, but was delayed whilst waiting for a pardon which never came. He was hung at Heavitree on the 16th of April the same year.
Pierce Mitchell*, for the murder of Vincent Beven a fellow French prisoner of war at the Sugar House prison, Topsham. Again, his execution had been due to take place on the 29th of March but was postponed until the 16th of April.
William Goddard and John Sackmore, for the highway robbery of Abel Croad; robbing him of a silver watch valued at forty shillings. They too were hung at Heavitree on the 16th of April and were buried at St. Sidwell, Exeter, the same day.

* I think his name was more likely Piers Michel or similar.

The great Fire of Plymouth.

A huge fire at the 'Three Crowns' on Plymouth Barbican near to the Custom's House which started in the early hours of the 3rd of March 1765, very nearly destroyed the town of Plymouth and the Citadel. Two houses were completely destroyed. Within the same premises were one hundred and twenty-three barrels of gunpowder which was being held in storage waiting for a French vessel bound for Guinea to come and collect it. Whilst the flames were being fought, terrified men swiftly assisted in the speedy removals of the barrels. An act of parliament had said that no more than four barrels containing over 100lb of gunpowder should be landed in any town in England. Had the gunpowder gone up in flames, thousands would have been killed. The question was, were the customs officers complicit in the barrels being stored there; they being next door?

The county's oldest man dies.

In 1777 it was reported that a farmer called John Brookey of Broadrush Common, Devonshire, was in his one-hundredth-and-thirty-fourth year and had had thirteen wives. He died in 1778 aged one-hundred-and-thirty-five [allegedly].

Poor Rebecca.

Rebecca Downing, a fifteen-year-old apprentice girl was found guilty of the murder of her master, seventy-seven-year-old Richard Jarvis at Rickham near Salcombe on the 25th of May 1782. Mr. Jarvis had employed young Rebecca to carry out work in the fields, such as picking weeds and stones and attending to cattle. Rebecca obviously hated the situation she found herself in and decided possibly on the spur of the moment, maybe not even meaning to kill the old man but to just make him sick; she put some arsenic which was used to wash diseased horses in the teakettle with the water that was boiled for Mr. Jarvis and his grand-daughter's breakfast. Rebecca's guilt became apparent when she refused to drink the tea herself. She was found guilty of the crime of 'petty treason' - the murder of a husband or master. [People allegedly set above the offender by God.] For this crime Rebecca was burned at the stake on the 29th July 1782 at Ringwell, near Exeter.

At her trial Rebecca was said to have claimed that she didn't understand the Lord's prayer and that she had heard of God but not of our Saviour and had never been told anything about a soul. It sounds as though poor Rebecca had a terrible upbringing, she had either been an orphan or a foundling, it isn't quite clear.

The first flight over Exeter.

In June 1786, Monsieur St. Croix ascended in his hot air balloon from the castle at Exeter. There had been a subscription raised towards the cost of the great display, but sadly only ten pounds had been pledged. Despite the heavy rain the previous evening which had continued late into the night and the wind blowing in the direction of the sea, M. St. Croix was not in the least put off. At around two o'clock in morning of Monday the 19th of June he proceeded to prepare his apparatus for making the inflammable air (extracted from vitriol poured on the borings of iron cannon) at which he worked with incessant labour till around eleven a.m. when the balloon was suspended in the centre of the castle ready to be inflated. All those that had subscribed towards the exciting display were present and watched as he proceeded to inflate it, which to the astonishment of every spectator was completed in less than an hour. Having fixed his car to the net-work of the balloon which took much longer time than the filling, he continued his task without a break even for refreshment.

At two o'clock on the firing of a gun, the balloon began to rise. It cleared the walls of the castle and ascended with a speed that was difficult for those witnessing it to describe. The number of spectators in the castle held no comparison with the enormous crowds assembled in the neighbourhood and the fields adjoining the city, who all joined in to make the air resound with their applause.

Within five minutes from his leaving the castle, M. St. Croix found himself at least fifteen thousand feet up in the air, and although there was very little wind at that elevated height the balloon continued to climb and a quarter of an hour later it attained its greatest height; nineteen thousand feet. M. St. Croix was able to take in the most enchanting view of Devonshire as well as parts of Cornwall, Somerset, and Dorset, appearing like one smooth verdant plain without hill or valley. The view was terminated on one side by the English Channel and on the other by the Bristol Channels, affording altogether the most extensive and brilliant scene that the eye of man had ever beheld.

The balloon, which measured seventy-six feet in circumference reached such an incredible height in just a few minutes that it had the appearance of a globe not more than five or six inches in diameter. It then stood stationary for ten minutes; the onlookers admiring the reflection of the sun's rays upon it which gave it a most beautiful appearance. A cloud then hid it from view for a short time after which it began to descend with great rapidity. M. St. Croix had experienced a great degree of heat and the balloon had become exceedingly dilated. The pressure from the blast of gas had forced out the wooden frame with the glass from the neck of the balloon and ripped part of the material. M. St. Croix threw himself from the car into the net around it and instead of giving way to any gloomy apprehensions of danger, he grabbed hold of the two pieces of fabric and twisting them together he then held the material between his teeth, his hands being afterwards employed in holding the two tubes which carried the gas into the balloon, as well as holding onto the neck of the balloon to prevent the very great loss of inflammable air which would have rendered his descent incredibly rapid as well as dangerous.

On his descent towards earth, he passed through a very thick cloud which deprived him of the sight of objects below. The cloud although dry from its great weight it accelerated his approach towards earth; the ground below only coming into sight seconds before he landed in a cornfield belonging to Farmer Whipple in the parish of Cadeleigh, about ten miles outside of Exeter. His coolness and intrepidness throughout the whole business certainly awarded him the greatest honour, sadly the subscription in no way equalled his expense – he was left ninety-seven pounds out of pocket. [Around three and a half thousand pounds today.]

Premonition in a dream.

Mr. James Champling, master of the windmill at Exmouth Point, was struck from the platform of the mill in April 1799 by the sudden movement of the vane, caused by an unexpected gust of wind blown in from the sea. He was so severely wounded that he died an hour later. What was so extraordinary about the incident was that a woman had not half an hour earlier cautioned him saying she was fearful some accident would happen on account of dream she had the previous night. She had only just returned to her home when the incident occurred.

Artist Francis Danby's sketch of the mill in 1826. The windmill was built on the dunes by the sea.

1800-1850

Oldest man in Devon.

Mr. John Cocker of Rattery, aged one-hundred and five years old, who to within two days of his death in 1800 had retained the full use of his limbs and faculties. He was carried to his grave by his grandsons and his coffin was followed by one-hundred and thirty-nine of his children, grand-children and great grand-children.

Murdered by his best friend and possibly love rival.

George Tapp (alias Godbear) was executed at Exeter gaol on the 16th of August 1808, for the wilful murder of his companion and good friend Robert Leach. Just as he was about to step on to the gallows, he threw forth into the crowd some papers on which he had written information, relating to a female who he attributed to his untimely fate.

George a tailor and Robert a butcher, both lived in the village of Morchard Bishop, about thirteen miles from Exeter. On the evening of Sunday the 24th of April, they were seen together at a public house in the village and were then later seen to leave together. Robert Leach was never seen again. Enquiries were made and by the following Friday, family and friends were becoming increasing alarmed at his disappearance. Strong suspicion fell on Tapp, he being the last person seen in Leach's company. He was also observed having more money than usual, added to which a neighbour said that a week preceding Robert Leach's disappearance, Tapp was seen very late at night digging a pit in his garden and on being questioned why he was digging in the dark and so late his reply was that he was burying some dung to make a cucumber bed. With this information at hand Tapp's garden was dug up and to the shock of all who witnessed it, they uncovered the mangled body of Robert Leach. George Tapp was then arrested and taken into custody where he freely admitted to what he had done. He said that on returning from the public house they had both gone into his garden where Leach complained of a pain in his head. [It appears there is some vital missing information here on his account.] Leach sat down on the branch of a fallen tree and whilst in the process of tying a handkerchief around his head, Tapp came behind and struck him a violent blow with an old axe which he had fitted up for the purpose. He repeated the blows until he had finished his bloody deed. He then went through Leach's pockets and took from them cash and bills amounting to around sixty pounds. He then threw his friend's body into the pit which had already been prepared. The axe handle he burnt on a fire, and the iron part he threw into a running stream to wash of the blood. He also burnt his hat and cut of the bloody marks from the tree with a hook. On being asked how long he had premeditated the murder, he replied, "about a week."

Devon Lent Assize.

The 1815 Lent Assize for the County of Devon commenced on Monday the 20th of March, before the Honourable Sir Robert Graham and the Honourable Sir Henry Dampier. The following individuals were some of those tried and sentenced.

Maria Jones for stealing a silver spoon, two blankets and a tablecloth from Mrs. Bullen of [Plymouth] Dock. Maria was sentenced to one month's imprisonment.

Jane Meredith was indicted for stealing forty-two pounds. Grace Davidson said she lived in Stoke Damerel with her husband who was a seaman. The previous October he had been paid off and he had given her forty-two pounds in notes which she put in a teapot inside of a cupboard. A short time later, Jane Meredith came to their room where she sat chatting. Grace Davidson left the room leaving Jane talking to her sister Catherine. When she returned Jane had gone and so had the money. Catherine Richards, Grace Davidson's sister said she remembered Jane and a young man coming to the room and her sister going out soon after. Mary Richards another of Grace's sisters said whilst she was out walking with a gentleman on the 31st of October, she saw Jane Meredith. The gentleman she was with knowing what had allegedly occurred took hold of Jane Meredith by the elbow and said, "You are the woman I've been looking for!" When Jane asked what he wanted with her, he replied that he would tell her by and by. Jane who appeared scared said that she would need to fetch her mother and rushed home. Mary Richards and the gentleman followed her. When they reached her house, Jane's mother came to the door and asked what her daughter had supposedly done. The gentleman explained about the missing money and on hearing this her mother put her hands together and exclaimed; "That's the money she brought home. Her father and I have been distracted ever since!" She said they had questioned their daughter as to where she had got it from. She first said she had been given it by a sailor and later off a gentleman. Hearing her mother say this Jane angrily responded by shouting; "Why do you make such a piece of work mother. Gathering such a mob around the door?" A policeman was then sought, and Jane was taken into custody. She was later sentenced to death though this sentence was likely commuted to transportation to the colonies as the death penalty was not carried out.

Mathew Fisher was indicted for stealing wearing apparel. Robert Mallett stated that he lived at [Plymouth] Dock. On the evening of the 1st of December 1814, he left his shop, locking the door behind him. On his return the next morning he found the door to have been unlocked and several articles were missing from the counter. A few days later he again found that the door had been unlocked and ten black silk handkerchiefs, fancy waistcoats and other articles were missing. Having his suspicions as to who the thief was, he had Fisher's lodgings searched and found some of the missing property.

Mathew Fisher like Jane Meredith was sentenced to death. His sentence was possibly later commuted to transportation as I can find no record of him being hung.

Peter White was indicted for stealing twenty-three pounds in Bank of England notes. Mr. R. Rickard, of Stoke Damerel, told the court that Peter White boarded at his house. In January of that year, he had gone away for a few days on business leaving White in the house with his wife. He had some money hidden in a white cotton stocking which he kept in a wooden chest. He had seen it there on the Sunday but when he returned from his trip at the end of the week, the money was gone. He immediately confronted White who confessed to the theft and handed back some of the stolen money. White was also sentenced to death, but like the last two cases, the execution was commuted.

Edward Raffin was indicted for stealing a watch on the 4th of November 1814. He had been at the house of Anne Grey, and soon after he had left, she noticed the timepiece which hung over the mantlepiece to be missing. Mr. Barnard a watchmaker then showed the court the watch which he had purchased from Edward Raffin. Raffin was sentenced to six months imprisonment.

Samuel Chadwick and George Hunt were indicted for stealing five coats, four waistcoats, two pistols, four silver spoons, two silver forks, a pocket compass and other items belonging to Captain Jones of the Royal Marines based at Stonehouse Barracks. Giving evidence Captain Jones said that Chadwick was his servant and Hunt was Captain Wilson's. On the 30th of November in his absence, the above-mentioned items were stolen from his apartment. One portmanteau which was locked had been cut open across the top. The other which was unlocked had simply been opened. Returning to his apartment he caught the two prisoners in the act of carrying out the theft. They fled on his discovering what they had been doing.
 Both men were sentenced to death but again the sentence was later commuted to transportation. [The Judge was obviously very fond of donning his black cap and putting the fear of God into the criminals who came before him.]

Ghostly visitor in a Church.

In a small parish Church not twenty miles from Exeter one Sunday in 1816 the Clerk and Sexton arrived early to prepare for the service that was to take place that day. On entering they found that a jackdaw had by some means or other gained entry. After some chasing, they soon caught it and rather than letting the bird go, they thought they would keep it until after the service as they felt it may well give some amusement to the congregation when they opened the doors and let it fly free. The sable-plumed bird was then safely placed in the vestry, from where he was to be liberated as soon as the service ended.
The parishioners once seated the sermon commenced, when suddenly a knocking was heard by all present. Fear and surprise were portrayed on almost every face and whispered speculation

was that something supernatural must be the cause. The pious Priest turned pale at the strange visitation. The sound then subsided and the congregation calmed their nerve. Suddenly the sound began again even louder than before. During the remainder of the sermon which might as well have been preached to the roaring waves of a wild sea than to the terrified congregation; the loud knocking was repeatedly heard. Many likely wondered if it was there to claim possession of their souls. No real clue could be found for the cause of the strange phenomenon. Word of the occurrence quickly sped through the neighbourhood, and it became for many weeks afterward the general theme of conversation; many folks attributed it to be the collusion of someone meddling with evil spirits.

The Clerk and Sexton kept secret the cause of the spectral sound, for fear of censure from their superiors or perhaps even worse, dismissal from the church altogether. This eerie story stayed a mystery until an anonymous letter writer contacted the editor of an Exeter newspaper and told him what had really produced the 'supernatural' sounds.

A Sailor's Pocket book.

In 1822, a sailor who had recently been paid off from 'H.M.S Superb' was about to leave Plymouth by coach, when he discovered that his pocketbook containing a considerable sum of money was missing. Suspecting who had taken it, he returned to the house in Plymouth Dock where he had spent the previous evening and found the woman with whom he had spent the night and who had the book in her possession. He seized it from her and gave her a mighty wallop knocking her to the floor. He then left immediately not wanting to get the police involved and started off again on his journey.

Seated on the coach he drew out the book in order to count the money, suspecting that the women may have helped herself to some of it, but to his amazement it contained ten pounds more than he had left in it! The coach reaching Ivybridge he instantly assembled the poor of the village and treat them all to beef, bread, cheese, and beer. Having enlivened the villagers with his sailor-like generosity he proceeded on his journey amidst the cheers of the people he had so pleasantly regaled.

Christmas Eve shooting accident.

Mr. Thomas Searle, a respectable yeoman of Dittisham near Dartmouth in South Devon, had the terrible misfortune of shooting dead his son, also called Thomas; a youth of just seventeen. The young man had returned to the family home for the Christmas holidays and whilst out on a Christmas Eve shooting excursion in 1828 the father's gun accidentally went off and poor Thomas died where he fell. The parent's distress was described as exceeding description.

Oldest woman in Devon.

In 1834 it was reported that there was a woman [un-named sadly] living in Cullompton, who was one-hundred and three-years-old and even at her advanced age she was still capable of attending to her duties at the family dairy, milking cows etc, and her faculties were still in perfect preservation. She lived in the same house as no fewer than four generations of her family.

Killed by a boy on a horse.

The inhabitants of Bishop's Tawton were thrown into state of indescribable consternation on the evening of Sunday the 20th of September 1838, when rumours began circulating that a murder had just been perpetrated at or near New Bridge about three miles away on the Exeter road. The report spread with the greatest rapidity and met the congregations as they were leaving their respective places of worship after the evenings religious services. Anxious groups crowded onto the streets especially surrounding the station house.

Arthur Bassett Esq., of Umberleigh House was returning from Watermouth at about quarter to seven when he met a woman of suspicious appearance around half to three-quarters of a mile beyond Bishop's Tawton. A short distance further on he came across the body of a man lying in the road and on examination he found him to be on the point of death; he breathed twice before expiring. He called to two local men for help and to bring a light. Realising that the man had come to his end by unfair means he guessed that the woman he had passed earlier was the murderer. He mounted his horse and retraced his path but couldn't find her. He then went to Barnstaple to inform the police. The body was removed to Bishop's Tawton and was recognized as being sixty-year-old George Slooman a servant with Mr. Ford, a yeoman.
From Mr. Bassett's description of the woman's appearance and dress, it was supposed that she was the wife of the deceased who had been separated from him for several years and was living in service at Ilfracombe. A constable was instantly dispatched but the gentleman (Mr.Vye) with

whom she lived as a cook, wrote a note which he gave to the police to show the Coroner, stating that she had scarcely been out of the house that day.

At twelve o'clock the following day the Coroner, Thomas Copner, Esq., and a jury composed of respectable men of the parish assembled at the 'Three Pigeon's Inn' at Bishop's Tawton to inquire into the circumstances attending the death of Mr. Slooman. After viewing the body several witnesses were then questioned.

Mr. Arthur Bassett described how he was on his way to Umberleigh when he came to a spot between Bishop's Tawton and New Bridge, when below New Bridge Cottage garden he saw the body of a man on the right-hand side of the road lying on his belly with his face downwards and his arms outstretched. He called out 'holloa' a number of times but receiving no answer he suspected something was wrong and looked about for assistance. He saw a young man in the garden above and asked him to bring a candle. Another man from the adjoining cottage then joined them with a lamp and a candle. He said that he had earlier recalled seeing two young gentlemen on their horses near Mrs. Chichester's gate at Pill. He had at first been able to keep up with them as they were riding quite slowly but then they galloped off at great speed. They would have passed the spot where the body was found around ten to fifteen minutes before he arrived there.

Mr. James Greenough of New Bridge Cottage was next to give evidence. He said how his son had heard a man on the road calling out 'holloa' and that he wished them to come down and bring a lighted candle. His grandchildren had been playing out in the garden and said they had heard a horse go past about five minutes before Mr. Bassett called out to them. Mr. Greenough's son corroborated his father's statemen saying his daughter who was with her brother and sister in the garden had said she heard a horse galloping fast a few minutes before Mr. Bassett called up.

Mr Joseph Coles a servant to Mr. Owen of Barnstaple, said that he passed a man walking near the hedge at New Bridge. He then saw two boys riding steadily and a little further on a man on a white horse [Mr. Barrett.] It had by now been ascertained that the two boys were the son and nephew of Mr. Moore a respectable farmer of Tawstock. The boys hadn't said anything that evening but the following morning when news of the murder began to spread, Henry Moore had apparently told his father that he'd seen the man's body at the side of the road. The nephew Edward Tyte said that he had seen the man's hat. The Coroner being told this information and thinking their evidence may aid the enquiry sent a summons for them to attend the hearing. Edward Tyte aged thirteen after having the nature of an oath explained to him said that he was the son of Mr. Tyte of Plymouth. The previous day he and his cousin had ridden from Tawstock to a green gate (Mrs. Chichester's gate.) At New Bridge he had seen a man's hat lying in the road. His cousin was riding ahead of him and when he caught up with him his cousin asked if he had seen a man lying in the road; he said he had not. His cousin said he didn't stop because he was afraid that the man might have been dead or drunk. Henry Moore was then brought into the witness box and it was explained to him that he must tell the truth and not to conceal any part of the truth. The boy seemed quite affected but went ahead and gave his statement. He said that when riding home the previous evening with his cousin he was riding past New Bridge when his horse hit a man and he ran over him. (A great sensation was manifested in the courtroom, as this information came quite unexpectedly.) He went on to say that his horse was at full gallop. He didn't see the man before hitting him and knocking him down. The man had been walking near to the hedge and it was quite dark. Henry said he didn't stop to see how the man was nor did he tell anyone about it.

Dr. Parker who examined the body said there was a wound on the scalp which resembled a horseshoe. There were other smaller wounds on the face. He didn't though feel that wounds were sufficient to have caused death. The man suffered from a hernia and had suffered fits, it was possible the shock of the incident had maybe brought on an apoplectic attack although there was no evidence to say this was the case. The Coroner expressed his readiness to adjourn the inquest for further medical investigation, but the foreman of the jury said there was no need. The jury then retired before returning with a verdict of 'accidental death.'

George Slooman was said to have lived in the neighbourhood all his life. He was a sober man and on the day of his death he had been to visit his sister in Tawstock and was returning home. The Coroner hoped that this sad event would be a salutary caution to all who were in the habit of riding furiously, and especially to the boy whose culpable heedless-ness, on a Sabbath evening too. He hoped it would be a lesson which he ought never to forget.

It was said a very strange fatality seemed to have touched the Slooman family. George was one of four sons; one of his brothers was drowned some years previously, another of them fell off his pony and broke his neck and the wife of the other was killed after a wall fell upon her.

Bideford Petty Sessions – April 1834.

Mr. John Saunders brought a charge of assault against Mr. Joseph Chidley. On the 12th of March, Mr. Chidley had thrown a knob of coal, a coal hammer, and a coal peck measure at him when on board his own vessel lying in the quay at Bideford. After both parties had respectively stated their case the court recommended them settle the matter amicably between themselves, to which they agreed with Joseph Chidley agreeing to pay all expenses.

Mr. Thomas Anthony made a complaint to the court against James Ball for quitting his service without his consent. Mr. Anthony stated that Ball made an agreement with him to serve him as a potter for twelve months at the wages of ten shillings a week. Ball had entered his service on the 14th of January and on the 15th of February quit his post. During the cross-examination it came to light that James Ball had left Mr. Anthony's service to work for his present master who gave him higher wages. The Magistrates having explained the law between master and servant and as many disputes had frequently come before them on that subject, they sentenced James Ball to fourteen days imprisonment in the house of correction.

Crockernwell Petty Sessions – April 1834.

Mr. John Arnold of South Tawton, complained that Mr. Mark Cann, and Mark his son, of the same parish, had assaulted him on Sunday the 23rd of March. Mr. Arnold said that the road from his house to the church went over land occupied by Mr. Cann. On the day in question, he had ridden his horse to church and consequently did not use the footpath, though he did send his brother and some others on foot to support the right of way to the church. When they came to the disputed path, Mr. Cann and his son were there to block their passing. Mr. Arnold who was not too far away rode over to the stile where the dispute was taking place and endeavoured to go over it, but Mr. Cann who was sitting on the stile, prevented him by pushing him away. Mr Arnold again got on to the stile and had his hand on it for the purpose of getting over when young Mark Cann, with a stick lashed out and brutally marked his hand and for this he now sought recompense for the assault.
The Bench fined Mark Cann the younger forty shillings to cover costs and compelled all three men to enter into sureties to keep the peace towards all the King's subjects and especially towards each other for the space twelve calendar months.

 * Crossing another farmer's land to access church on a Sunday seems to be something which was often disputed.

Run-away apprentice.

The following article was placed in a local Devon newspaper in April 1836, threatening legal action against anyone who employed the young run-away.

'Widecombe in the Moor. Run away from his Master (John Leaman, of Bittleford Farm, in the parish of Widdecombe on the Moor, on the 23rd of March.) John Edward Lloyd, his apprentice, aged fourteen years. Wearing a short smock frock, corduroy trousers, fustian coat and waistcoat, and black hat. He has light hair and a fair complexion. Whoever labours or employs him after this public notice will be prosecuted according to Law. Dated 1st of April 1836.'

Dreadful fire at Cullompton.

A most devastating fire occurred in Cullompton on Sunday the 7th of July 1839. Just as the congregation were about to leave church after the close of the morning service the alarm was raised, and flames were seen coming from the chimney of a house near to New Street. The fire when first discovered was slight; and had aid been quickly in arriving there was little doubt it would have been extinguished without much trouble but before any measures could be taken, the sparks from the chimney settled on the thatched roof, which instantly went up in full blaze. The conflagration then rapidly extended itself to New Street and from there ran with fearful rapidity to all the adjoining houses. The local fire engines were soon on the scene, but the brisk wind carried the sparks to a great distance and flames broke out simultaneously in various quarters of the town to the alarm of the inhabitants, and those engaged in extinguishing them.

Picture courtesy of wikisource.org

An express pony was sent to Exeter appealing for assistance, and the fire engine of the West of England fire brigade under the superintendence of Mr. G. W. Gumming was the first to arrive at Cullompton, followed very shortly afterwards by more engines from surrounding towns. By this time the scene presented was truly awful. From New Street the flames had extended to Town Green, from where they spread more or less all over the town. Houses in the neighbourhood of the 'Half Moon' were seen to be on fire; a quarter of a mile from the where the original fire had broken out. Upwards of one hundred houses were destroyed and many others to a great extent damaged. It wasn't until late in the evening that the fire was completely extinguished, and the engines continued to spray water on the smoking ruins until five o'clock the following morning. The loss of buildings and property amounted to well over ten thousand pounds. Hundreds of families lost everything they owned. Whole streets were burnt down, in fact nearly two-thirds of the town were said to have been destroyed. A great number of the homeless were accommodated in the old Workhouse.

The Wacky Races.

With the introduction of the fast-growing railway lines across the country for freight and public transport, there was competition from various companies to win the contracts. Amidst the immense rush to secure the lodging of documents with the Clerks of the Peace, a number of incidents and escapades occurred amongst employees rushing from London to Exeter, to fulfil the important missions of depositing their documents before the cut off hour. On Sunday the 30th of November 1845 on the Great Western Railway alone no fewer than seven special trains were despatched from Paddington on separate undertakings connected with the West of England, and such was the demand for locomotive engines that security appears to have been disregarded.

One special train carrying Mr. Barton of the Taw Vale railway, Mr. Sanders of Plymouth, and Mr. Wollaston of Brixham, was careering along at great speed when just beyond Maidenhead the bottom of the firebox came loose and soon brought them to a standstill. Two of the gentlemen got out and wiled away some time smoking cigars whilst they awaited the arrival of an engineer. The third gentleman stayed onboard and pondered on the necessity of reform for the Great Western Company. The engineer arrived and quickly found the problem. He clambered under the engine and got on with repairing the fire-grate. A short time later, the cry of "a train is coming!" was bellowed from one of the gentlemen standing at the side of the track. The engineer jumped up from underneath the engine, and the gentleman who was sat inside quickly sprang out. He had barely done so when the roaring locomotive heading towards them, which was a special train carrying Mr. Bremridge of Barnstaple, and other gentlemen connected with the North Devon scheme, came upon them. The second engine although the steam had been shut off, was going at such a furious rate it literally smashed into the first carriage driving it up on end with all its important contents of plans, sections, justice etc. So there they were, the Taw Vale engine and part of a North Devon carriage, with inmates not much hurt but almost speechless from fright. The situation was resolved when both parties proceeded to the next station in the first engine; the fire-box of which was soon put into working order again. They all had to crowd together in the tender. Before this could happen though it was necessary to recover the Taw Vale documents which was done by Mr. Barton crawling through a hole in the bottom of the carriage. Once the important papers were properly secured, a temporary amalgamation of the rival companies was affected and at the next station a new carriage was procured by which the respective parties were able to reach Exeter at around half-past eleven at night, less than thirty minutes before the cut off hour of midnight, at which time the necessary deposit had to have been made.

Tragic double suicide by two factory girls.

In October 1846 two young factory girls residing in Ottery St. Mary; Mary Ann Oldridge and Jane Smith, during their lunchbreak met with a man whom it is supposed they knew and from who, Mary Ann convinced to give her a half-a-crown with which she would go and buy the three of them some liquor. Having not returned the man went in search of them and eventually caught up with the young women. When he realised that they had never intended to come back he demanded they repay him the money. He then threatened to tell their employer Mr. Newberry, the proprietor of a silk factory in Exeter. Having spent some of the money and no longer having sufficient funds to repay him the threat hung heavily on the minds of the two girls. They decided to go to a nearby chemist where they purchased three-pence worth of arsenic with which they were determined to destroy themselves rather than face the shame of their deceit. They then went back to the factory and carried on their afternoons work. At the end of their shift, they went to a public-house kept by a man named Taylor, and there they mixed the poison and pouring it in to some cider to disguise the taste, drank it.
The poor girls died a long agonising and lingering death. Mary Ann Oldridge several days later and Jane Smith twenty-four after her friend. The inquest into the unfortunate girls' deaths held at the 'Red lion Inn' Ottery St. Mary, recorded a verdict of 'felo de se' – suicide. Both girls were then interred in Ottery St. Mary parish churchyard.

Spring-heeled Jack visits Teignmouth.

Spring-heeled Jack was an entity in English folklore of the Victorian era, and who was known for his startling leaps from rooftop to rooftop, and his ability to cover many miles in a short space of time. He also reportedly could breathe flames and had cloven hooves. The first claimed sighting of Spring-heeled Jack was in 1837 in London. Later sightings were reported all over Great Britain.

There were those who tried to imitate 'Jack' and play on the fear of folk especially women and played mischievous tricks on the vulnerable. Captain Finch, an elderly military man residing at Shaldon, near Torquay was charged in April 1847 at Teignmouth Magistrates Court, of replicating the disgraceful character of Spring-heeled Jack. During the previous winter, several women had at night, been assaulted and made terrified by an 'apparition' dressed in bull's hide and wearing a skull-cap, horns and a mask. In two such cases the person in disguise was proven to be Captain Finch and he was fined in both instances, followed by a suitable lecture from the Bench.

Some of the cases heard at Woodbury Petty Sessions June 1847.

The quarter sessions were held at the 'Globe Inn,' Woodbury, on Monday the 31st May 1847, before the Rev. J. Huyshe, G. Smith, Esq., and J. Garratt, jun., Esq., Magistrates of Devon.

Removed to the asylum.

The first person to be called into the dock was Joel Budd, an elderly man who was brought before the Magistrates as a candidate for admission into the County Pauper Lunatic Asylum. Charles Fox a surgeon, stated that he had examined Mr. Budd, who gave reasonable answers on some points though he considered his mind to be unsound as the gentleman had told him that the previous night he had heard from the Almighty by post, and that the letter had been published in the newspapers. Also, that he was to be freed from going to the Devil. Dr. Fox said he thought that Mr. Budd was not capable of taking care of himself although he was unable to say that he was a danger to himself or others.
Mary Ann Budd, daughter of Mr. Budd, said that her father was seventy-two-years-old and had been out [of the asylum] since Christmas. She said he had complained of being troubled at night with the idea that the Devil was walking in his room. On the previous two days he had made his escape from the home they shared, taking a knife with him. The knife was an old rusty iron one which he had sharpened until he had brought it to cut. He had also made a sheath of leather for it. She stated that her father had the knife on his person now. Mr. Budd when requested took the knife from his pocket and showed it to the Magistrates, who agreed that it could be used to inflict a serious injury. Mr. Budd declared that he had no intention of using it as God had forgiven him and he [God] and scores of other people had read about it in the newspaper. The Magistrates directed the Clerk (Mr. Coleridge) to make an order for the committal of Joel Budd to the lunatic Asylum.

Who was the father of Sarah's child?

Sarah Piggott, a widow for the past eighteen months, applied to have an order made against John MacMahon of Exmouth for the maintenance of the child she had given birth to on the 29th of March that year. The Magistrates declined making the order on evidence stating that Sarah Piggott had repeatedly stated another person as to being the father of the child.

Bread Riots in Exmouth and beyond.

In 1846 and 1847 there were widespread crop failures in Devon leading to poor harvests, this resulted in the price of bread rising steeply. This in turn led to a number of riots breaking out across the county. On 17th May 1847 bakers' shops and flour stores in Torbay, Dawlish, Oakhampton, Cullompton, Crediton, Tiverton and Exmouth, were attacked and plundered by angry men and women. Their main targets being bakers who were thought to have sold underweight bread or had refused to give credit to the poor.

Henry Hayman was charged with having disturbed the public peace at Exmouth on the 17th of May, in the company of others. He was also charged with breaking a window at Thomas Halse's house. Thomas Halse a baker, stated that just before eleven o'clock in the morning when he was busy at his oven a disturbance took place outside and two panes of glass were broken. At nine o'clock that evening another disturbance took place and this time nine panes of glass were broken. The whole damage amounted to seventeen shillings and sixpence.

Thomas Mills, a thirteen-year-old boy working for Mr. Ellis of Exmouth, stated that on the night of the 17th, he saw a crowd of between three and four hundred people standing outside of Mr. Halse's house making a great disturbance. He saw Henry Hayman throw stones at the upstairs windows. Many of the crowd had sticks but some men made them throw them away. Cross-examined he denied being a part of the mob.

Ann Taylor a greengrocer, said that two of her windows were also broken that day but she didn't know who had done it. Ellen Cook, the wife of a baker who lived next-door to Mrs. Taylor described the terrifying scene of the mob on the street and that she saw Hayman throw something; though what it was she could not say as there was such a melee taking place.
 Mr. Trenchard, an attorney of Exmouth, said that immediately after the occurrence, Mrs. Cook came to see him and told him that it was Henry Hayman who she saw throwing things.

Aaron Wheaton was also charged with having taken part in the riot and with breaking the windows of Mr. John Dyer, another baker of Exmouth. Mr. Dyer said that the damage done to his glass by Wheaton amounted to ten pence, although the whole damage to his property amounted to three shillings. His son William Dyer said that at about ten o'clock on the night of the riots a dozen men had come to their house and he saw Aaron Wheaton pick up a stone and throw it through the window. During the whole day he had been aware of the riotous mobs in the street. Aaron Wheaton denied that it had been he who broke the window and said that William Dyer must have been mistaken. Wheaton's master came to his apprentice's defence and said that the lad had lived with him for three years and was a very good boy and that a woman he had spoken to could swear that it was another boy who had thrown the stone. William Dyer in retaliation insisted that it was Aaron Wheaton who he had seen throw the stone. He knew him well and saw that it was him by the light coming from the window of the 'White Hart Inn' which was directly opposite. Several persons present stated that the Wheaton was 'a very good boy'.

Henry Perry was charged with committing a riot at Withycombe Raleigh on the same day along with others who obstructed the highway and prevented Abraham Bolt who was trying to take vegetables to market from passing. Bolt stated that as he was going through the streets of Exmouth near the Parade the mob stopped his cart and took some of the potatoes and then a group of them followed him into the marketplace. He had fixed the price of his potatoes at two shillings a score, but a great noise and disturbance then took place in the market and his potatoes were sold at one shilling and sixpence a score. Had it not been for the disturbance the potatoes would not have been sold at that price. He declined to admit [through fear of reprisals] that Henry Perry was standing by his side in the market when the potatoes were sold. When asked if Perry had had words with him regarding what had taken place Abraham Bolt declined to answer. When asked if Perry had threatened him if he was to give evidence against him Bolt again declined to answer – even under oath. Eventually he gave in to the questioning and said that he had met Henry Perry in a field at Colaton Raleigh. After a great deal of perseverance on the part of the Magistrates, Abraham Bolt then admitted that he had promised Perry not to swear against him but eventually said he himself had not weighed out the potatoes sold but was given the money afterwards by Perry. Bolt was then threatened with prison if he refused to answer the questions put to him. He continued to attempt to evade answering but after being cautioned admitted that it was Henry Perry who had weighed and sold his potatoes. In answer to further questions, he admitted that he brought around two pounds worth of potatoes to Exmouth for which he had only received seventeen shillings. He would not have sold them at that price had he not been intimidated.

John Corder a coal-factor, said that he saw Abraham Bolt's cart on the Parade. He saw around fifty people standing around the cart buying the potatoes. He also saw Henry Perry there handing a basket of potatoes to another man. Later that day he saw Abraham Bolt at the turnpike and Bolt said to him that he should have lost many more of the potatoes if it had not been for Perry who protected him. Bolt was re-called to the stand and admitted that the person who had interfered with him on the Parade was the same person who sold his potatoes in the market. He then produced a testimonial to his character which was numerously signed by the inhabitants of Exmouth.

Mr. Foster, the keeper of Exmouth market, said that when Abraham Bolt came into the market, Henry Perry had assisted him, and his conduct was there very proper. After the sale of potatoes was over, he asked Bolt how much he had lost as many people had expressed their thanks to Perry and at least two to three hundred people had followed the cart into the market. Mr. Foster said that it was the women who kicked up the riot. One woman had taken Bolt's hat from his head and another took his whip from his hand and was showing off with it in front of the crowd. Another witness named Elliott, stated that some of the women pulled Bolt off the cart and under Henry Perry's instructions, the potatoes were sold at one shilling and sixpence a score, but the mob had wanted them to be sold for nine pence or one shilling a score. He believed that if Perry had not caused the potatoes to be sold for one shilling and sixpence then Bolt would have got nothing at all. Cross-examined, Henry Perry denied having stolen the potatoes, though a witness commented that they had heard him say that it was wrong that the poor should go without and he would do it again if he had to.

Aaron Wheaton was ordered to pay nine shillings for the damage he had caused, plus costs. Henry Hayman was ordered to pay the amount of damage done by him, plus costs and to give his own recognisance of twenty pounds for his good behaviour for a year. Henry Perry was ordered to pay the expenses and find sureties of thirty pounds for himself and fifteen pounds for two others for his good behaviour during the next year. The Chairman observed that the defendants ought to feel that the Bench had dealt very leniently with them.

Thomas Burrows a labourer in Sir John Kennaway's service was summoned to show cause why he should not be required to find sureties for his good behaviour, and in default be committed to prison. The defendant had been charged with being concerned in the riot at Ottery St. Mary. This he denied; he said he merely went from his work to Tallaton, where bought two loaves of bread, one of which he put in a handkerchief and the other he stuck upon his stick. He was asked by one the Magistrates if that was a usual way of carrying bread and by another if he collected a crowd of people at Cadhay Bridge? In reply the defendant expressed his sorrow for what he had done.

Joseph Moray a pit-sawyer, was charged with making a riot in the town of Ottery St. Mary on the 15th of May. The Ottery policeman stated that on that day he met Moray in Mill Street with a penny loaf stuck upon a pole with a wallflower stuck in it. He then stopped at every baker's shop he passed and said that they must either drop their bread prices or raise the wages. A great number of people joined him, and it was with great difficulty to disperse them after having taken the bread and pole from the defendant who the officer said was the worse for liquor. Moray in his defence said that he was in the employ of Mr. Marker of Coombe. His wages for the last four months had been ten shillings a week on average. Mr. Huyshe, one of the Magistrates, said that he knew what wages sawyers could get; he had paid too many bills not to know that and he was assured that Moray was receiving twenty-four shillings a week not ten. Moray like Burrows admitted to being drunk at the time of the offence and was also very sorry for what he had done. Thomas Burrows and Joseph Moray were bound over to keep good behaviour for the following year, and were ordered to pay the court expenses.

Defaulting on maintenance.

Robert Foster was charged by Ann Rouse with non-payment of nine shillings for the maintenance of his child, under an order for bastardy. Ms. Rouse told the Magistrates that three times she had gone to his house to ask for the money and each time was told to "come again." The Chairman said that it was Robert Foster's responsibility to bring the money weekly and Ann Rouse nor the child should have to wait or to have to go and ask for it. It came to the Bench's attention that the original order was for one shilling and six pence a week but Ann had been pressured into only accepting nine pence a week under the intimidation of the father's family and out of this she was charged three-pence every time she received the money for the writing out of a receipt. The Magistrates made an order for the whole amount due without reference to the woman's agreement and her expenses for bringing the case before the Bench. Ann was awarded sixteen shillings and six pence in total. The Bench instructed the young woman that she was not bound to go for the money, nor any receipt, but that the money was to be paid weekly to her.

Like something out of Punch and Judy.

Mary Braund was charged by Caroline Willis with having assaulted her in her own home at Sowton on the 15th of May 1847.

Caroline Wills stated that Mary Braund broke open her door and forcibly took possession of the house. She then tore off her cap almost choking her. Mary's sister in-law who had followed her through the doorway then joined in the assault. Charles Wilson, a youth who was in the house at the time had come between the women and broke up the fight. The outrage had apparently arisen after a 'few words' had been exchanged between Braund's sister-in-law and Caroline Wills, though Mary Braund was vehement in her protestations of absolute innocence of having been the perpetrator.

Charles Wilson was then called as a witness. He stood between the two women, looking from one to the other with a vacant stare. "Didn't you see her bust open the door?" said Mrs. Wills. "The door was open before," replied Charles. "Oh fie! How can you say?" remonstrated Mrs. Willis. "Didn't you see her at [hit] me?" The youth replied; "No, I didn't see her at thee."

"Lor ha mercy upon me!" exclaimed a bewildered Mrs. Willis, wringing her hands in vexation. "You had got the baby and parted us!"

"The baby was on the table," replied the youth in a petulant tone as though he considered that the poor woman had lost both her memory and her wits. The Chairman enquired if Charles Wilson had actually seen the women fighting. "No, they wasn't fighting," he said. "They was only pulling one another about." At this point Mrs. Willis became near hysterical in her rage and the two women began to throwing vexed accusations at one another. The Magistrates dismissed the case as it was impossible to decide who was the worse of the two women, and the expenses were to be divided between the two of them.

Exeter Police Assizes.

These are some of the cases heard at the Exeter Police Assizes in the week beginning Monday the 7th of February 1848.

William Norris and Mary Ann Vereo were charged with assaulting a police officer whilst in a state of insanity caused by intoxication. The previous evening the couple had been drinking and when they met with a policeman in the street who attempted to arrest them for being drunk and disorderly. But the alcoholic spirit having got into their system they resisted with all their might and another officer was called to give assistance. Whilst trying to place the couple in handcuffs to which William Norris objected most forcefully, he knocked one of the officers to the ground. The other officer then applied the twitch which immediately put a stop to further hostilities and the prisoners were taken to the Police Station. Norris was fined one pound and Vereo five shillings. Neither being able to pay, they were both sentenced to a week's imprisonment.

John Rew, was charged with begging in the streets. He stated that he had some time previously been discharged from the Workhouse in Plymouth and had since then been going about the county in search of employment. He soon spent what money he had and was obliged to beg. The previous day he had been so engaged in South Street when he was arrested and taken into custody. The Magistrates allowed him to go, on his promise to leave Exeter immediately.

The Orange Barrows - Several people, both male and female who although held licences, were charged by the police for obstructing the public causeway with their one-wheeled barrows. They were told that unless they were attending to a customer then they should be perpetually on the trot. The Bench appeared indisposed to fine on this occasion and instead gave the offenders a caution. One of the accused said that he was the father of five children and his living depended on his selling a little fruit. Mr. Woolmer said that if they wished to sell fruit, they should get a stall in the market which was the proper place. The Police Superintendent stated that several tradesmen had complained that the access to their shops were being obstructed by these persons whilst horses continually shied at the barrows.

Thomas Procter was charged with begging in South Street, Exeter. Young Procter told the court that he was originally from Wellington in Somerset. His father had told him that he needed to go in search of work. Sharpened by seven years' experience in school he went off in search of a future profession. Work was scarce and begging amongst the upper classes was all the fashion but people not being so charitable nowadays as they used to be, he took to thieving and in consequence of this was very soon apprehended in Taunton for stealing money and sentenced to ten days' imprisonment plus a whipping. When the ten days had expired, he ventured on his travels again and came to Exeter, where he again resorted to begging. It was here whilst deluding the charitable with tales of woe and suffering that a police officer took him in to custody for vagrancy. The Magistrates ordered the relieving officer to send the boy back to his own parish.

George Morrish was charged with not keeping his wife. It appeared that he had not worked for three weeks but had been frequently to an alehouse. The previous Thursday his wife had resorted to asking for a charitable donation of food and she was given bread, meat and groceries. George Morrish was sent to the House of Correction for two weeks.

Thomas Southcott of the' Britannia Inn' South Street, was charged with allowing disorderly persons to assemble in his house. The superintendent stated that on the previous Sunday night people coming out of church and passing by the Britannia Inn were shocked at the blasphemous language that came out of the building. Then on the on the Monday night there were a number of men and women fighting and screaming and disturbing the neighbourhood. Southcott was fined one pound plus expenses.

Three beggars who had been brought in from streets were committed for one week's hard labour. The Mayor commented that a great deal of time was spent by the Bench with cases of vagrancy.

Sad suicide of a young policeman.

On Saturday the 15th of July 1848 a railway policeman called Richard Farley, a twenty-three-year-old single man from Denbury near Newton Abbot who had been in his post at the new station in Ivybridge for the past six weeks, destroyed himself whilst on duty. He sat upon one of the transoms of the railroad just as the seven-thirty a.m. train was approaching the station. He had deliberately chosen a position on the Plymouth side of the Slade viaduct where there was a curve in the line and which was only visible by an approaching train at a very short distance away. The engine driver only spotting him at the very last second was unable to bring the train to a halt in time. The guard-iron on the engine struck Farley on the head, killing him instantly and flung his body under the carriages. The train was then backed up and his broken body removed and conveyed to Ivybridge. In Richard's pocket was found a document filled with biblical references and stating the intended act to end his life. It was also said that he had recently been unsuccessful in an attachment [with a young woman.]

*Up until the Suicide Act of 1961 being passed in Parliament, attempting to take one's own life was a criminal offence. Even those who succeeded in the act could find family members being prosecuted.

The cost of being drunk and disorderly.

Thomas Newcombe of Throwleigh, was brought before Exeter Police Court in September 1848 for having been so drunk the previous evening between six and seven o'clock and that he could neither steer his course correctly nor see his way clear and in his ramblings had fallen against and smashed a pane of glass at Mr. Spencer's house in Sidwell Street. He had then proceeded to use foul language when the police were summoned. Thomas was placed in cells overnight and the following day fined five shillings for drunkenness, one shilling and sixpence for the pane of glass and three shillings and sixpence in expenses.

A case of Careless poisoning.

Farm labourer John Dymond, who worked for Mr. Charles Brown at Lakes Farm near Holsworthy was making his way to the farmhouse for dinner on the 20th of November 1848 when passing a hedge, he noticed a half-hidden bottle containing some liquid. He picked it up and when later joining with the people with whom he was about to dine and not thinking the bottle contained anything which might do harm, he offered a boy called Willian Reece a drink. The boy being thirsty immediately drank from the bottle, but he and very soon afterwards began vomiting violently. Mr. Brown arrived soon after and being told what had taken place he recognised the bottle and knew it to contain a solution of corrosive sublimate something which a long time before he had used on his sheep and had quite forgotten that he had hidden the remainder under a hedge. William Reece was taken to Holsworthy for medical aid, unfortunately he continued to decline and died a few days later. An inquest was held which resulted in Dymond being committed for trial on a charge of manslaughter. On the 17th of March 1849. Twenty-year-old John Dymond was acquitted of the charge at the Devon Assizes.

1850- 1899

The witch of Woodbury.

In the village of Woodbury, a few miles south east of Exeter in 1851 resided an old woman called Mary Toby who was by locals said to possess the power of communicating evil to her neighbours. There were allegedly many instances according to the villagers of such events having occurred. Her company was shunned by the elders and the youth of both sexes were said to have had their hearts filled with fear at the sight of the old woman as she hobbled along using a wooden staff for support. In the same village lived a woman called Maria Stone towards whom the old woman had of late appeared to show much interest. Mrs. Stone who was fearful as to the powers of Mary Toby had taken care so as not to offend her fearing the consequences. This wise precaution on the part of Maria Stone did not have the desired effect as it appeared to her that Mary Toby was determined to wish her harm. The old lady made a number of visits to the Stone's family abode and on one occasion said that she understood Mrs. Stone to have a 'purty pig' and asked to be allowed to see it. Maria granted the request and when the old woman went to the sty she said, "what a fine pig 'tis," whilst at the same time poking the animal with her stick, laying it across the animals back. This poking was then said to have been repeated on a second and third pig owned by the family. From that moment on the pigs refused to eat and soon after died.

The old woman was then said to have held the hand of Maria's youngest child an eight-month-old baby and called it a "purty little dear," and from that moment on the child was also said to have ailed and become weakly and sick. Maria Stone said that from that day onwards as soon as the clock stuck midnight the little soul would sit up in bed and turn topsy-turvy until four in the morning and neither she nor her husband could get any sleep. She told her husband that she thought Mary Toby was a 'reeker'[witch] and said that she should never be allowed near their house again. A short while later Mary Toby once again knocked at the Stone's front door regarding some straw she wished to purchase. Maria Stone ordered her off the premises but when the old woman refused to leave Maria took hold of her by the shoulders and pushed her out. In doing so the old woman tripped on a cabbage stump and fell down. For this assault Mary

Toby summoned Maria Stone before the Bench at the monthly petty sessions held at the 'Globe Inn' in July 1851. Mary in her evidence swore that Maria Stone threw her, and afterwards kicked her assisted by four or five others, each of whom also kicked her when she was on the ground. She offered the Bench to examine her back and sides but this they very politely declined, it not being their 'profession or practice' to do so. Mary Toby called as witness a female named Mary Stump, but she denied that the complainant was used as she had described and said that she had accidently fallen over the cabbage stump when Mrs. Stone had taken her by the shoulders to take her off the premises. The Bench in delivering their judgement said it was painful in the present day to find people so extremely unreasonable and so excessively ignorant as to have the idea that a person could bewitch another. After cautioning Mary Toby they fined Maria Stone fifteen shillings including costs.

*It would appear that the Bench fined the defendant for believing in witchcraft and not for the assault. The evidence being that no more violence was used than necessary in removing the complainant from the defendant's premises.

The Devil's footprints (or Spring-heeled Jack?)

During the night of the 8th of February 1855, the fields, gardens, roof tops and tops of walls in various parts of Devonshire including Woodbury, Dawlish, Torquay, Totnes etc, bore in the snow the impression of mule or horses hoof prints in a single line, eight inches apart. They even crossed the estuary of the river Exe which was two miles wide and extended a length of the county for over forty miles. The actual distance of the hoof prints reported across the southern counties seemed to show the individual had progressed at least one hundred miles in one night. Apparently, a group of tradesmen in Dawlish were so unnerved by the prints that they armed themselves with guns and bludgeons, and on the morning of the 9th of February set off in pursuit of the tracks.

A letter sent to the Editor of the Exeter and Plymouth Gazette reads as follows:

Sir, Thursday night, the 8th of February [1855] was marked by a heavy fall of snow, followed by rain and boisterous wind from the east, and in the morning frost. The return of day-light revealed the ramblings of some most busy and mysterious animal, endowed with the power of ubiquity, as its foot-prints were to be seen in all sorts of unaccountable places – on the tops of houses, narrow walls, in gardens and court yards, enclosed by high walls and palings, as well as in the open fields. The creature seems to have frolicked about through Exmouth, Littleham, Lympstone, Woodbury, Topsham, Starcross, Teignmouth, &c. &c. There is hardly a garden in Lympstone where his footprints are not observable, and in this parish, he seems to have gambolled about with inexpressible activity. Its tracks appear more like that of a bi-ped than a quadruped, and the steps are generally eight inches in advance of each other, though in some cases twelve or fourteen, and are alternate like the steps of a man, and would be included between two parallel lines six inches apart. The impression of the foot closely resembles that of a donkey's shoe, and measures from an inch and a half to (in some cases) two inches and a half across, here and there appearing as if the foot was cleft, but in the generality of its steps the impression of the shoe was continuous and perfect; in the centre the snow remains entire, merely showing the outer crust of the foot, which, therefore, must have been convex. The creature seems to have advanced to the doors of several houses, and then to have retraced its steps, but no one is able to discern the starting or resting point of this mysterious visitor. Everyone is wondering, but no one is able to explain the mystery; the poor are full of superstition, and consider it little short of a visit from Satan or some of his imps old.

From the Ellacombe papers: a comparison of the two drawings published in The Illustrated London News *(above), with two further sketches (below) of the footprints.*

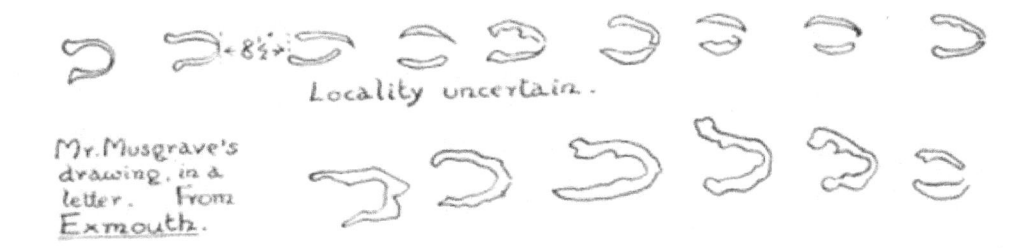

Image courtesy of Peter Moore – The curious case of the Devil's foot prints (or the great Devon mystery 1855)

* The winter of 1855 was particularly cold and the temperature stayed around freezing from January through to March. The river Exe and Teign froze over. The hoof prints measured from an inch and a half to two inches across. The phenomenon has never been explained and there are various theories as to what could have caused the marks over such a wide area. There have been a number of explanations put forward; from an experimental balloon released from Devonport Dockyard with trailing shackles, hopping wood mice to badgers. It's very possibly the marks were not made by one animal, but from a number of different animals. No one would have been able to have travelled the length of the trail to verify that they were all of the exact size and pattern.

Bigamy at Totnes.

Francis Dalley a seaman, was charged with having on the 1st of May 1858 feloniously marrying Elizabeth Julyan, his former wife still being alive.

Mr. John Jones the governor of the county gaol in Anglesey, Wales, said that in 1843 Francis Dalley had married in his presence, his sister *Sarah Jones, in the church of St. Nicholas, Liverpool. Charles King Heale, A police constable in Brixham, said that Dalley's first wife had been living in the town up until the time she had been sent to the Union Workhouse where she died on the 17th of November. Samuel Parnell, the registrar of marriages at Totnes, produced a register of the marriage between Dalley and Elizabeth Julyan a widow, residing in Brixham. Mr. Bere acting on behalf of the defence, submitted that it was not clearly proven that Sarah Jones to whom the prisoner had married in 1843, was the same person as the Sarah Dalley who died in the Totnes Workhouse.

On the evidence provided, the jury found Francis Dalley guilty. Elizabeth Julyan was then called to give evidence, she stated that she had married Francis Dalley on the 1st of May and that his conduct towards her since their marriage had been that of the best of husbands. His Lordship in passing sentence remarked that the prisoner had already been incarcerated since the 12th of November [over a month previously] and considering the first wife was now dead, and that the second wife had not been deceived, he considered the punishment already undergone was sufficient and he discharged the case.

* What is strange about this case, is that marriage records show that Francis Dalley married Elizabeth not Sarah Jones on the 5th of February 1843. Possibly she was 'known' as Sarah and not by her real name of Elizabeth? [See image.]

Ruined by the temptation of pretty things.

Seventeen-year-old Emma Stoneman the daughter of respectable but humble parents had entered the service of the Crediton postmaster to work as a domestic servant in July 1858. She was also to assist in stamping the letters mornings and evenings when not engaged in the household duties. Being young and naive and likely never owning very much the attraction of money, trinkets, and goods that were beyond anything she had ever owned – became too much and within a few weeks of her beginning her employment items were being reported as missing or having not reached their destination. Coming under suspicion as the thief her room was searched and inside was found a number of items that were more than sufficient as to establish her guilt. There were no less than thirty charges against Emma for stealing articles of various kinds.

On the 15th of September, Mr. Moule of Crediton had marked two half-sovereigns which he enclosed in a letter addressed to Jane Hannaford, care of Mrs. Smithers, 3. Stonehouse Cottages, Plymouth. He also enclosed a pair of gloves in a letter which he addressed to Miss. Grantley of Wellington Place, Hastings; and posted them at Crediton Post Office. The following day he returned and saw Emma engaged in stamping letters. He asked her if she had seen the two letters in question and she said she hadn't. She said that she never read the addresses; her duty was merely to stamp the letters. Mr. Moule then asked if she had any objection to his searching her room and she said she did not but that she should like to 'put it right' first. Mr. Moule however insisted on going to her room before it was 'put right' and accompanied by Mr. Smee, a police officer belonging to the General Post Office and Sergeant Budden of the Devon County Police, a purse was found in the bedroom which Emma opened and threw out from it some silver coins. Noticing that she kept her hand on an inner clasp Mr, Moule then said; "You have got gold in there, put it out." Emma opened it and produced three sovereigns and two half-sovereigns. On examination Mr. Moule identified the latter as the two half-sovereigns which he had marked and enclosed in the letter he had posted the previous day. The gloves were also found in a box as well as a Honiton lace veil which Miss. Thorpe of Crediton later identified as the one she had sent to Mrs. Robertson of London, but which had never reached its destination. A brooch, riband, and a box of pills were also found. All later being identified by the owners as having been stolen in their transit through the Post Office. When asked how she pleaded at Crediton Court, Emma wept bitterly as she pleaded guilty and expressed great penitence for what she had done. She was then remanded to on placed on trial at the Devon Assizes held at Exeter on the 16th of December 1858.

Mr. Willesford who appeared as her defence counsel, said that a young ignorant country girl ought never to have been placed in such a position of temptation, and he had several certificates as to her previous good character. The Judge in passing sentence said that it had been a very distressing case to all who had presided upon the trial for perhaps without knowing the gravity of the offence, Emma had done something which must subject her to a very heavy sentence. She had pleaded guilty to several indictments, and to stealing public property with which she had been entrusted in the full confidence that she would behave honestly. He then said he would not distress her feelings by making further observations and sentenced her to be kept in penal servitude for three years.

At the same Winter Assizes that Emma Stoneman was found guilty of theft, a number of other difficult cases were heard:

The fraudulent mute.

Joseph Smith was indicted for trying to use a Bank of England ten-pound note knowing it to be forged. The prisoner when called upon to plead did not answer but stood mute. Mr. Kingdon, a doctor at Exeter Prison then took the stand and said that Smith had been in his care since the end of November. Up until the previous Sunday he had been like any other person. On that day he became very wild; in an excited state and talking to himself though there were no other signs of him being attacked with acute mania. His pulse was quiet, his head cool and nothing unnatural in the pupil of his eyes. If it had come on without previous indication it might have been acute mania, but there was still the absence of any other insane symptoms.
Mr. Warren, the doctor at the city Workhouse was next to give evidence. He said that he had been called by Mr. Kingdon to see Joseph Smith on the previous Sunday, with a view of ascertaining whether he was feigning insanity. When he arrived, the prisoner was sound asleep, but still he felt he showed no signs of insanity.
The learned Judge then summed up this part of the case. It was clear the prisoner stood mute. The question was whether he did so with an endeavour to deceive or whether it was through actual insanity. The jury found the prisoner stood mute by fraud and malice. A plea of 'not guilty' was then entered and the indictment was proceeded with. The facts of the case were very simple. At about six o'clock in the evening of the 20th of November the prisoner went to the shop of Mr. Silverton, a silversmith in Exeter. He saw Mrs. Silverton and requested to look at

a silver watch. One was shown him, the price of which with a chain attached, was three pounds. He said he did not want the chain and agreed to buy the watch for two pounds and ten shillings. Upon that he produced the forged ten-pound note. Mrs. Silverton said she had no change and he said he had none either. She requested him to write his name on the note and he wrote upon it 'Joseph Smith.' Mr. Silverton came in and upon looking at the note he took it to show it to other persons, one of whom was a Mr. Linscott. This was done in the presence of Smith. Mr. Linscott then took it away saying he was going to show it to another person, but in fact went to the police, one of whom was accompanying him back to Silverton's shop when they saw Joseph Smith running into the street another way (showing him to be a stranger to Exeter.) They spoke to Smith who said he had been looking for Mr. Linscott, as he had run away with his note. Smith was then escorted to the superintendent of police, who asked him where he had got the note from. He said he had got it in exchange for a pony he had sold on the previous day. He was then asked where he came from and he replied Barnstaple. When asked which street he lived on, he gave the name of two different streets – neither of which were in Barnstaple. Asked his occupation; he said he was a tailor. It was then discovered that he had within twenty minutes of going to the watchmaker's shop, he had tried to purchase items for a small amount with the same note at a draper's and at a gunsmith. The note was proved to be a forgery. The jury found Joseph Smith guilty and he was sentenced to four years penal servitude.

Accused through spite.

Harriet Short, a fifty-two-year-old farm servant, was indicted for setting fire to a barn and other buildings on the 8th of August 1858, tenanted by her employer William Brownscombe, a farmer of Bratton Fleming, near Barnstaple. The fire which started in the barn soon spread to the dwelling house and several of the outhouses. The premises, which belonged to Sir Arthur Chichester, was totally consumed and a quantity of wheat, furniture and other items valued at one hundred and fifty pounds was destroyed. The evidence against Harriet Short was purely circumstantial. In her defence, she said that Mr. Brownscombe had brought her forward out of spite and envy. The Jury acquitted her.

Eliza Murray the bigamist.

Eliza Murray was indicted for bigamy; her second marriage being clearly proved. The poor woman had finally found happiness. Her first husband had frequently appeared before the Magistrates for assaulting her, and on one occasion had been imprisoned for six months due to the violence he had shown towards her. He had kept her without food and had neglected his children. He had even been fined fifty shillings for an assault upon a policeman. Eliza herself had raised the money to pay the fine.

The jury found Eliza Murray guilty, but recommended her to mercy. The Judge said that although Eliza had undoubtedly offended against the law of the land, and it was quite clear that that this must be followed by some sentence; but he had seldom witnessed a more distressing case, and he could not help feeling that she stood there an object of great commiseration. The sentence of the court was that she should be imprisoned for two days, and that time having expired, she would at once be discharged. Eliza clasped her hands and thanked the Judge; she was then removed from the court in a fainting state.

Manslaughter of a friend.

John Lidstone was indicted for the manslaughter of thirty-nine-year-old William Blake, at Kingsbridge on the 21st of November 1858.

The deceased and another man had gone to the 'Anchor Inn,' there they came across two men fighting, Lidstone being one of them. William Blake got between them and broke up the scuffle. The four of them all sat down and in good humour they drank beer from the same cup. Lidstone then mentioned some old gripe that had existed between himself and Blake. William Blake said; "Surely you are not going to bring up old grievances?" To which Lidstone replied; "No, here's my hand and my heart," and they shook hands. It appeared in all respects to everyone around that there were good friends. But suddenly, Lidstone challenged Blake to a fight. Blake refused saying he didn't want a fight and would never strike a man first. Upon which Lidstone threw a punch at Blake, who reactively threw a punch back; but Lidstone expecting this retaliation stepped to one side and they both fell against a wall. A scuffle then ensued and Lidstone struck Blake another punch, this time on the back of the neck, and they both fell to the ground. Blake didn't move – he had fallen on his forehead and was dead.

The surgeon who carried out the post-mortem on William Blake was of opinion that death arose from the fall to the floor. There were no external marks of a blow. He pointed out that William Blake was one of the finest and fittest men he had ever seen.

Mr. Carter for the defence urged that this had been a fair fight and no unlawful weapon had been used, and that juries were in the habit of saying when knives were used, that the parties should have had recourse and only to have used their natural weapons i.e., their fists. In his opinion William Blake's death had been accidental. The Judge responded by saying there could be no doubt that all fights were unlawful and all persons present, if death ensued, were guilty of manslaughter. The prisoner would therefore be guilty if the jury thought any of the blows led to the man's death, either by a blow or a fall arising from it. If the blow did not cause the death, but caused the fall which led to the death, then the prisoner would be guilty. The jury found the John Lidstone guilty. He was sentenced to be imprisoned with hard labour for six months.

The sleepwalking servant.

In early December 1858, Mr. Bagstaff, an ornithologist of Brixham, was startled to see his servant Grace Banks a young girl of eighteen, enter his bedroom and put down at the side of his bed a bird which she had taken from his shop. She then left the room and shortly after returned once more, this time with a stuffed pheasant which she deposited in the same place she had put the first bird, smoothing it down and saying, "here's a beauty." Leaving the room again her master hastily dressed himself and followed her. She went outside, walked up the street a short distance still in her night-clothes, and then returning went into the house. Her master tried to waken her; he shook her by the arm and called her name but she was so securely wrapped up in her sleep that she took no notice and at once retired to her bed.

Kidnapped by her loving husband.

An audacious kidnapping was carried out in early August 1861. The names of the individuals involved were kept private from the public due to the sensitivity of the case; though the newspaper strangely still felt that they should print the story!

A young married woman who was said to have lately become insane, and her relations believing that she would be better kept away from her husband, placed her in a house in Coburg Street, Plymouth, under the medical care of an eminent physician. The husband, a man in a respectable position in the middle class of society and connected to great public work in the neighbourhood not approving of this arrangement and having found out her location made arrangements for his wife's removal. Knowing the precautions taken to prevent her from leaving the property, he came up with a plan. He hired two men and a cab. On the evening of Thursday the 8th of August, one of these men dressed in livery knocked at the door of the house and on it being opened he said he had brought a letter from the eminent doctor. He also mentioned the name of one of the lady's trustees and her own name and that he would wait for an answer. As the person who answered the door went into the house with the letter the liveried messenger followed them in and entering the room where the lady was sitting, he threw open the window into which sprung the husband and before any words were exchanged, he took his wife under his arm and swept her back out through the window, across the garden and into the waiting cab which headed off in the direction of Lipson. The accomplice then made good his escape on foot. A search ensued for the abducted woman and two days later on the Saturday, her location was found but seeing as she appeared quite well and happy it was felt best to leave her reconciled with her husband for the time being.

Duped by Cinderella, the fortune teller.

An elderly woman named Cinderella Small who described herself as a gypsy fortune teller was indicted in March 1862 for stealing thirty-two pounds from a labourer named Thomas Field Horswell, at Sokenham on the 8th of February that year. The previous October Cinderella [yes, her real name] had visited Mr. Horswell's home saying she wanted to tell his sister's fortune. She then asked Thomas if she could tell him his. She took from her basket a book and read some passages from it. She then told Thomas that she didn't see him working for his master at Christmas and that some evil would befall him. For this information she asked for five shillings which he gave her. She said that if he were to give her gold, she would be able to keep the evil intent away from him for good. In accordance with her directions, he put a gold sovereign on a book of planets that she had with her, and placing his hand upon it, knelt down and said the Lord's Prayer. Cinderella put the sovereign in her pocket and left assuring Thomas that all was now well.

At around Christmas time Thomas's sight began to fade very fast and he became nearly blind. He was not an elderly man; he was only thirty-two. Thinking that this was the evil Cinderella Small had said was about to befall him he contacted her, and she again came to visit. She said; "Young man, I must touch your flesh" and she made the sign of the cross on his hand before reading aloud a prayer. She called him into the small back kitchen of the house and told him to kneel down and say the Lord's Prayer and again asked for some gold to put on the book. Thomas placed a gold sovereign on the book. Cinderella then rubbed his nose with a stone, after which she asked for another two pounds.

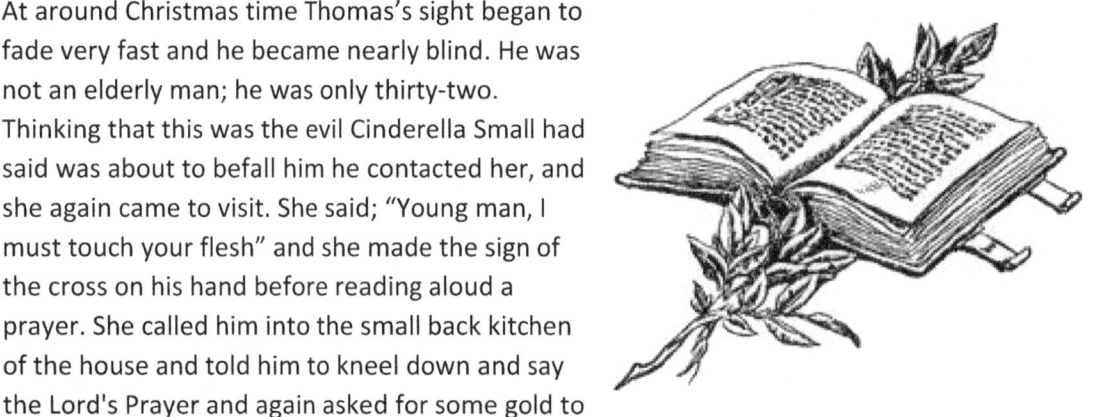

On the 21st of January Thomas gave Cinderella another one pound and seventeen shillings. On the 7th of February she called on him again and asking how his eyesight was and demanded more money. Thomas told her that he didn't have much money and what he had he needed but Cinderella told him that she knew he had money and that she must have it otherwise there was nothing more she could do for him and he would go blind. Fearing this to be true, Thomas went to the bank and withdrew the last of his money; fifty-seven pounds [nearly five thousand pounds in today's money] and when the gypsy woman next came to his house, she again made him kneel and say the Lord's Prayer after which she asked for thirty-two pounds stating that the following Thursday, she would repay the money and with it his eyesight would be returned. Thomas patiently awaited her return but nether she with his money nor his sight returned. Finally realising he had been duped, he informed the police of what had occurred.

Cinderella Small was soon after arrested in Cornwall and brought to the Magistrates Court in Exeter where her case was put forward to be heard at the next Assizes. It was here that Thomas told the court that prior to the woman calling at his house the previous October he had never seen her before in his life. He didn't believe her at first but when she said she was the seventh daughter of a seventh daughter (laughter in the court) he thought that she if anyone would be able to turn the evil away from him. He went on to say that his eyesight began to fail just before Christmas. He had previously lost an eye and when the sight in his one good eye began to fail, he felt he had some faith in what the woman had told him.

The Judge Mr. Justice Blackburn summing up the evidence, said that until reading the testimonies of the witnesses he did not believe that any person living in the kingdom could have been so foolish as to have believed in all that the young man seemed to have put his faith in. The jury after a few minutes' consultation found Cinderella Small guilty of fraudulently converting the money which was given to her as a loan, to her own use. Falling to her knees Cinderella begged his Lordship to be gracious to her saying that the money had been given to her and that she had eight dear little fatherless children [She was sixty-one.] The learned Judge said the offence had been very clearly proved. He did not think however that it would be necessary to pass a very severe sentence to operate as an example; therefore, the sentence would be six months' imprisonment with hard labour.

Suicide of a Royal Marine.

Sergeant George Kirkwood, a twenty-five-year-old divisional muster clerk with the Plymouth division of the Royal Marines, committed suicide in early January 1866. Having not shown up for duty he was discovered in his barrack room with his throat cut after the door to it had been broken down, having been locked from the inside. His habits were said to have been temperate and he was considered by many to be a 'jolly fellow.' He frequently took part in the theatrical performances put on by the Royal Marines, and the night after he committed the rash act, he was set to play the character of Cox in the farce; 'Box and Cox.'

At the inquest into his death a bandsman named Lucas said that he was stage manager of the Marines Amateur Theatre. At rehearsal on the evening prior to his death, Kirkwood who was usually quick in learning his lines, read portions of his part incoherently, talking to himself and speaking over other people's lines. He also kept putting his hand to his head. Lucas thought he was under the influence of drink and told him so jokingly. Kirkwood responded by saying he hadn't been drinking. He then began walking around the stage and when asked for the book of lines he was holding he stared at Lucas in a strange way and pulled such a horrible face that

Lucas actually felt afraid. Mary Ann Brooks, Kirkwood's fiancée said that on the evening prior to his death, George accompanied her to the home of Major Gray where she worked as a servant. He had appeared rather dull and out of sorts. Another witness a fellow marine said that Kirkwood told him that he had recently received a letter which had sorely confused him; but what the letter was about or who it came from he didn't say. The Jury returned a verdict of 'suicide during temporary insanity.'

* Box and Cox is the story of a landlord who lets a room to two lodgers, one who works nights and one who works days. When one of them has the day off, they meet each other in the room and tempers flare.

Cured by a witch.

In the early part of 1869 three young women living at Dittisham fell ill. Their mother's thinking they had been 'ill-wished upon' consulted a wizard at Teignmouth. He came to the conclusion that the women had been 'deeply wounded' and promised a cure for a sum of money which was duly handed over. The girls continued to remain unwell and the wizard said that nothing more could be done for them. The mother's not giving up, next consulted with a witch at Dartmouth and many pounds it was said were expended on her to ensure success. This money was handed over through a secret friend of the witch. The three young women in time did get well and the cure was attributed to the witch, who demanded four pounds as a final sum. The mothers unable to raise that amount of money got a friend to have words with the witch, who alarmed her by threatening to bring the case before the Magistrates. She not only relinquished her claim to the four pounds, but returned part of the money she had previously received.

Tragedy of two brothers, near Barnstaple.

Two young boys; William and Thomas Hearn, aged nine and four years old, disappeared on 29th of October 1869. They were sent to school as usual, but for some reason decided not to go and nothing more was heard or seen of then till the following day when the elder boy, William, was discovered sitting at the side of a mill-leat near Landkey, with his younger brother Thomas lying by his side. The elder boy when asked what he was doing there, said that couldn't get his brother home. A quick examination found the younger boy to be quite dead. The little boy had sadly died due to exposure to the cold and exhaustion, after having spent the night out in the open. William Hearn was at once taken care of and conveyed to his home where he lay in very weak state. The body of Thomas was taken to the nearest house at Landkey to await an inquest. John H. Toller, Esq., the Deputy County Coroner, that evening arrived at Landkey to hear the evidence. Mr. Henry Martyn Bryant, a shopkeeper at Swymbridge, said that he was on his way to Harford to help his brother take down a hedge. After crossing a stream, he picked up a child's cap which was behind one of the posts of a stile. He went back to the stream to see if he could see who the cap belonged to. He saw two boys, and asked one if the cap belonged to him, he said it did and Mr. Bryant threw the cap towards him. Noticing another child lying on the ground, he asked what the matter was. William replied saying that his brother was dead adding that he had fallen into the water. After questioning William some more, he discovered that the boys lived in Davie's Lane, Barnstaple and that their parents didn't know where they were. Henry Bryant then went off to get help before returning with a neighbour, Mr. Verney, and several others. They carried William and the body of Thomas Hearn to the 'Castle Inn' at Landkey.'

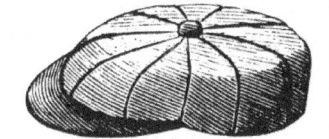

John Hammet, the son of Stephen Hammet, a shoemaker in Swymbridge said he had seen the boys the previous evening at half-past five walking along the road near Harford Water. He noticed the younger boy was crying and the elder was leading him. When he asked where they were going, William replied that they knew where they were going and they then carried on going in the opposite direction to himself.

Mr. John Hearn, the boys' distraught father was next to speak. He said how the boys had been at home the previous day until just after two o'clock when they had finished their dinner. The boys left the house together heading towards the school at Hardway Head. In the morning they had stayed home to look after the baby whilst their mother went to market, as was their custom. There was nothing said or done that he felt would have compelled them to run away. He said Willy, the elder boy had often absented himself from school and taken his brother with him, though he hadn't done it for several weeks. Returning home from work at half past five there was some concern as they boys had not yet returned. After his wife had given him his supper, he sent her out to look for them. Unable to find them she returned home and they went out together; they didn't come across anyone who had seen they boys. At ten o'clock he informed the police that the children were missing. At daybreak he again went out to search and shortly after ten o'clock when he was at Newport turnpike gate, he was informed that the boys had been found at Landkey. He made his way there, where he found Thomas dead and his brother very exhausted. He added that the boys had never been ill-used, but Willy had always been afflicted.

Mr. John Hawkes Jackman, a surgeon living in Swymbridge said that morning he had been informed that a child had drowned at Landkey. He immediately rode over on his horse and carried out an examination. It was his opinion that Thomas had died from exhaustion and congestion of the lungs, consequent upon exposure to the weather and having fallen into the water he would have felt the exposure more. The Coroner passed a verdict of 'died from exhaustion and congestion of the lungs consequent upon exposure to the weather.'

   * Young Thomas was the third child that John Hearn and his wife Emma had lost. Their son John died aged two in 1861. Their first-born child daughter Grace died age six in 1863. Willy sadly died in 1876, aged fifteen.

Sudden death in a house of ill-repute.

Mr. Alfred Southby Crowley, doctor on board H.M.S. Indus, on Monday the 27th of December 1869, after having spent Christmas with his father, left his house in Torquay and travelled to Plymouth by train. He left his luggage at the railway station and proceeded to 6. Summerland Place, a well-known brothel where he was met by previous appointment by a woman of ill-fame. Mr. Crowley remained at the house for quite some time and saying he didn't feel very well he went for a lie-down. Within half an hour of him going to bed he suffered a fit, from which he never recovered. The unfortunate man remained speechless up to the time of his death, which took place at three o'clock the following morning. Dr's Prance and Reynolds were in attendance shortly after he was seized with the fit, but all their efforts were futile.

Cat up a lamppost.

One evening in early March 1871 a policeman walking his beat in Regent Street, Teignmouth noticed one of the gas lamps appeared to be giving a much more brilliant light than any of the other streetlamps in the town. He approached the lamppost to ascertain the cause and to his astonishment around the gas-burner itself, he saw coiled a cat. Some of the fur on one side had been singed, and to avoid being burnt all over the cat had curled herself into a very cramped position. The difficulty now presented itself as to how he could dislodge the cat from her warm but uncomfortably situation. A man happened to be passing who was adept at climbing and he quickly reached the slowly roasting cat. The poor animal wasn't too keen on being disturbed and every time she got to her feet, her fur was singed and began to flare up. After a minute or two's excitement she was released and lowered to the ground. The mystery was as to how and why she got into the lamp in the first place. It was supposed she took refuge in the lamp through the lighting-rod, in consequence of being chased either by dogs or children.

Infanticide.

The following three very sad stories are those of infanticide – the murder of new-born children or those under one year of age. It's a sad fact that mothers have been taking the lives of their newly born offspring for thousands of years. Historically infanticide was used as a form of contraception by our early ancestors in nomadic tribes when civilisations were at war and food supplies scarce. Many cases in the Victorian age were the result of young single women having been seduced who then hid the bodies of their illegitimate child to 'hide their shame.' There was a degree of sympathy with mothers in such a predicament and those charged with infanticide were often found guilty of the lesser offence of 'concealment of birth' or reprieved if convicted. Nineteenth century Britain saw a fascination with infanticide cases. The horrors of child-murder were sensationalised in the press and horrifying cases were often published in local and national newspapers. These three women were all convicted and sent to trial at the Devon Summer Assizes held in Exeter in July 1871.

Concealment of birth at Walkhampton.

Mary Ann Martin had originally been brought before the Roborough Petty Session in April 1871 charged with concealing the birth of her illegitimate daughter at the small village of Walkhampton on Dartmoor. Mary Ann had been working as a domestic servant and living in the house of Mrs. Susan Adams, a widowed farmer at Walkhampton for upwards of seventeen months. She was forced to leave her employment in early March after Mrs. Adams had questioned her as to her condition, something which Mary Ann denied. Mrs. Adams told her she had better go home, and in the meantime her sister Jane Martin took on the role as domestic servant to Mrs. Adams. On the 29th of March Jane went into the cellar of the house to look for a pair of old boots and whilst there she saw a bundle in an old disused tub. She called to Mrs. Adams and together they unwrapped the bundle, only to discover it to contain the decomposing body of a new born child. A constable was sent for and after examining the body and the surroundings, P.C. Grigg proceeded to Huckworthy Bridge, where he found Mary Ann Martin. He took her back to Walkhampton, and showing her the body of the child, charged her with being the mother. She burst into tears but made no reply. P.C Grigg then escorted her to Roborough Police Station. The following day the body of the child was examined by Mr. Richard Willis a surgeon. He found it to be that of a fully developed female child but in such a state of decomposition that he was unable to say whether the child had been born alive or not. He did though believe that the child had been born over a fortnight previously. The following day he made an examination of Mary Ann and found marks of more than one delivery.

At Mary Ann's trial at the Roborough Petty Sessions, Mrs. Adams said that she was aware that Mary Ann had an illegitimate child previous to taking her into her service and that child was now alive. The Bench expressed their regret at seeing the prisoner in such a position. They had paid considerable attention to the case and could only come to one opinion in the matter - that she had violated the law in not making preparations for the birth of the child. She therefore was committed to take her trial at the next Assizes at Exeter, on a charge of concealment of birth. At her trial at the Assizes, Mary Ann Martin was cleared of all charges the jury throwing out the charge of manslaughter against her.

Suspected child murder at Westward Ho!

Infanticide was a very rare occurrence in Westward Ho! But in May 1871, Zena Maynard, a single woman in her late thirties who had been living at a lodging house called 'Rowena' on the road between Westward Ho! and Northam where she was employed as cook, was accused of murdering her new-born child. Her mistress a Mrs. Murray had been suspicious that her cook was 'with child' but these accusations were strongly denied, even right up until the day before Zena gave birth.

Whilst the family were having tea Zena went missing for about an hour, and on her making her re-appearance at around six o'clock, it was noticed that she was looking ashen and haggard. Being asked what pained her she replied; "Oh, nothing in particular." Mrs. Murray herself being several months pregnant at that time and being of the opinion that her cook was shortly about to become a mother, ordered a young lad to drive Zena in a pony and trap to her aunt's house (Miss. Dennis) who resided at 46. Honestone Lane, Bideford. When she left the Murray's residence, Zena took with her a bundle.
After her departure from 'Rowena,' Mrs. Murray went up to Zena's bedroom and looking around she noticed spots of blood. The following morning a closer examination of the bedroom confirmed Mrs. Murray's belief that the cook had been pregnant and had given birth in the room. She made her way to the aunt's house in Bideford and accused Zena of having given birth to a child, something which she was unable to deny. Mrs. Murray then went to Superintendent Vanstone of the Bideford Borough Police, and informed him of what had transpired. He immediately made his way to Honestone Lane and going into one of the rooms he saw Zena sitting on chair near the fireplace, in which there was no fire burning. He charged her with having given birth to a child, which she again freely confessed to and added that she had destroyed part of it by burning it in the stove at 'Rowena.' Superintendent Vanstone then asked her what had become of the other part of the body. She rose from her chair and went to the fireplace, lifted a screen, and took from the chimney a bundle (identical to the one she had brought with her from Westward Ho!) On opening the bundle, the outer part of which consisted of a dirty black rag Superintendent Vanstone was horrified to find part of the body of a new-born male infant - minus its head and right leg. So far as could be judged from the state of the body the missing parts had evidently been severed with a not very sharp instrument. Zena admitted to having cut them off with a knife. The remains were taken to the Police Station by

Vanstone. He also ordered that Zena Maynard be taken from her aunt's house to another in Union Street where she was given into the custody of a female attendant and placed indirectly under the supervision of a police officer. That evening, Superintendent Vanstone went to 'Rowena' and examined Zena's room, but failed to find any trace of the missing portions of the child.

Had not Mrs. Murray's suspicions become aroused, there is a high probability that the whole horrible affair would never being brought to light. Zena Maynard already had two other illegitimate children aged six and thirteen. Up until six or seven months prior to giving birth she had been in service for the Reverend Edward Vincent of North Down Cottage, Bideford, and on him leaving the area she then went on to work as a cook at the 'Globe Hotel' in Torrington. That job only lasted a few weeks and afterwards she spent some time without work before being taken on by Mrs. Murray, whom she had previously worked for in the summer of 1869.

The jury at the Assizes returned a verdict of manslaughter, accompanied by a recommendation to mercy. His Lordship Mr. Justice Brett thought the time had come when judges and juries should harden their hearts against the pity which prompted them to deal lightly with women who had murdered their offspring. He then sentenced Zena Maynard to ten years' penal servitude.

Found in a shoe box under the bed.

Eliza Flaye was a mother of seven and kept a dairy at Sowton. She was put on trial for the 'concealment of birth' of her baby son born on the 31st of May 1871. In the days leading up to her confinement it had become apparent that she was about to have a child, and the clergyman of the parish, no doubt with the best intentions, went to her house and pressed her to admit that she was in the 'family way.' He told her that her character was at stake and there was suggestion that she may lose her dairy. He then told her she would need to submit herself to being examined by a doctor. However, before a doctor's examination could take place, the baby was born. A midwife was sent for and was present within minutes of the birth. She dressed the child and attended to it for a time. She then left, and that night, or the night afterwards, the child was found to be missing; eventually being found in a box under the mother's bed.

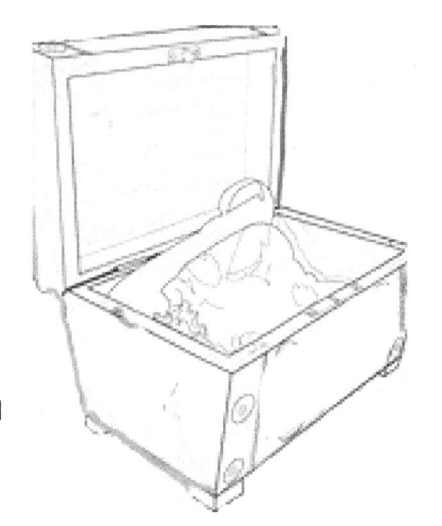

At Woodbury Petty Sessions on the 8th of June, Eliza Flay, described as an elderly widow [she was no more than forty] was charged with the concealment of birth of her male child. Mr. Friend appeared for the prosecution and Mr. Toby for the prisoner. Mr. Friend in opening the case said the prisoner resided in the parish of Sowton and had been a widow for about eighteen months. On Wednesday of the previous week, she had given birth to a male child which had since died. A Coroner's inquest had been held and the jury had returned an open verdict that the child died from suffocation but how or by what means they could not say. It was a fact that just a fortnight before her confinement there were rumours going around about the woman, and they having come to the clergyman's ears he questioned her regarding her being 'in the family way,' something she strongly denied. In consequence, she had not attempted to provide any necessaries for her confinement. He intended to proceed under sections 24 and 25 Vic., Chapter 100, section 50, which said, 'If any woman shall be delivered of a child, every person who shall, by any secret disposition of the dead body of the said child, whether such child died before, at, or after its birth, endeavour to conceal the birth thereof, shall be guilty of a misdemeanour and being convicted thereof shall be liable at the discretion of the court to be imprisoned for any term not exceeding two years with or without hard labour and etc.' Mr. Toby for the defence, said concealment of birth meant concealment from the world. Eliza Fraye had not done that, but as was usual in little country places, they had called in a midwife. He submitted that there was not the slightest evidence of any jury in England convicting her in the case.

The first witness called was Sarah Harris who said she was a servant at Mr. Ashford's of Honiton Clyst. She said she had practised as a midwife for the past five years. On the Wednesday evening Mrs. Flaye's son had come and asked if she would go and see his mother who was very ill. She immediately went and arrived there about twenty minutes later. Mrs. Flaye was by the side of the bed on her knees and said to her; "Oh Mrs. Harris I have been let fall to have a child." Mrs. Harris asked where the child was and was told it was on the bed. Mrs. Flaye also told her she had taken a drop of brandy and had given the child some. Mrs. Harris picked up the baby, which was a very five one; breathing and in good health. She washed and dressed it and heard it cry. Whilst she was carrying out the task of dressing it, Mrs. Flaye told her that the clergyman, Mr. Sanders, had been to see her twice and confronted her about being in the family way, which at the time she had strongly denied. She said that she 'would not have it known for the world' if she could help it. Her mother and sister were coming down the following morning and she should send the child home with them to take care of it. Mrs. Harris said she then heard nothing more of Mrs. Flaye until the following Sunday evening when Mr. Wolland the schoolmaster came to see her and mentioned the rumour that Mrs. Flaye had given birth to a child, but that the doctor had said it was a false report. Mrs. Harris told him it was nothing of the kind because she had washed and dressed the child and that it was sent to Mrs. Flaye's mothers. The following day, P.C. Hurson brought to her the dead body of the infant boy and she recognised it by the clothes it was wearing.

The Rev. Prebendary Henry Sanders, Rector of Sowton, admitted to going to Mrs. Flaye and asking her about being in the family way, which she had strongly denied. Dr. Gibbs who was next to be questioned, said that in consequence of information he had received from Mr. Sanders, he went to see Mrs. Flaye. The result of his examination was that he did not believe she had been confined. After having the first witness's statement read out to him, he withdrew his opinion.

P.C Hurson when questioned by Mr. Friend said that on Monday the 5th of June he went to Honiton Clyst and saw Mrs. Harris. From what she told him he then went to Mrs. Flaye's house. He told her he was a Detective Constable from Exeter and had come to make enquiries about certain rumours that she had given birth to a child. She admitted having given birth and when he asked her where it was, she said that it was 'all right'. He asked whether it was dead or alive and she replied that it was dead. She went upstairs and he followed her. In the bedroom he found the body of a child in a box under the bed. The child was wrapped in a linen sheet. Mrs Flaye said that after Mrs. Harris had left she took some more brandy and went to sleep, and when she awoke the child was dead. He asked if she had told anyone about the child's death and she replied; "No, I don't think I have. No, I haven't." He went back to Exeter and returned a few hours later. He saw Mrs. Flaye sitting in her bedroom and told her he was there to take her into custody on a serious charge, but before he did so he cautioned her that whatever she said in answer to the charge he would be bound to repeat in evidence against her. He then charged her on suspicion of having wilfully caused the death a male child born on the 31st of May. She made no answer for a minute, then said; "I didn't kill it I only gave it some brandy and I should not think that harmed it." P.C. Hurston called for a doctor to examine Eliza to ensure she was in a fit state to be taken into custody. Receiving the affirmative she was taken to Constable Ryall's house at Honiton Clyst.

Mr. Sommer, the doctor who P.C Hurston called to examine Eliza on the 5th of June said that after attending to her he found the body of the dead child. The following day he carried out a post mortem examination on it alongside Mr. Edye of Exeter. This he described in detail to the court. He considered the cause of death was congestion of the lungs and heart and the state of the blood vessels generally which had brought on suffocation. In reply to Mr. Toby, he said if the mother had overlaid the child in her sleep then that would account for the appearance of the child. If the child had been too closely wrapped up in the bedclothes or if the child had changed its position in the bed and got its head downwards, this would also have produced the same effect. The jury after short deliberation returned with a verdict 'that the child was suffocated, but how or by what means there was no evidence to show.' This concluded the enquiry which lasted about five and a-half hours. The Bench decided to send Eliza to take her trial at the next Devon Assizes. Bail was accepted.

At the Devon Assizes in July, the Judge said, as had Mr. Toby, that as a midwife had attended to the child; the very best person who could be present at a birth, and that this fact had been made public, there was no 'concealment of birth.' The mere secreting of a child's body, if not for the purpose of concealing its birth, was not an offence within the Act of Parliament. The case was at this point thrown out.

Manslaughter in King Street.

Emma Creed aged twenty-five, was also on trial at the July sitting of the Devon Assizes. She had been indicted for the manslaughter of James Reblin* in King Street, Plymouth, on the 3rd of July that year.

Emma, a woman of 'ill fame' was drinking in a beer house in King Street when Reblin who was fifty-five, came in. Another woman who was also in the house asked him to buy her some ale, which he refused. Emma swore at him for his refusal and he replied calling her a bad name. In response she slapped him across the face. Reblin then left the beer house and Emma decided to follow. Grabbing hold of him she struck him several times, knocking him down and striking him again as he lay helpless on the ground. James Lay a baker, witnessed the assault from his shop window and saw Emma Creed grab hold of James Reblin by the smock frock he was wearing and begin to beat him about the neck and face with clenched fists. When he saw the man unable to get to his feet, he went to help. Reblin complained of his leg hurting and James Lay on examination found it to be broken. He called for assistance and had Reblin conveyed to the South Devon and East Cornwall Hospital.

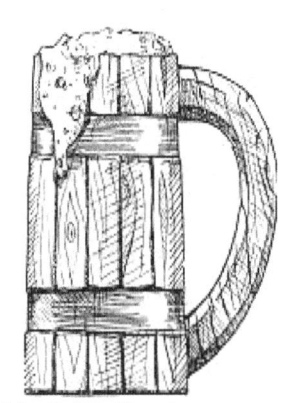

Mr. S. Wolferstan, a surgeon at the hospital, said that he found Mr. Reblin to have suffered a compound fracture of the left leg and that he passed away the day following the attack. When carrying out a postmortem he found that the deceased had advanced diseases of the heart, lungs, liver, kidneys, and brain. It was the disease of the heart that was the cause of death, which in turn had been accelerated by the injury to his leg.

P.C. Lamerton who also witnessed the attack was advised by the Judge to in future run and try to prevent such occurrences in preference to walking towards it to take the delinquent into custody. The jury found Emma Creed not guilty and in discharging her the Judge said that if she had been taken before the Magistrates for assaulting the man, she would no doubt have been sent to prison. Notwithstanding the great respect he had for the opinion of the medical man, he did not think the jury could say the woman was guilty of manslaughter. The deceased was a man who ought not to have died when he did but lost his life through his own intemperate habits.

* In various newspapers, the journalists appear to have had trouble over the exact name of the victim, and having searched the deaths for that year, the above-named gentleman who was only correctly named in one newspaper article. Most newspapers named him Joseph and his surname variations included Rebbin/Rebelin/Roblin/ Rebbens/Roblin/Rubleim/Rublum.

The lost cow.

On Friday the 7th November 1871 a spotty cow, giving milk from three teats and with a halfpenny in each ear as a mark, was reported missing near Modbury. A reward was offered for her recovery and anyone with information as to her whereabouts was asked to contact Mr. N.P. Oldrieve of 'Southwood House' near Dartmouth, or Charles Ferris of 'Dunstone,' Yealampton.

The mysterious death of Elizabeth Brown.

The body of young woman almost naked and whose clothes were discovered neatly piled up on a rock was found floating in the water beneath the Citadel at Plymouth on Wednesday the 8th of July 1874. Inquiries were at once made and it was discovered that the deceased was Elizabeth Jane Brown the daughter of parents occupying a respectable position in life and living near Truro. Elizabeth had left home and led what the newspapers described a 'bad life' and had been residing at a property in Lower Lane, Plymouth, but had recently moved to Fore Street in Stonehouse. The house in which she was living was next door to that in which a woman called Bridget Welch* had been murdered the previous Monday.

Elizabeth was said to have attended the Sutton Harbour Regatta on the Tuesday the day before her body was found. At around half eight in the evening she had left a female companion and gone off with a man who was described as having the appearance of a navvy. She was not seen again until her body was found floating in the water the following day. Was it suicide, murder or mishap? Her death remained unsolved.

* The shocking murder of Bridget Welch is covered in my book 'Dark Tales of Victorian Plymouth.'

A Christmas Ghost.

On the morning of the 21st of December 1876 whilst the choir was engaged in practising for the Christmas services at the village of Kingston in South Devon a door suddenly opened, and through the dimly light church, a figure draped in white slowly made its way down the aisle and mounted the pulpit. On being challenged the alleged apparition slowly retraced its steps and vanished through the same door from which it had entered. The terrified choir fled in dismay. Some said they thought they recognised the features of the ghost of those of a deceased popular former minister of the church. The following day at least one member of the choir required medical assistance.

The White Witch of North Devon.

Considerable excitement was manifested in South Molton in October 1877 in consequence of eighty-six-year-old John Harper, a White Witch from West Down near Barnstaple, being put on trial, charged with using certain subtle craft, means or devices, by palmistry and otherwise to deceive and impose on people. Harper had for quite some time made a significant business as a herbalist and quack doctor. He was commonly known as the 'White Witch of North Devon.' When visiting patients, he usually took with him a number of rods made of wood or metal with small pieces of parchment attached on which were inscribed the names of the planets in the solar system. These rods were supposed to have some mysterious instrumentation.

For some time previously a woman called Elizabeth Saunders, living at Bishop's Nympton had been very ill and doctor's being of no help, her husband had sent for the 'White Witch'. When Harper arrived at the house, he felt Elizabeth's pulse and said he didn't know if he could do her any good as he was only a humble instrument in the hands of God. He gave her four or five iron rods to hold which he asked her to tap in succession on a piece of manganese. On the end of each rod was the name of a planet. He asked her age and the hour she was born so he could work out under which planet she was born and then spoke some words in a low voice. For this service he charged twenty-five shillings and was amply provided for by his host, staying at the house for five hours and whilst there drank rum and ate biscuits. Before he left, he gave Elizabeth some bitters to take and told her husband that although his wife was very weak there was no reason why she shouldn't recover. Sadly, Elizabeth died a few days later. The post-mortem confirming her death was caused by fatty degeneration of the heart and bronchitis. The defence stated that the rods were struck by the patient on a piece of manganese and this produced an electric shock. It was further said that the different planets actually did exercise a powerful influence over the human body and the electric currents permeated through the body. Some people who had been healed by Harper's work were called to give evidence. They spoke as to the cures effected by him, in some cases after medical men had given up all hope of a recovery. Harper told the court that he told the man and his wife when he entered the house that he was simply a humble instrument in the hands of God, and he was not sure he could do anything. He denied that he said that there must be three persons of the same faith in the room before he could do any good.

The Magistrates sentenced John Harper to one month's imprisonment, but owing to his age they did not impose hard labour. The sentence was then quashed.

The murderous baby farmer.

Annie Tooke, a forty-five-year-old widow and mother of five, was executed within the Devon County Gaol at Exeter on the 11th of August 1879 for the murder of Reginald Hyde a child of just six months old. Little Reginald had been placed into her care by his mother, a young woman named Hoskins, the daughter of a person of independent means living in Cornwall. Miss. Hoskins had left her family home the previous summer under the pretence that her health requiring a change of air; the real fact was that she had been seduced and was now pregnant. She left Cornwall so that she could give birth to the child somewhere that she was not known and so as not to bring shame upon her family. The only people who knew of her condition were her brother and sister. She made her way to Exeter and took lodgings in the suburb of Ide taking on the name of Mrs. Hyde. The child was born in October and a month later her brother arranged with Mrs. Tooke that she should undertake the charge of the child. The mother and sister then took the infant to Mrs. Tooke's house in Exeter. A lump sum of twelve pounds was paid with the promise of a further payment of twelve pounds to be paid in one years' time. Mrs. Tooke however, was given neither the name of the child or its parents.

A few months having elapsed Mrs. Tooke wrote to her daughter complaining of the great burden of looking after the child; she also mentioned that it had an enormous appetite and spoke of in very derisive terms of it. Soon afterwards she started telling people that the child had been taken from her by a stranger who had said that she had been sent by the mother to collect the child. A few days later the headless torso and mutilated bits of a baby's body were found in the mill-leat followed soon after by the head being found lower down the stream. Mrs. Tooke at first denied that the murdered child was the one she had nursed, but later admitted that it was the same child, although she stuck to her story of the child having been taken from her by a stranger. The mother was then discovered and apprehended as being an accessory to the murder, and Mrs. Tooke gave evidence against her. Miss. Hoskins however was cleared of any crime and Mrs. Tooke was then solely accused of the child's murder. Whilst being held in police cells, she finally acknowledged that she had smothered the child with a pillow and a few days afterwards dismembered his body with a hatchet and a knife before taking the remains to the mill-leat. Later, before the Magistrate's Court, she denied ever having made such a confession, but finding her guilty and telling her that she was to stand trial, she acknowledged that she had made the confession and that it was a true one.

During her trial Annie Tooke maintained an almost unmoved demeanour, and when sentenced to death, she directed that no visitors were to be admitted to see her except her children and one female friend who had taken on the care of her youngest child. Her execution was carried out a little before eight o'clock on the morning of August the 11th. The black flag was hoisted over the entrance to the gaol before the prison clock commenced to strike the hour. Annie Tooke left a written statement. In it she acknowledged her guilt.

Sensational arrest at a boarding house.

On Sunday the 25th of January 1880 two men were arrested at Plymouth in connection with the murder of Sarah Jane Roberts, a domestic servant living at the home of Mr. Greenwood in Westbourne Grove, Harpurhey near Manchester, which had taken place on the 7th of the month. Two men answering to their description, were seen loitering in the neighbourhood of the house where the murder had been committed. The whole nation was gripped with the dramatic reports of how poor Sarah, aged eighteen, had been brutally murdered.

Mr. Greenwood had received a letter which had been put through his door requesting to meet the writer at a certain hour in the evening at a public house in order to arrange for the purchase of some land of which he was the owner. He arrived at the public house named in the letter but found no one there to meet him. He returned home to find that a shocking tragedy had occurred in his absence. His wife who was in poor health had been in her bedroom when soon after her husbands' departure she heard a knock at the front door and then on it being answered she heard someone going into the kitchen. The door was then closed and Mrs. Greenwood thinking that some acquaintance or neighbour had come to see the servant, thought nothing more of the matter. A few moments later she heard a terrible scream coming from the kitchen. She made her way to the top of the stairs and called out "Jane?" but getting no answer she came down the stairs yelling "murder!" assuming the servant was in a fit or that her clothes were on fire. A neighbour, Mrs. Cadman heard Mrs. Greenwood's cries and went into the house to see what was the matter. Entering the kitchen, she was horrified to see poor Jane lying on the floor. She was bleeding from two wounds to her head, one over the right eye and another on the back of the head. One theory was that she had been murdered by a person with whom she had formed an acquaintance and for whatever reason wanted her to stay silent – possibly a sweetheart, a married man? Another was that the letter sent to Mr. Greenwood was merely intended to lure him away from his home and that the writer or his accomplices intended to rob the house in his absence.

The Leeds Mercury on Monday the 26th of January 1880 detailed a seemingly important breakthrough had been made - "Our Plymouth correspondent telegraphing last evening, states that the local police assisted by two Manchester policemen, yesterday arrested two men, one of whom is named Robert Haild alias Thomas Wait, and has been charged with the murder of the servant girl Sarah Jane Roberts at Harpurhey, Manchester. Wait who is a coal dealer in a small way of business in Manchester had tramped to Plymouth in order to emigrate. Several days ago, the Plymouth Police received a communication from Manchester Police giving a description of a man who was supposed to be about to emigrate from Plymouth for Australia and who was wanted for perjury. It appears that the warrant held by the Police charged the man with perjury which consisted in having given his name in the emigration papers as Robert Haild, whereas his real name was ascertained to be Thomas Wait."

Thomas Wait using the alias Robert Haild, and a companion named John 'Jack' Laycock, had made their way to Plymouth in hope of getting passage to Melbourne on an emigrant's ship. Unfortunately, the vessel they were hoping to board had left two days prior to their arrival in the town. They decided to take up residence in a lodging house until the next passage became available. Haild as stated in the newspaper article had indeed given the false name of Wait in his declaration to the Emigration Commissioners as he was unable to afford his passage to Australia having been there previously, he had used a false name in hope of being given free or assisted passage.

Officers from Manchester Police arrived at a lodging house run by Mrs. Sprauge near to Millbay Dock and made their arrest. When taken to the Police Station and the warrant read out to him, Haild said that he supposed they wanted him for the murder and that it was all 'a mare's nest' and he'd never heard anything about it until he read about it in the papers the previous evening. The lodging-house keeper Mrs Sprague at whose house the men were found, a few days later gave a reporter for the 'Western Morning News' a detailed account of the men's stay with her. She expressed a willingness to tell the truth on oath if necessary, although was anxious to avoid being brought forward as a witness. She said; "The two men arrived here on Sunday last week. They looked like very poor but respectable sort of men saying they were emigrants and very tired. I let them have a room which they occupied until Mr. Stone and the other gents [the detectives] came and took them away. There was a third man besides these two, he slept here on the Saturday night and said he was going to stay too. He had his breakfast here on the Monday morning and then slipped off without anybody knowing; never even said a word to me that he was going." She said that the men had appeared seemingly hard up as they hardly ever went out. They went to bed very early and got up late. She also remarked that they were very pleasant and when her clock stopped working, they put it right. She went on to say that sometimes the little one [Haild] got excited and damned the steamers and about them not being able to go away. The men had told everyone that they were from Liverpool and had walked all the way to Plymouth. They also told her that they didn't go by their own name. After the police had come to the house and arrested Haild, Laycock told her that they hadn't really come from Liverpool but from Harpurhey and that Haild was much upset at having missed the ship to Australia which had sailed a day or two before they had reached Plymouth. She said that Laycock had told her that they had left suddenly in the middle of the night and both of them had expressed a wish to sail on the next steamship which was due to leave in the early part of February. Asked about any washing she had done for the men Mrs. Sprague said that she had noticed a sour and disagreeable smell in the men's bedroom and there was a bundle from which the smell appeared to be coming from. She said she had told the men that if they had any dirty or wet clothing in the room then to kindly put it outside to dry. The smaller man had brought down some shirts, cuffs, and other items for her to wash. She said that they looked like they had been dragged through muddy water; they were dirty and damp. The shirt sleeves had heavy stains underneath which she had to scrub for a long time get out. Regarding the arrest Mrs. Sprauge said that when the police arrived, both men were in bed. "They took the little man [Haild] and when they brought him down, he stood by the table and I thought he would drop; he could hardly stand. Holding on to the table he gasped for breath when he asked what he was charged with, it was as much as he could do to dress himself. After the police had taken him off the tall dark man came down. He was nearly as bad as the other. In a big powerful fellow like him I never saw such a change - white as a sheet and trembling most violently. "Ah! Missus" he said, "Missus, damn me; I knowed what the police wanted as soon as they came in." Mrs. Sprague said she urged him not to get so excited, saying it was only for giving a wrong name his mate was wanted. "Damn me, missus," he replied, "No, t'aint that I know what they wanted him for, 'tis that Manchester murder."

"Murder!" Mrs Sprague said surprised. "Do you say he's mixed up with a murder?"

"That's what he's took for, it's the murder," Laycock repeated.

"What murder was it?" she asked. Laycock who appeared to be in a frenzied state said "T'was a servant lass that was murdered in her master's kitchen at Harpurhey. He started off an hour after the murder was done. I knows that be what they wanted him for. It's a sorry day for me that I ever saw him. Tom come to me an hour after that murder was done and he said; "Jack, come out of this. The farther away we can get away the better for us, and we started off there and then. I had eighteen shillings and six pence in my pocket. He never wished nobody good-bye. We walked all night." He then told Mrs. Sprague that he thought the police would be back soon to arrest him. He asked her if he should give them the slip, but she advised him that that would only show guilt and recommended that if he hadn't done anything wrong, then to stay where he was. Laycock told her that his companion had sold a horse and trap for six pounds the day before the murder but had left the money with his wife. He said that he had heard Detective Stone remark that the men could not have walked from Manchester in the time they said it had taken them. Laycock admitted to Mrs. Sprague that they had ridden part of the way. Laycock continued to declare that the police would come for him which they eventually did and he and Haild were escorted back to Manchester by train to stand trial.

The murder made headlines across the country and two hundred pounds was offered as a reward for the capture of the killer. This offer was then raised to three hundred. Thousands of people travelled to visit the scene of the murder and the poor girls' grave. Newspapers were full of stories about Haild and how he was the main suspect in the case. He was in fact never charged with the murder and also cleared of the charge of trying to gain assisted passage to Australia using a false name. Acquitted of all charges he was allowed to leave the court a free man.

In January 1882 Edward Lynch, a private of the 4th King's Own Regiment stationed at Colaba in India, was charged with the murder of Sarah Jane Roberts. Private Lynch told Sergeant Edward Jarvis, Corporal John Jones and two or three others that he had murdered her and desired to give himself up to the authorities. He didn't explain the motive for his crime but declared that its recollection burdened his conscience and troubled his sleep. His confession was later dismissed as it was made when drunk and he gave the wrong date for when the crime was supposedly committed. Several other individuals also came forward confessing to the crime including a licensed pedlar from London and a labourer from Stockport. Ten years later, thirty-one-year-old John Williams was arrested in Chicago, Illinois, after admitting he was the actual killer. He had been living with his parents in Harpurhey at the time of the murder - his confession turned out to be merely a ploy to gain free passage home. The murder of Sarah Jane Roberts remains an unsolved mystery to this day.

A great snow storm befell the South-West in January 1881. On the high ground at isolated Princetown the storm was felt in all its severity. At the prison farm twelve sheep were dug out dead from the snow drifts and another seven were missing. Mr. Skinner the contractor who supplied all the meat to the prison set off along the road from Tavistock but was foiled in his endeavours and the prisoners in consequence had pea-soup and salted pork for dinner. The establishment due to its isolated location always had a reserve of stores in case of such emergencies. The inhabitants of the village for safety travelled for food in organized parties.

The county authorities commenced cutting through the road to Princetown on Thursday the 20th of January, starting from Merrivale bridge at Yelverton. Inmates from the prison began cutting in from the opposite direction. Mr. Davy the highway surveyor said that his men had encountered drifts from around ten to twelve feet deep, and for more than a mile they had to cut through four feet of snow. Two days later on the Saturday a gang forty-five men proceeded from Tavistock to make another attempt to open the road towards Princetown in order to relieve the convicts of the arduous task. Unfortunately, when they arrived, they found that the gale which had hit the area the previous evening had completely undone the work of the preceding day. After nine hours of hard and laborious work they succeeded in clearing the road to Merrivale bridge, and a very strong body convicts were seen at work the other side.

Mr. Skinner the supplier of provisions for the prison again set off from Tavistock with a supply of meat; the first that has been taken out for many days. He set off in a waggon drawn by three horses. With great difficulty he made some headway but found it impossible to proceed any further than the Tavistock side of Merrivale bridge. The convicts who had not by that time cut through the road on their side sufficiently wide enough to enable them to bring down their carts carried the provisions up the hill to a point where carts could be brought to. There was also a great fear that the occupants of the many isolated houses on Dartmoor which were completely snowed under may have run short of provisions.

In South Devon at Modbury, the town was in such state of destitution that gangs were sent out to cut a passage through the snow to Ivybridge so as get coals for the poor not a hundredweight of which was left in the town; the coal dealers not being prepared for such a blockade. Business was at a standstill and several of the shops were forced to close. A soup-kitchen was opened up for those who had ran out of food supplies. At Plymouth there was a water famine and the Mayor ordered pumps to be sunk in places where wells were known to exist. At Exeter the river Exe was frozen, the ice being six inches thick. On Sunday the 23rd of January four thousand people skated upon it.

A party of visitors snowed up in Kingsbridge since Tuesday the 18th, tried to get away on the Saturday morning on horseback. They were however compelled to return with the mail-bearers who had left three hours previously and were also unable to proceed any further. In the afternoon the party again left after a body of thirty labourers having preceded them had cut a path about two feet wide in which they were able to ride along, enabling them to reach Totnes.

The Earl of Devon and Lord Courtenay were at Salcombe unable to move. At Torquay a great many of the large villas were entirely without water and to these a daily supply was carried by the watercarts of the Local Board. Nevertheless, the strictest economy has to be observed and some of the Torquay bakers were struggling to obtaining sufficient quantities of water to enable them to properly carry out their business. In Newton Abbot men were being paid between three and six pence a time to bring pails of water to houses on the hills.

Don't drink and drive.

An inquest was held on Saturday the 24th of September 1881 into the death of John Baker a fifty-eight-year-old drayman employed by Messrs. Norman and Pring, Brewers of Exeter. The first witness called was a labourer named John Dinham living at Tedburn St. Mary, who said that he had last seen John Baker at the 'Traveller's Rest Inn' Whitestone on the Thursday evening at about nine p.m. Baker had stopped there with the waggon he was driving and in the company of another drayman he partook in two three-pennyworths of gin. He said that whilst Baker was under the influence of drink when he arrived at the Inn, he wasn't drunk.
Thomas Pyle a fellow drayman said that he had known John Baker for a considerable time and that he was of temperate habits. He had seen him in the 'Red Lion Inn' on the Thursday evening. He and Baker were both on their usual country round. He saw Baker drink a pint of beer at the inn before leaving. He appeared slightly intoxicated but was still able to control his horses. Both he and Baker then travelled separately to the 'Traveller's Rest Inn' at Whitestone as the previous witness had said there, he saw Baker again drinking. This time he supped two three-pennyworths of gin saying that he felt rather cold. They both then left the inn and went off in different directions on their respective waggons.
David Thomas, the toll-collector at the Dunsford Gate at the end Cowick Street, St. Thomas, said that at about quarter past ten Thomas Pyle passed through the gate and then half an hour later John Baker's waggon drove down the hill towards him. The gate was open and not knowing who was in charge of the vehicle he shouted out but receiving no answer he stopped the horses. There was a lamp nearby and he was able to see a leg hanging over the front of the waggon. Thinking that the driver was asleep he poked him with an iron rod, not being tall enough to

reach him with his hands. There was no response. He then shouted out to the driver again but still there was no response. Several men had now gathered around the waggon and a doctor and policeman were sent for.

Richard Burnett, living at 101, Cowick Street, said that his attention was caught by the noise made by David Thomas calling out to the waggon driver. He went out into the roadway and saw the man lying in the waggon and so he clambered up to see what was the matter. He put his hand upon the face of the man and found him to have been foaming at the mouth. He dragged the man from the waggon and laid him on the pavement. Restoratives were applied but even though his body still felt quite warm he was dead. A doctor was immediately sent for and the body removed to the nearby 'Falmouth Inn.' On searching the body four half-sovereign's, one half-crown and a few pence in coppers were found. It was later ascertained that that was about the sum expected from him by his employers.

Dunsford gate, unknown artist.

Mr. R. Andrew a surgeon of St. Thomas, stated that at ten thirty p.m. on the Thursday evening he was requested to go to the Dunsford Gate near to which the deceased was lying. He found the man's life to be extinct and later on an examination of the body he found no marks of violence. In his opinion the deceased died from a coma accelerated by drink. After a few comments from the Coroner the jury returned a verdict of 'found dead.'

A warning to housemaids in want of husbands.

The following tale was published in December 1881 with a warning for housemaids to take heed. Miss. Ellen Holley, a twenty-year-old housemaid appealed to the Magistrate at Marlborough Street, Devonport after having made the casual acquaintance of a gentleman calling himself Mr. Henry Cook, a well-dressed man wearing a heavy moustache and with hair beginning to turn grey. The friendship quickly progressed and Henry proposed marriage and was readily accepted. The next proposal of Mr. Cook was for a loan of forty-five pounds. Poor Ellen never saw the money again, or her watch which she had also entrusted to Mr. Cook's keeping.

*Two years later, on accepting another marriage proposal, Ellen Holley married Charles William Cross in Plymouth and they went on to have a happy marriage and two children together.

The mysterious injuries of a South Brent man.

After an evening's dining in Totnes, a gentleman having missed the last train in May 1882 decided to walk to his home in South Brent. With his stout stick he set off in the darkness.... the following morning when daylight broke, he made his way to a farm just outside of the town. He was in a semi-conscious state and his clothes were covered with blood. His eyes were blackened, and he had various other wounds. He was conveyed home and attended to by Dr. Handle of Ivybridge. His condition was so serious that the doctor thought it likely he would lose his sight. Strangely the gentleman could give no explanation as to how the injuries had occurred other than to say he fell into a quarry. The police made inquiries but no new information came

to light. The quarry he alluded to was searched but its structure did not corroborate with the man's explanation. The fact that none of his bones were broken and that he had no bruises on his body was enough to discredit his story. His hat and stout stick were both missing too even though a thorough search had been made. His injuries remained a mystery – what was the gentleman hiding?

A week later the mystery was solved when his missing hat and stick were found by a gentleman named Thomas Hodge who lived at Rattery. He found the items on the top of a railway cutting at Ashbridge, a few miles from Totnes and nearly midway between there and South Brent. The cutting had a sheer descent of upwards of forty feet and marks were still visible that looked as though someone had fallen down it.

Bewitching of a Brixham boat.

A case which caused considerable amusement came before Mr. H. Studdy and Mr. N. Baker, Esq, at the County Magistrates who sat at the Churston Petty Sessions on the 13th of December 1882. John Thomas Wotton a smack owner of Brixham, was summoned by Harry Hurrell his apprentice for non-payment of three pounds in wages alleged to be due, and also for three pounds in damages for non-payment of the same. Mr. C. F. Nelson of Dartmouth appeared for the complainant and Mr. Grove of Brixham, for the defendant. It was said that in July of that year Harry Hurrell was suddenly taken ill while at sea his eyesight becoming affected and suffering such intense pain that the Captain was obliged to take the boat back to Brixham. Hurrell was seen by a doctor who said that he was unfit to continue going to sea and that unless he was attended to promptly, he would lose his eyesight. Hurrell told his master what the doctor had said and Thomas Wotton recommended that he should visit a 'white witch' called Edwin Burley, who lived at 20. Gibbon Street, Plymouth.

Acting on his master's advice, Hurrell went to Plymouth and saw the white witch who informed him that he could do nothing for him as it was not he [Hurrell] that was bewitched but the vessel. The witch also said he wanted to interview the boat's Captain. Hurrell then returned to Brixham and told his master of what the witch had said. Both Hurrell and the Captain went to Plymouth and a second visit was paid to the witch. At this point Captain Wotton advised Hurrell to go to the Plymouth Eye Infirmary which he did and had been under their treatment ever since. His claim for unpaid wages was he explained at the rate of ten shillings per week during the period of his illness. Mr. Nelson submitting that wages were due to an apprentice although incapacitated by illness. Mr. Grove opposed the defence and said that no wages were due and that while in Plymouth the complainant performed other work which exonerated his master from paying him anything. The Bench however awarded Hurrell the full amount claimed; three pounds for wages and three pounds for doctor's fees, railway journeys and solicitors' fees. The Bench also recommended that his apprentice indenture should be cancelled to which Mr. Nelson consented.

The murder of P.C. Creech.

In the little village of Georgeham about nine miles northwest of Barnstaple, on Saturday the 29th of July 1883, P C. Walter Creech of the Devon Constabulary was murdered by an elderly gentleman named George Geen who was known to the police as a drinking man. He had on more than one occasion been convicted of drunkenness and while in that state had exhibited behaviours of a most eccentric kind, almost amounting to madness. For the last two years however, he had been tee-total though sadly he had recently began drinking again. That evening at about seven o'clock, Geen was in the 'King's Arms Inn' a public house near to the village church. He was not drunk but he had taken sufficient ale to excite him to the extent where he was making a lot of noise. P.C. Creech hearing the hullabaloo, went to the door of the inn and politely asked him to keep the racket down as he could be heard across the village. George Geen's response was to invite the officer to join him in a drink. Creech replied; "Not from the likes of you." Which annoyed Geen, and he retorted with a volley of abuse. P.C. Creech then left the scene.

Mr. Bale of Barnstaple, who was also drinking at the inn, succeeded in quieting the old man down and encouraged him to go home. When they got outside, Geen seeing P.C Creec, again spoke to him in an argumentative way. Mr. Bale knowing that the old man was fond of beekeeping enticed him away by saying he wanted to speak to him about some bees. On the way to his cottage, Geen remarked to Mr. Bale that he had a knife at home and that he should kill the b_____, meaning P.C Creech. Mr. Bale, not taking the threat in earnest casually remarked "Don't kill him, let him live another Sunday." The old man then became very irritated and continued ranting and swearing. Arriving at his cottage, Mr. Bale persuaded Geen to go inside and get to bed. He then returned to the village and went to friend's house for a cup of tea. A short time later a young boy ran in and said that George Geen had stabbed the policeman. Mr. Bale immediately rushed out and discovered that Geen had indeed stabbed P.C. Creech, using an old butcher's knife. There were several people about, but nobody seemed to have been able to stop the assault. George Geen had approached the constable with the knife hidden in his pocket and as soon as the officer turned to face him, he drew out the knife and stabbed him. He then walked up and down the road with the knife in his hand shouting that there were two more people he was going to kill.

Apparently when Geen had inflicted the wound to P.C. Creech, stabbing him in the left-hand side of his body, Creech had retaliated by felling Geen to the ground, but he suddenly lost his strength and Mr. Bale with the aid of another gentleman assisted him to his house. Walter Creech sat upon a chair and began vomiting. Becoming worse he was helped upstairs and put to bed. His tunic was taken off and it was seen that there was a clean cut in his side about inch long, just under his ribcage. On the arrival of Dr. Lane of Braunton, an examination of the wound was made. He then informed Mary, the wife of Constable Creech, that he did not believe her husband could recover. Walter Creech lingered through the night until six o'clock on Sunday morning when he died.

Sergeant Rich of Braunton, along with a constable arrived soon after the stabbing had taken place with the intent of apprehending George Geen. They were accompanied by Mr. Bale, who found Geen sitting behind his garden wall brandishing the knife in his hand and threatening to kill any who came near him. Mr. Bale rushed forward, leant over the wall and laid firmly hold of Geen by the collar of his coat with both hands. Geen's hand was then extended with the knife in it. Mr. Bale then pulled him over the wall onto his chest from where the police took hold and secured him and the knife. The knife was said to have been very worn with a fine point and had the appearance of having been recently put across a stone for the purpose of sharpening it. George Geen was taken to Braunton Police Station and locked up.

Walter Creech was thirty years old; he had been a police officer for the past five years and left behind a wife and one child. He had a brother who was also at that time a serving officer with Devon Constabulary. Geen lived with his sister, who was also known to be very eccentric. No reason was given for the brutal attack, other than Geen had an abhorrence of policemen generally. He was charged with the murder soon after the Walter Creech passed away. Geen aged sixty-nine, passed away in prison on the 8th of November 1883, the day he was to stand trial for the murder of Walter Creech.

The questionable death of Laura Dimes.

Hugh Shortland of Modbury, who had recently returned to England from New Zealand, where he had practised as a barrister, was apprehended in the town in May 1884 charged with having murdered his wife. Hugh Shortland and Miss. Laura Dimes, daughter of a gentleman living at Oldstone House at Blackawton near Totnes, had married a month previously at the Registrar's Office in Kingsbridge, on the 8th of April. Two days later Hugh Shortland bade his wife and her parents farewell saying he was going New Zealand and would return soon. On Monday the 28th Mrs. Shortland who was still residing with her parents at Oldstone House went out for a ride, leaving the house at ten o'clock in the morning and returning soon after noon. She then changed from her riding habit into a walking dress and went out again accompanied by her favourite collie dog who she was fond of taking to a nearby pond for a bathe. She was never again seen alive by any member of the household. The following morning Mrs. Elizabeth Lucraft, wife of Mr. Dime's hind, went in search of the missing woman. She had suspicions that Laura might have accidentally fallen into the pond and going there she was horrified to find the body of the unfortunate woman standing upright in the water about three feet from the edge; her hands held up in front of her and the water covering her hat by an inch or two. Mrs. Lucraft at once called to her husband and a man named Langworthy, who helped to take the body out of the water. Laura's body was examined by Police Sergeant Mills of Blackawton and also by Mr. R. W. Soper a surgeon of Dartmouth. Both men agreed that the deceased's clothing showed no indications of a struggle having taken place. A close scrutiny of the path around the wall of the pond also failed to detect any traces of a struggle. The only marks of violence on her body were slight scratches on the left temple and on the right tip of her nose and these the surgeon thought might have been caused by contact with the wall of the pond. His theory was that she might have fainted when near the edge of the pond and fallen in. He could not say positively that death had been caused by drowning as the body had been so long in the water but by appearances it was consistent with the theory that Laura Shortland was still alive at the time of immersion. An inquest was held and a verdict of 'found drowned' was returned.

The same morning a letter addressed to the newly wed Mrs. Shortland was received at Oldstone House purporting to come from her husband in Brindisi, Italy. In the letter he said, "I am hurrying on at the fastest rate and shall soon be home again." The envelope bore a Plymouth postmark, but this was explained by Mr. Shortland who said he was enclosing the letter with some other documents to his solicitors in Plymouth and had asked those gentlemen to post it on to Oldstone. It later transpired that that this was simply a ruse and that Mr. Shortland has not left England at all but had all the time been within a few miles of his wife's home, and his apprehension together with a man named William Ryder; also known as 'Modbury Bill,' who was suspected of being associated with him in the crime, caused considerable excitement throughout the whole district.

At Kingsbridge Magistrates Court on Wednesday the 7th of May 1884, Mr. Hugh Shortland was charged with the wilful murder his wife Laura Dimes. The Superintendent of Police said that when the inquest into her death had been held two letters were produced one in the prisoner's handwriting stating that he was then at Brindisi on his way to Australia and that his wife might next expect to hear from him from Sydney where his father Dr. Shortland was in practice. The officer stated that he went that morning to the cottage of a labourer in Modbury named Ryder and there found Mr. Shortland. The officer stated at that the inquest it was proved that the deceased was found dead in an ornamental pond attached to her father's garden. During the hearing it also emerged that Shortland had visited his wife at her parents' house after their marriage but had never cohabited with her. He had been staying with William Ryder in Modbury since the 10th of April. It was said to be common knowledge that whenever Hugh Shortland visited Modbury rather than stay in one of the respectable hotels there, he would lodge with William Ryder who lived in a back street near to a tannery. He was seen however going through some fields early in the morning of the day his wife's body was found. It was also said that the letter supposedly sent from Brindisi had been written in Ryder's house and that William Ryder had sent his son to Plymouth to post it. Ryder, whom Shortland sometimes called his clerk and sometimes his solicitor, had been driven handcuffed from Modbury to Kingsbridge in the custody of the police. He was then brought before Mr. Herbert the Magistrate and charged with being an accessory both before and after the murder of Mrs. Shortland. Constable Dunford stated that on May the 4th he had interviewed Ryder at his house in Modbury where it was later found that Shortland had been hiding. Ryder told him that Shortland had gone to New Zealand via Brindisi and that he had received a letter from him addressed from the latter place. He further stated that the postmarks on the envelopes were Brindisi, London and Plymouth. The constable also said that after the inquest into Mrs. Shortland's death he had shown a report from a newspaper to Ryder who said he knew all about it and appeared rather distressed. When asked, Ryder said he had no questions to ask the policeman; but he then commenced to make a statement where he admitted that he had told the officer a lie when saying that there was a Brindisi postmark on the letter. The Magistrate's clerk (Mr. Square) advised him not to say any more and hold his tongue.

Police Superintendent Dore applied for a remand, but the Magistrates decided that although Ryder had placed himself in a questionable position with regards to the letter there was not sufficient evidence to justify remanding him. The decision was received with loud applause and the prisoner was discharged.

On the 1st of June 1884 before the Kingsbridge Magistrates, Hugh Shortland was again brought before the court charged with the murder of his wife. The Solicitor to the Treasury stated that after an exhaustive analysis they were of the opinion that there was no evidence and therefore he would withdraw from the case. The Bench said they had no knowledge of any letters and therefore could give no information. Hugh Shortland was a free man. In September that year he sailed to a new life in New Zealand.

A follow-on strange tale...This is an abridged version of an article that appeared in the Totnes Weekly Times in November 1891.

In the spring of 1884, I met Hugh Rutherford Shortland for the first time. He had suddenly made his appearance in the neighbourhood of Modbury, when he created much discussion about schemes he was supposed to be promoting no less than by his eccentric manner which led me to doubt his sanity. It was in connection with these plans and projects that I came in contact with Shortland. He was anxious to secure the support of the press, but it was very difficult to take his proposals seriously. He wanted to form one company to run a tram line from Plymouth to Modbury, and to form another for the purchase of land to raise and grow meat and cereals for Australia. Whilst he was actively engaged in making speeches and writing letters on these subjects, and generally advertising himself freely and as cheaply as possible, Shortland was no less busy in affairs of gallantry, with the too obvious object of capturing an heiress. His family was one the best in the district. His father had emigrated to New Zealand many years before, but the Shortland's were so well-known throughout the South Hams, that Hugh had no difficulty in securing access to the society of the county. He soon commenced a policy of pursuing eligible young ladies with good financial prospects. In one case, as admitted to me afterwards, the friends of one such lady sought the protection of a ward of Chancery appeal to the Lord Chancellor; Shortland was not easily discouraged.

He came to know in the manner that will be described hereafter Miss Laura Dimes, the pleasant but guileless daughter of a county gentleman who lived at Oldstone near Blackawton. It was difficult to understand how Miss. Dimes fell as to the wiles even of Shortland. He was not a fine or attractive man in any sense. He was gentlemanly in demeanour but was lean favoured with a sharp face, and shrewd expression, strongly flavoured with cunning. He was very far from being the Adonis with whom an impressionable young lady might fall distractedly in love at first sight. A visit to Oldstone House which I made later accounted for much that was otherwise inexplicable. An olde-worlde mansion to which admission could only be gained after heavy locks and bars had been removed. Then there was a large quadrangle to be passed, and after that, more locks and bars which admitted one to a hall dingy in itself and rendered gloomier by its armour and antler-clad walls. It was here that Miss. Dimes had lived with her aged father and her mother and a still more aged housekeeper, receiving no visitors and visiting no one.

Miss Dimes was possessed of property in her own right and Shortland prevailed upon her to accompany him one day to Kingsbridge. Here they married at the registry office. Miss. Dimes returned to her home and Shortland went back to his lodgings in Modbury. He next caused it to be given out that he was about to leave the country to develop his plans in Australia and simultaneously the body of his young bride was found drowned in a pond in the grounds around Oldstone House. Her body was buried without internal examination. Later it was exhumed on the order of the Home Secretary after it was discovered that a letter in her possession which her husband had purported to have despatch in Brindisi, Italy, had really been posted in England.

On the day of the trial, I journeyed to Kingsbridge and was present in court. Hugh Shortland was placed in the dock and accused of the murder of his wife. He looked a little haggard but was impassive and apparently indifferent. There was no touch of sorrow about him. Ever and on he stared steadily at me but there was no symptom of recognition. The proceedings lasted only a few minutes the detective confessed himself as baffled and Shortland was dismissed from custody. He left court in the company of his solicitor and if he despatched a look in my direction it was one of curiosity rather than of acquaintance. Shortland was determined not to know me that day. The following evening, Sunday I went to the Mercury office in Plymouth shortly after six o'clock. I found Shortland patiently sitting in my editorial room - the only other person in the establishment. The front door had been left unlocked for the employees and he had entered. I took Shortland's presence in very matter of fact way and jocularly twitted him for not recognising me at Kingsbridge Court. "That would never have done," he remarked with a laugh. "Well, and what can I do for you?" I asked. "I want you to communicate the case to the public" he responded. "But tell me, what do people think of the charge against me?"

"So far as I can gather, they think that you pushed your wife into the water" I said. Shortland looked at me with his hard foxy expression and then said; "And what do you think about it?" "It looked very much like it, does it not?" was my reply. Shortland laughed and remarked; "Well, we will publish a story that will make the others [newspapers] wild to think they have not got it. Their reporters will be hunting me all over the town tomorrow."

My impression at this time was that Shortland feared that I knew and suspected more than I cared to reveal and that he might bribe me into silence by furnishing me with material for a journalistic 'boom.' "Tell me then, I asked, how you first met Miss Dime?"

"Oh, it was in a lane near Oldstone, a nice little Devonshire lane with overhanging brambles. She was riding through on horseback and I was going the same way. Her hair caught in the brambles and fell in a cloud over her shoulders. I went to her assistance and then we rode on together. Quite romantic, wasn't it?" Shortland laughed out loud. With that a shiver went through me; for the man who could laugh under such circumstances was evidently insane or callous to the point of madness.

"And so, you were married soon afterwards?"

"Yes, we were married, clandestinely of course, for I wanted to be married before my departure to New Zealand. The marriage was never consummated for that would have led to discovery and I told my wife that there must be no evidence of that kind for the world to look on." Shortland laughed again that weird harsh laugh and then he produced a painting from his pocket; a picture of his wife which he passed to me for inspection. "Charming girl don't you think so? If you'd have asked me, I would have lent that to you so that you might put a sketch of her in your paper. My cell at Kingsbridge looked out on to the churchyard and if you had slipped in at the back and tapped at my window, I would have supplied you with all kinds of copy."

"What do you wish me to say in the paper?" I asked.

"You may begin this way, take it down in shorthand if you please; We are in position to give this morning, on authority which our readers need not question, certain information in reference to this remarkable case which adds considerably to that already in possession of the public." Reciting a passage from a letter sent from his wife, Shortland said "You are your own good angel. Hugh, if there were no Hugh, I think I should die, because I love you so dearly." He was not in the least moved as he recited this pathetic passage to me.

"But what am I to say about the death of your wife?"

"Put it down this way; with regard to the circumstances under which Mrs. Shortland met her death, Mr. Shortland has repeatedly asserted that the absence of all marks of a struggle in the pond, or in the locality of the pond, disproves the theory of the accident and the suggestion of suicide. He declines to hazard any theory as to the cause of death but says he has been struck by the fact that the body was found upright in the water. Upon this he wants to know if the body was found suspended in the water what point did the body start from where there any footmarks? If it was murder, where were the marks to the body ever touching the ground? I understand that in Mr. Shortland's opinion, the chloroform theory would best reconcile with the circumstances under which the deceased met her death. The first time Shortland heard anything of chloroform was when he saw allusion to its possible use in one of the daily papers, and it struck him the time very acutely indeed."

"You believe your wife was really murdered?" I asked. Shortland jumped from his chair, stretched out his arms and shouted across the table; "You have put that down in shorthand. Strike it out, strike it out!" He resumed his seat calm and impassive as before, recovering immediately his subtle and icy demeanour. Bidding I resume writing, he continued; "Mr Shortland believes an accident has not been proved, he believes a suicide has not been proved and to use a phrase that has been attributed to him, he believes murder has not been disproved."

(Shortland then told the journalist he had more to tell him and could they meet the following evening at eleven p.m. by the hollow at Compton, near to some trees and his aunt's residence, adding that it would be quiet and no one would be about. The writer turning down the offer was then informed that Shortland would instead return to the office the following evening which he did.) Exalted with the sensation of the statements he had already made he went on to come up with further ingenious ideas for diverting public attention from the beaten tract. On one occasion he asked me to state that; "a hooded, young, and beautiful widow who bears title showed considerable feeling towards Mr. Shortland near the turnpike at Kingsbridge shortly after his release…… Mr. Shortland will shortly be on his way to Rome, to take a course of training at the Holy College, preparatory to being admitted to the ministry of the Holy Father. The Holy Roman Church is always clever and prompt to enlist talent and energy her service."

Such was the man who married Miss. Dimes, such was the husband who believed that she was murdered, such were his views on the subject of her death. He hung about my office like a nightmare; suddenly and noiselessly entering my room and renewing the familiar theme - until at length he vanished, without the formality of leave-taking, and I learnt, not without relief, that he had booked his long-deferred passage to New Zealand.

*The fact his first wife had died in suspicious circumstances in England and that he had been tried for her murder was again brought to the fore when eight years later he was found guilty of criminal libel and sentenced to two years in prison. He was said to have lived the life of a libertine in New Zealand and had taken advantage of a young woman in Auckland. He had endeavoured to seduce her to gain possession of her savings, and not succeeding, deliberately defamed her.

Theatrical entertainment between two Gentleman.

At Teignmouth Petty Sessions in January 1884, the Magistrates were engaged in hearing a charge of assault brought by Captain W. H. Saunders against Mr. C. W. Toogood, both gentlemen and residents of the town. The assault was not one that had brought about bodily injury, but was regarded by Captain Saunders as a deliberate insult. After attending a stage show of the opéra-comique of 'Les Cloches De Corneville' at the towns Assembly Rooms a few days earlier, at which both men had been in attendance. At the close of proceedings, Captain Saunders was outside on the pavement and while in the act of seeing some ladies into their carriage, Toogood, without in any way explaining his conduct, pushed Captain Saunders against the wheel of the carriage. Getting back onto the pavement, Toogood once again pushed Saunders towards the carriage. Captain Saunders called out to him and asked what he was doing. "You're a _____ liar and I'll kill you!" responded Mr. Toogood. Such conduct was described as unbecoming of a gentleman said Captain Saunders and was calculated to lead to a breach of the peace. He had taken out the court proceedings to put a stop to it. He had made a complaint to Sergeant Bright saying that Mr. Toogood had twice assaulted him and if it was to be repeated, he should bring him up on a charge. Sergeant Bright then ordered Mr. Toogood to leave the area and he did as he was told.

Unknown artist.

Mr. Templer acting for Toogood, said that the case should never had been brought to court. He had written Captain Saunders a letter without prejudice in which he stated that he considered it great pity that a quarrel between two gentlemen in their position should be allowed to come before the court. Saunders replied saying that an apology or explanation would be refused and although he was perfectly willing to make an *'amende honorable'* he felt that the only way was to bring the case to court. He went on to say that although the assault itself was of a most trivial nature and admitted that Mr. Toogood had made use of a strong expression towards Captain Saunders it was done in the heat of passion and until Captain Saunders had referred to the defendant in a slighting manner when complaining to the Sergeant the case was not, he considered one which called for a conviction but would be better met by a few words of advice as to the future. A Mr. Stiles was then called as a witness for the defence, he stated that there had been a large crowd outside of the Assembly Rooms. On leaving the building he saw Mr. Toogood with his hands in his pockets. He then saw him 'touch' Captain Saunders, but it could not be helped. He saw no attempt on the part of the Toogood to insult Captain Saunders.

The Chairman said that the Bench regretted that the case had been brought before them, but they could now only do their duty. Had the simple act of pushing been unaccompanied with the language stated then they should have viewed the case more leniently, but due to the accusation, they fined the defendant twenty shillings plus expenses.

The murder of Miss. Emma Keyse.

This shocking crime is sadly remembered more for the fact that Emma Keyse alleged murderer; John Lee, became infamously known as 'the man they could not hang' after three attempts to execute him failed rather than for the brutal way in which Miss. Keyse died.

Emma Anne Whitehead Keyse, was an elderly lady who lived in a chalet called 'The Glen' set in an idyllic thirteen-acre estate overlooking the beach at Babbacombe, with three female servants and a young footman named John Henry George Lee. Miss. Keyse had been a former lady-in-waiting to Queen Victoria and was visited at her home in 1846 by the late Prince Consort, and more recently by the then Prince of Wales.

John Lee, originally from Abbotskerswell, had been a servant at 'The Glen' since leaving school, but left in 1879 to join the Navy as a boy sailor. After being invalided out of the service, he returned to Torquay to work as a footman. He then spent three months in Exeter prison in 1884, having been found guilty of stealing a plate from his then employer, Colonel Brownlow. Miss Keyse had kindly taken him back into her service after his release in hope that he might redeem his character.

On the morning of Saturday the 15th of November 1884, the cook Elizabeth Harris, who was John Lee's half-sister, was awoken between three and four o'clock in the morning by fumes and smoke and opening her bedroom door she saw that the house was on fire. Raising the alarm, the coastguard, fishermen and a few neighbours succeeded in extinguishing the fire. A full examination carried was out in daylight and it was discovered that the fire had been started in

The Glen, looking onto Babbacombe Beach. Picture courtesy of wisconsinfrights.com

three different places. The body of Miss. Keyse was found in the drawing-room lying in pool of blood with the back of her skull fractured and her throat cut from ear to ear. Her clothing had been burnt off and her body was badly scarred. It was believed that Miss. Keyse according to her habit, often came downstairs for a cup of cocoa and had been attacked. No motive for the crime could be found and although many valuable items were in the house none of them were taken. John Lee the footman, soon came under suspicion and was arrested for her murder. His right arm was bandaged, an injury he said that he had sustained when breaking a window to let the smoke out of the house.

The inquest into Emma Keyse death was opened on Monday the 17th of November in the music-room of The Glen and afterwards the jury adjourned to St. Marychurch Town Hall. To the surprise of the Coroner and the jury they found over six hundred people awaiting their arrival. Miss. Keyes body was identified by George Whitehead of Victoria Park, London. He said that she was his step-sister and was nearly seventy years of age.

Elizabeth Harris told the inquest that she had heard no sound but was awakened early on the Saturday morning by the smell of smoke. Exiting her bedroom, she saw John Lee on the landing; he was partially dressed and assisted her in putting the fire out. She noticed that there was blood on his clothing. Jane Neck the parlourmaid said that when she was alerted to the fire she rushed to her mistress's bedroom and called out to her but found the bed to be empty and the furniture on fire. She said that John Lee afterwards told her that he had cut his arm breaking a window to let the smoke out. [This window was later found to have been broken from the outside.]

Lee sat throughout the proceedings quite unconcerned whilst he was listening to the witness's evidence. The inquest was then adjourned and resumed the following day again at St. Marychurch Town Hall where William Gasking was the first witness to be called. He said that on the Saturday morning John Lee had asked him to help to remove Miss Keyse's body, which he felt hesitant in doing, but reluctantly carried out the grim task. He noticed Miss Keyse's burnt clothing smelled strongly of paraffin and John Lee's trousers were oily. He said Lee mentioned that he had cut his arm although he didn't see any blood on him.

William Richards a postman, said that about two months previously he had a conversation with John Lee who said; "I'm tired of this place. If missus don't soon get me a good place, she will soon wish she had. I will put an end to someone in the house before I leave." Richards told Lee he had better be careful because if anyone got hold of his words he would be locked up if anything occurred. He then related a later conversation on the 29th of October when Lee told him that he had had a quarrel with his mistress the previous day and said he would not have stayed any longer in the house but for the prospect of him being engaged by the gentleman to whom Miss Keyse hoped to sell her estate.

Dr. Steele was then called and asked to describe the wounds on Miss. Keyes body. He described the burns and wounds and how her skull had been fractured and compressed; the bones of the skull having been driven into the brain. Such a wound he said would have proved fatal in a very short space of time. He had examined the hatchet thought to be the murder weapon and found on it and also on a small table knife found in the prisoner's pantry stains of blood. The knife had been rubbed on fresh earth in an attempt to clean it. The blood was that of a mammal, but the evidence was not positive as it being the blood of a human. There was also a stain of blood of the same kind on the hilt of the handle of the knife, but he was unable to say if it was of a more recent date than six weeks. The knife was blunt, but it could possibly have produced the wound on Miss. Keyse throat. He did not think that wiping the knife on paper would have effectually removed blood stains but rubbing it in earth might have done so. There was a slight sign of soil remaining near the hilt of the knife. He had also examined a nightdress covered with smears of blood, but again was unable to say if it was human or animal blood. John Lee's shirt was also smeared with blood on the arms and over the shoulders the stains being similar to those on the nightdress. The marks were chiefly on the outside and appeared to be of a recent date. A pair of men's socks belonging to Lee were saturated with oil and on which he found several hairs, similar in size length and colour to those belonging to the deceased. Dr. Stevenson was then called, he too had made an examination of the scene and said he found bloodstains along the seam and beneath the handle of a paraffin can as well as on the bottom of it. No attempt appeared to have been made to rub out the stains which appeared to be of a similar date to the stains on the other articles examined by Dr. Steele.

Sergeant Nott stated that Jane Neck the parlourmaid slept in the pantry and it was not possible to have access to the cupboard where the paraffin can was kept when the bed was down without climbing over it. Jane said that between eight and nine o'clock on the morning after the murder, she found the cork of the paraffin can on the floor of the pantry. The knife which Dr. Stevenson had examined was shown to her and she recognised it as the knife which was kept on the table in the hall [to open letters] and she believed that it was there on the day prior to the murder.

The evidence having been heard, the jury retired to deliberate and returned after a half hour's discussion with a verdict of 'wilful murder' against John Lee, who next appeared before Torquay Police Court on the 3rd of December. The courtroom was again crowded. Sergeant Nott of Devon Constabulary described the condition of the premises when he arrived at The Glen on the morning of the murder. In the presence of another officer, he questioned Lee as to his movements on the previous night. Lee stated that he went to bed immediately after prayers, and heard nothing until aroused by the other servants shouting that the house was on fire. He explained away the presence of blood on his shirt by saying he had broken the dining room window to let out the smoke and in doing so cut his arm. Lee stated distinctly that he received the injuries before going to fetch William Gasking. Sergeant Nott said that he had noted that Lee's overcoat was stained with blood on the inside of both sleeves and the left sleeve smelt strongly of mineral oil. On being charged on suspicion with the murder of Miss Keyse, Lee had said to him; "Oh, on suspicion, all right." He went on to add that Lee had changed his socks just before his arrest and on the discarded pair human hairs were later discovered. On lifting the blood-stained carpet in the hall, Sergeant Nott found a slipper and a burnt stocking belonging to Miss. Keyse. Two doormats and the carpet itself must have been raised to place the slipper and stocking there.

Two Coastguard men named Searle and Phillips confirmed that John Lee produced a hatchet almost immediately on being asked for such an instrument. Superintendent Barber stated that in his opinion the premises had not been broken into. The fires in various parts of the premises were all separate and distinct. Medical evidence proved that the depression in the skull of the deceased lady fitted the head of the hatchet which was stained with blood. The Bench at this point in the proceedings remanded the prisoner until the following morning, it being found that several witnesses whose evidence ought to have been gone over had left the court under the impression that they were no longer required. At the continuation of the proceedings the following day more witnesses were called and again the public gallery was packed. When the hatchet with which the deceased was supposed to have been knocked down with was produced there was profound sensation in the courtroom. When John Lee stepped into the dock to hear the decision of the jury, he exhibited the same self-command that he had shown throughout. He stared at the Magistrates and then gave a searching look at his fellow servants at The Glen. He scanned the faces of the witnesses and then looked around the courtroom, giving a slight smile to his sweetheart Miss. Kate Farmer. He was dressed in a clean collar, black bow-tie and had carefully groomed his hair. Although looking pale and anxious, he spoke with promptness and decision when addressed by the Magistrates. The Chairman read out the charge; "John Lee, the charge against you is two-fold. First is that you did murder Emma Ann Whitehead Keyse and the second is that you did set fire to her house in which persons were living. You have heard the evidence?"

John Lee replied, "Yes Sir." The Chairman then continued; "Having heard the evidence do you wish to say anything in answer the charge. You are not obliged to say anything unless you desire to do so." John Lee; "I wish to…." The Chairman then interrupted him. "Wait till I have finished. But whatever you say will be taken down in writing and may be given in evidence against you upon your trial. And you are clearly to understand that you have nothing to hope for from any promise or favour and nothing to fear from any threat which may have been holden out to you to induce you to make any admission or confession of your guilt; but that whatever you now say be given in evidence against you your trial.

John Lee: "I wish to reserve my defence." The Chairman then informed John Lee that he was to take his trial upon the two charges the next Assizes to be held at Exeter. Lee heaved a deep sigh and was then whisked to the cells below. The witnesses, twenty-four in total, were then bound over on the sum of twenty-five pounds each to appear at the Assizes to give evidence.

John Lee. Picture courtesy of winsconsinfirghts.com

At the Devon Assizes in Exeter in February 1885 Lee was found guilty of the murder of Miss. Keyse. When he entered the dock to hear the verdict of the jury he was busily chewing on a mouthful of food and appeared quite indifferent to the importance of the occasion. When the Chairman asked Lee if there was any reason why the sentence of death should not be passed, Lee simply replied that he was innocent. His Lordship having assumed the black cap said, "You have been found guilty of as cruel and barbarous murder as ever was committed and the jury have found you guilty of that murder upon evidence so clear and to my mind conclusive that I am sorry to say that I cannot entertain a doubt to the correctness of their verdict. It is not my habit to dwell upon the details of a case so painful, nor do I think my doing so would affect any good either to the public or yourself. You say you are innocent; I wish I could believe it. You have throughout this case undoubtedly maintained a calm appearance and at this moment you appear to be calm. All I can say is that the jury have found that you did commit that crime. I am not surprised that a man who could commit that crime could maintain the calm appearance that you have maintained. I have only one duty to perform and that the law imposes upon me to perform, and that is to pass the awful sentence of death. You have undoubtedly broken the law, both human and divine, and by that law you must suffer the penalty of death. It is this: That you be taken from the place where you now are to the prison from whence you came and, on the day, appointed, that you be taken to the place of execution and there be hanged by your neck until your body be dead and that your body when dead, be buried within the prison where you were last confined after this sentence. I cannot hold out any hope so far as I am concerned that any mercy will be extended to you. I advise you to spend the short time remaining listening to the advice which will be given to you, and such comfort as can be afforded in preparing for your end. May Lord have mercy on your soul."

As Lee was about to be removed from the dock, he placed his hands on the framework of the dock and addressing the Judge said; "The reason my Lord, why I am so calm, is that I trust in my Lord and he knoweth I am innocent." Lee, smiling, was then taken to the cells.

On 23 February 1885 three attempts were made to carry out Lee's execution at Exeter Prison. All ended in failure as the trap door of the scaffold failed to open on each occasion despite being carefully tested by the executioner beforehand. At this point the medical officer refused to take any further part in the proceedings and they were stopped. As a result, the Home Secretary, Sir, William Harcourt commuted Lee's sentence to life imprisonment. After an investigation into the failure of the apparatus, it was discovered that when the gallows had been moved from the old infirmary into the quadrangle of the prison, overnight rain had caused the trap door to swell so when the bolts were pulled the door failed drop.

From his prison cell Lee continued to petition successive Home Secretaries and was eventually released from Portland prison in Dorset on the 19th of December 1907 after serving a twenty-three-year sentence. He immediately returned to his mother's address in Newton Abbott. On the 22nd of January 1909 he married Jessie Augusta Bulled, who until recently had been the chief nurse on the female mental wards at Plympton and Newton Abbot Workhouse's. In 1910 she gave birth to a son in Newcastle upon Tyne [likely whilst on a lecture tour with her husband.] The following year she gave birth to a daughter in Lambeth Workhouse having been callously abandoned by her now 'famous' husband. John Lee having fled to America with another woman who pretended to be his wife.

*Was John Lee the killer? There is a certain amount of speculation that he may not have been, but without the wide-ranging forensic testing we have available today we shall never know the truth. After serving his sentence, Lee went on to make a lot of money from his story of 'the man they could not hang.' He wrote a book on his life released in 1908, though what was fact and what was fiction is pure speculation. His demise – no one quite knows for sure, he simply disappeared into obscurity though there are reports that he was still alive at the beginning of the Second World War. There is another man who it has been suggested could have been the real killer - Reginald Gwynne Templer, a young solicitor from Teignmouth who was a friend of the victim and defended John Lee at the inquest into Miss. Keyse death and at Torquay Magistrates Court. Due to 'a fit of insanity' he was unable to defended Lee at his trial and his brother Mr Charles Templer acted in his stead. Reginald Templer was also rumoured to be the father of Elizabeth Harris's then unborn child.

Tiverton wife assault.

John Sanders a fifty-one-year-old master builder of Castle Street, Tiverton, was charged on the 28th of February 1885 at the Borough Police Court with unlawfully and maliciously wounding his wife Mary Sanders on the 18th of the same month with intent to do her grievous bodily harm. the couple had only been married three months. Two weeks previously they had quarrelled in the evening but had settled their differences before retiring to bed. In the early hours of the morning, Mrs. Sanders was awoken when she heard her husband getting up. She asked him the time and he said it was quarter-past-five. He then returned to the marital bed and dealt her three blows with a slater's pin hammer to the head. Before doing so he said, "I am dying, and we will both die together." In shock and excruciating pain, Mary took the hammer from him and ran from the house screaming. She knocked up the next-door neighbour Mr. Henry Fewins, a stone mason and a police constable was sent for. On entering the Sanders bedroom, he found John Sanders bleeding from several stab wounds to the throat and head. Both Mr. and Mrs. Sanders were removed to the Infirmary. Mr. Sanders lay in a precarious condition for a number of days. It was on his recovery and after spending five days in Exeter gaol that he was called to court. Mrs. Sanders said that in the short time they had been married they had not lived happily. Her husband had threatened to take her life on two or three occasions and had struck her with his fist. He had been in drink more or less the whole time. The quarrel on the night of the attack arose after a woman who lived close by came to the door. John Saunders had gone out to speak with her and when Mary had objected, he assured her there was nothing going on and she had only called to collect a receipt. After further questioning of both Mr. and Mrs. Sanders, Mr. Sanders admitted that his wife had been nagging him about this other woman and he had 'lost it' and hit her with a hammer to which she had retaliated and knocked him senseless. He said he could not recall anything after that though the previous evening her had lent his wife a pen knife to remove the cork from an ink bottle and he had not seen the knife since.

The doctor who examined the couple said that Mrs. Sanders injuries were light and superficial whereas Mr. Sanders injuries were more serious and looked as though they had been inflicted by someone else though he could have administered them himself. As well as the cuts to his throat, he also had a number of blunt instrument injuries to his head. After further questioning, Mrs. Saunders said that she most certainly didn't strike her husband with a weapon nor that she knew of another hammer being found in the bedroom [it was smaller than the one she had grabbed and taken with her when she fled the room.] She said she knew her husband had a hammer in his coat pocket a month previously which was hung up behind the bedroom door. The coat was in the same position on the morning after the assault, but the hammer was no longer in the pocket. She also denied her husband giving her a penknife to take the cork from a bottle of ink. The bottle of ink she had used the previous evening to sign some receipts had been opened by herself with a small knife a few days previously.

Ernest Norrish aged sixteen the son of Mrs. Sanders, said that on the morning of the 18th of February he was awoken by hearing his mother screaming. He stayed upstairs as he was afraid of what had happened and stayed in his room until the police arrived. Mr. Fewins, who lived next door to the Saunders in Castle Street said that he was woken up by Mary Saunders screaming 'murder!' and hammering on his front door. When he looked out of the window she asked to be let in and he went down and opened the door. He said her nightdress was covered with blood. She asked him to go into her house but instead he went to find a policeman; P.C. Rhodes who he found in Newport Street. Returning to Castle Street they both went to the Saunders property where they found John Saunders lying on the bed with his head hanging over the side. He had a bowl on the floor and blood was dripping into it from his wounds. A bottle found under the bed was stained with blood. It contained a small drop of whiskey. When P.C. Rhodes asked Mr. Sanders what had transpired, he replied that 'they had a comfortable home, and it ought not to have happened.' A doctor was then sent for. A hammer was later found on the bedroom floor by the side of the bed which was covered with blood. A penknife was also found after a search and blood was traced on the opposite side of the bed as well as on the door and at the back of the house.

Mr. Arthur Edwin Mason, a doctor at the Infirmary said that said when Mrs. Sanders was brought in on the Wednesday morning at half-past seven he examined her and found fresh blood on her face and night dress. There was also one wound on the left top of her forehead and another on the back part of her head on the left-hand side. Neither were very extensive and blood had ceased to flow from them. They appeared to have been caused by a pointed instrument such as the hammer produced in court. She appeared to have lost a good quantity of blood. She was later discharged from the Infirmary on the Saturday morning when the wounds were in such a condition that she was fit to leave. Her husband was also brought to the

Infirmary and examination showed that he had numerous wounds across his neck and a swelling from a blow by a blunt instrument to the right side his forehead.

The Bench spent some time critically examining the evidence and on returning into court they said that they were referring the case to the next Quarter Sessions. On the 2nd of April 1885 John Saunders was charged with common assault when under the influence of drink. He was bound over to keep the peace for three months with a bond of one hundred pound and two separate sureties of fifty pounds.

Tragedy on the beach at Dawlish.
This is a most harrowing tale of what should have been a pleasurable day out at the seaside. A most dreadful incident occurred in Dawlish on the 29th of August 1885 when a one-hundred-and-fifty-ton chunk of sandstone rock fell from a cliff, crushing a number of people who were sitting beneath it. Three people were killed and several persons injured. The rock had slipped from the face of a cliff near to the bathing cove. The cove was separated from the public beach by two spurs of rock. Each of these were pierced by a small tunnel with a bridge on the one side of the main tunnel and a walled footpath on the other which ran beneath the overhanging cliffs. Each winter the seas had gradually washed away more and more of the foundation lessening the support of the great mass of red sandstone and allowing large quantities of rock to fall onto the shore. Two or three years previously there had been a large slip in the cove itself and earlier that year there had been a considerable fall from the cliff above the walkway which connected the tunnel with the cove.

The action of the sea, winter frosts and the vibration caused by the running of the trains through the railway tunnel in the heart of the rock had occasionally led to rock falls and although these facts well-known to locals, it was unlikely that many visitors were aware of them.

Dawlish was full of visitors on the 29th of August, and amongst them were the Dowager Lady Sawle of Honiton as well as a party of her guests who included Miss. Watts and Miss. Kempthorne; nieces who resided with her ladyship. Six of the children of Colonel and Mrs. Watson [niece of Lady Sawle] along with Miss Matthews who was in charge of the Watson children. She and five of the children had arrived in the resort ten days earlier taking up lodgings at 2. Portland Terrace, just off the Esplanade. Lady Sawle, Violet Watson, Miss. Kempthorne and Lady Sawle's maid; Elizabeth Radford, had arrived the day prior to the fateful incident. They had delayed their trip due to Violet not having been very well. The Watson family resided at Clifton near Bristol but had come to visit their great-aunt Lady Sawle. The Watson children were; Eleanor aged thirteen, John aged eleven, Violet aged nine, Margaret aged six, Frank aged four and Alice aged three.

On the Saturday morning the party were on the Esplanade, but soon after eleven o'clock Lady Sawle returned home accompanied by Miss. Kempthorne who intended re-joining the children but was detained by the arrival of a letter. At about a quarter-to-twelve, Alice, the youngest of the Watson children was being looked after by Miss. Watts who was seated on the beach almost beneath the shadow of the cliffs. Miss. Matthews and the nurse, the lady's-maid and Violet were all close by. Margaret and Frank were playing with their buckets and spades at the water's edge, while Ellie and Johnnie, the two eldest children were midway between the cliffs and the sea, but rather nearer the wall than the water. Without any previous indication the face of the cliff was noticed by Ellie to be falling. She shouted an alarm and Miss. Matthews who grabbed little Alice from Miss. Watts's lap and ran towards the sea. One fragment of the rock struck her on the head inflicting a scalp wound and a stone struck her on the ankle. Another stone fell so near the face of the little Alice who she had in her arms that the child's face was scratched but she was otherwise unhurt. Ellie then caught her brother by the hand, and they ran down the beach, Johnnie stumbled, and Ellie tried to pull him up but seeing the rock falling directly towards her she was forced to abandon the effort. She leapt to one side and managed to escape the enormous chunk of sandstone which fell upon her brother. Miss. Matthews and the lady's-maid, Elizabeth Radford, who had Violet between them, ran in-shore - unwittingly putting themselves in greater danger as all three were struck down by falling rock and buried by the cliff. Miss. Watts, the children's aunt who had just before been nursing Alice on her lap before being relieved of her by Miss. Matthews, didn't have time to get to her feet before fragments of the rock reigned down upon her and the injuries sustained rendered her insensible.

Postcard from a private collection.

A large gathering quickly assembled. The danger of further rock falls did not deter men from promptly carrying out a rescue. Miss. Matthews and the four injured children were first removed from possible further danger. Attention was then turned to Miss Watts who although not crushed beneath the rocks was still very badly hurt. After about twenty minutes of hauling heavy rocks aside. Johnnie Watson was also rescued though had suffered multiple bruises and a compound fracture of the right thigh and broken right arm. The rescue work continued but there was still no trace of the nurse the lady's-maid or Violet Watson and there was considerable doubt as to the exact number of people who were actually trapped beneath the rock. The rescue party working in two gangs each taking one end of the mass of debris continued to labour for another hour until the body of nurse Keen was found. Her skull was crushed and was of course she was quite dead. Almost immediately afterwards the body of little Violet was discovered. An indentation in her temple was apparently the only visible injury to her body. Another half an hour passed before the rescue party came upon the remains of the lady's-maid Elizabeth Radford who had been in Lady Sawle's service for twenty-six years. She appeared to have been crushed between a rock already lying on the beach and a piece that had fallen from the cliff. Her body was in such a terrible state due to the injuries she suffered that it put identification almost out of the question. One side of her face was the only part of the unfortunate woman that had not been injured.

Although still alive, Miss. Watts injuries were so severe and she was not expected to survive. Johnnie on the other hand despite the severity of his injuries was expected to live. Lady Sawle when informed of the tragedy was almost prostrate with grief. Colonel J. Watson who was in the Bombay Staff Corps and was the political agent at Kolapore, India, where he was living with his wife, formerly Miss. Watts, a niece of Lady Sawle who had accompanied him there in the autumn of the previous year with their youngest child a baby; was also telegrammed of the terrible tragedy.

The Assembly Rooms at Dawlish were used for the purpose of the inquest into the most awful event which lasted several hours. It was said that Violet Mary Watson, Elizabeth Radford the lady's-maid along with Elizabeth Keen the nurse were all killed by the fall of cliffs at Dawlish the previous Saturday. Two of the injured persons a young lady named Watts and a boy named Watson still lay in a very precarious state. There was at times a considerable display of public feeling especially when the witnesses expressed opinions that the Local Board of Health should have taken steps to warn visitors to the bathing cove that the cliffs above were dangerous. After the identification of the bodies by Colonel Watson's brother, Lady Sawle's medical man and the brother of the nurse Elizabeth Keen. Frederick W. Short a chemist, living at 17. Bloomsbury, London, was the first witness called forward to give evidence. He said that he had been on a visit to Dawlish and had been sitting on a ledge of the cliff in the cove where the accident occurred. He was reading and watching the children at play. The cove he said was next to the bathing cove and at this side of it he noticed a group of people under the cliff. He also saw two ladies dressed in black whom he now believed to be deceased sitting on a ledge in the cove formed by the overhanging of the cliff. At about half-past eleven he heard a rumbling sound and looking up saw the face of the cliff fall on the group of people below. The cliff he said fell in very large fragments with a lot of rubble. He said that he didn't see any train passing by at the time of the fall and hadn't noticed any pass just before, though a train may have passed without him noticing it. When he saw the rocks begin to fall, he immediately ran across and did what he could to help. He saw a woman partially trapped; it was Miss. Matthews who was caught by her dress. He pulled her out leaving part of the dress behind. He then took Alice who was uninjured and placed her on the beach a safe distance away. He went back and saw that another lady was trapped under the rocks, only her head and shoulders sticking out. This was Miss. Watts who he was also able to pull clear. He saw other people who extricated another of the Watson children. At this point he left with Miss. Watts to help her back to the house where the party were staying at and to inform those there of what had happened. After informing Lady Sawle of the tragedy he returned to the beach to see if he could be of any further help.

Mrs. Caroline Boston of 14. Upper Winchester Road, Kensington Bridge, London, was also on a visit to Dawlish when the tragedy occurred. She told the inquest that she had started off from the town at half-past eleven to make her way to the cove. Finding several people bathing she made her way back to where the accident happened. She was within two yards of it when the rock fell. She said she remembered a train having just gone past and another passing whilst efforts were being made to get the bodies out from under the fallen rocks. She said she saw the piece of rock fall, that pitched near the little boy.

George Bond a boatman residing in Dawlish said, "I was standing by a boat in the cove at about half past eleven when the nurse who was killed came and asked me whether the tide was rising or falling. As soon as I got to the bathing cove, I saw two ladies sitting down and a little boy with a net in his hand. I heard a noise and on looking up saw the rock falling. I saw a lady under the rock and a little boy. The rock began to fall from the bottom and went right up. I cannot say whether it fell on the persons. I caught a lady by the hand, helped her out and ran for assistance to get the rest of the bodies out.

The Rev. Richard Harris-Doulton then spoke up saying; "There have been three falls within the last six months and one in March last. One was at Bowley Hole and the other was of minor importance. On the second fall taking place a notice was put up over the archway warning people not to pass under; but this remained a few weeks only and it was then removed. Shortly after its removal the bridge was constructed immediately under the place where this notice was put up. I remonstrated with the local authorities and directed a letter to them in which I stated it was an absolute insanity to construct a bridge in a place where the notice had been placed."

Mr. Whidborne the clerk to the Dawlish Local Board was then called and stated that they had never exercised any jurisdiction over the beach as the Great Western Railway Company claimed the entire right under a lease from the Commissioners of Woods and Forests. He however admitted that when the townspeople had made representations concerning the beach to the board, the latter held communication with the railway company to get the cause of complaint remedied. He also admitted that the board owned the pleasure-ground on the top of the Cliffs at the foot of which the accident happened, but he did not admit that the right of the board went down the cliff to the beach.

Mr. Delbridge the surveyor, said although he visited the cove and mentioned to the committee of the board any matters he saw there, he did not make any formal report as it was always understood the board had no authority on the beach. He did however admit that on the suggestion of the committee, he had put up one danger board a short time ago which had since disappeared and he didn't know what had become of it. The board had byelaws regulating the bathing on the beach, but those byelaws were under a special Act and did not indicate the ownership. After further evidence the Coroner summed up the case and the jury returned a verdict of 'accidental death' adding a rider, calling on the Local Board to ascertain with whom the ownership of the beach really rested and to consult a proper authority to secure the safety of the public. Pending this inquiry three notice boards were put up alerting beach goers to the danger of falling rocks.

* Miss. Watts did eventually recover. Nurse Elizabeth Keen was buried in the adjacent grave to Violet Watson in the churchyard at Awliscombe, Devon.

Bigamy in Tavistock.

William Parkhouse was brough up before Tavistock Petty Sessions in March 1888 accused of bigamy. Parkhouse had been working in Tavistock. A week previous to his appearance in court, a woman claiming to be his wife presented herself at the place where he was working. As soon as he caught sight of her, he bolted out the door and was later traced to Gunnislake in Cornwall where he was apprehended. It also came to light that Parkhouse had been a deserter from the Royal Marines in 1883. Mrs. Parkhouse told the court that she had married William Parkhouse at Torquay on the 1st of May 1877 and they had two children together. She was now living in Totnes. It was also asserted by the court that William Parkhouse had married Elizabeth Ann Dodd at Tavistock registry office in 1885 and they had one child together. The case was remanded for two days whilst witnesses were sought and brought to Tavistock. The case created great interest as both wives appeared in court.

Elizabeth Heard the wife Frederick Charles Heard, a cab proprietor of Totnes, and sister in-law of the Parkhouse's wife, said she had known William Parkhouse for many years and was present at his marriage to Emily Heard which had taken place at St. Luke's Church, Torquay, in 1877. Samuel Heard also of Totnes said he had known Parkhouse for around sixteen years and identified him as the man who had lived in Totnes with Emily Heard as her husband, and she was known as Mrs. Parkhouse.

Elizabeth Ann Dodd stated that she lived in Barley Market Street, Tavistock, and was a charwoman. She knew the prisoner and had married him under the name of William Frederick Bailey at the register office in Tavistock the 9th January 1888. Parkhouse had presented himself to her as a single man. They had lived as man and wife from the time of their marriage up until the day of his arrest when she was told that he had was already married. Mr T. H. Cranch the registrar of marriages at Tavistock, said he knew the prisoner and saw him write down his name as William Bailey on the notice of marriage to Elizabeth Dodd, in it he stated himself to be a bachelor. He also saw him write his name in the register book. Copies of the entries in the register books of both marriages were then produced, bearing out the evidence of the respective witnesses.

P.C. Bright of Morwellham, stated that he had apprehended the prisoner at Gunnislake the previous Saturday based on the suspicion of him being a deserter from the Royal Marines. After bringing Parkhouse to Tavistock, he received further information which led to the charge of bigamy. When asked by the Magistrates if he had anything to say in answer to the charge, Parkhouse stated that five years previously he had deserted from the Royal Marines then being on board 'H.M.S. Minotaur.' He was working up country when he received news that his wife was dying in Totnes. He was afraid to go there for fear of being arrested as a deserter. Sometime afterwards he came to Tavistock and married his present wife not thinking he was breaking the law. William Parkhouse was then committed to take his trial at the next Assizes in Exeter. In July 1888 he was found guilty of the charge and sentenced to eighteen months hard labour.

Never leave a boiling kettle unattended.

Poor little Alfred Ernest Burt aged three, of Castle Street, Barbican, Plymouth, was also involved in a tragic accident on the 3rd of April 1888. His mother had left him in the kitchen whilst she went to another room in the house. A few minutes later she heard a terrible scream and hurrying back into the kitchen she found her little boy soaking wet and with steam rising from his body. The kettle she had left boiling on the stove was now lying upset on the floor. Albert was taken to hospital but the shock and extent of his injuries which extended over his back and arms was too much for his little body to take and he passed away in the early hours of Thursday the 5th at the South Devon and East Cornwall Hospital.

The Professor and the Gatekeeper.

At Bideford County Magistrates Court on the 10th of April 1888, a charge of assault was made by Michael Foy a professor of phrenology, against an old man named John Smale; keeper of the town gate leading to the 'Hobby' drive and grounds at Clovelly. The plaintiff who appeared in court carrying a coat which was said to have been torn during the alleged assault, addressed himself to the Bench in very excited and eccentric manner, so much so that scarcely a word he said was understood. John Smale denied the assault and stated that Mr. Foy had refused to pay the regular fee for entering the Hobby grounds but had instead offered him the price of pint of beer, which he refused. John Smale said that at the time of the alleged assault (March 27th) when Mr. Foy approached him, he was in the act of sharpening the end of a broom-handle with a hook. Mr. Foy made use of bad language, rushed at him and endeavoured to strike him by taking hold of the hook. Thereupon he held out the broomstick in order to defend himself.

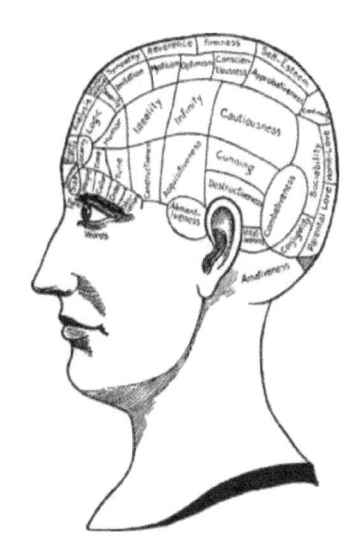

Michael Callaghan a witness, said that he was present and did not see John Smale commit an assault, but Mr. Foy seemed to have got into a violent temper at the refusal of the defendant to accept the offer of the price a pint of beer and rushed at him. Smale had kept him at bay with the broom handle. The Bench dismissed the case.

Devon summer Assize 1888.

The Devon Summer Assizes held at Exeter in 1888 had a number of interesting cases. The Assize commenced on Monday the 23rd of July, before Mr Baron Huddleston in the Nisi Prius Court and Mr Justice Day in the Crown Court at the Castle and also at the Guildhall.

James Adolphus Pearce aged thirty-three, a clerk at Devonport Post Office, pleaded guilty to stealing a postal package containing five cheroots and packet of tea on May 12th. Also, a postal package containing two half-sovereigns on June 22nd, the property of her Majesty's Postmaster General. The judge sentenced Pearce to eighteen months imprisonment with hard labour.

George Northcott a thirty-one-year-old gardener pleaded guilty to forging an endorsement to a cheque at the Three Towns Banking Company, East Stonehouse, in January of that year. He was sentenced to twelve months imprisonment with hard labour.

Mary Crapp, a twenty-two-year- old servant previously residing at 19. Cheltenham Place, Greenbank, Plymouth, pleaded guilty to attempting to conceal the birth of her female child on the 3rd of April. Mary had been five months in the service of the lady of house; Mrs. Radford. On the 3rd of April saying she felt unwell she went to her room to lie down. The following day her mistress highly suspicious as to her condition made a search of the bedroom and discovered the wrapped-up body of a baby girl hidden at the bottom of a trunk. A doctor was immediately called to attend and he found Mary to be in a critical condition. When he questioned her, she denied all knowledge of having previously known that she was pregnant. He later carried out a post-mortem on the body of the child and found that it had breathed. Its death had been caused by lack of attention at birth and a verdict of 'found dead' was returned. His Lordship sentenced Mary to two days imprisonment.

John Dymond a seventeen-year-old labourer pleaded guilty to a charge of burglary at the house of James Lavin, at St. Thomas, Exeter, on the 4th of July and stealing one cake and three tarts. In passing sentence, the Judge said that Dymond had already spent time in the reformatory, but his reformation did not appear to have been successful. He said if he could have it his way, he would have the young man whipped and then sent out to earn himself a livelihood. As those who were whipped rarely ever came back for the same offence. The more prisoners he said that were whipped, the fewer there would be. He was not at liberty to have the prisoner flogged and gaol in his opinion should not be used to confine one of such a young age. But as that was the only option available to him, he sentenced Dymond to three months' imprisonment.

Attacked for her purse at Modbury.
At the Assizes held later that year in early December, Robert Shaw aged thirty-two and described as a chairmaker of imperfect education, was charged with assaulting Ethel Pearse at Modbury on the 23rd of October with the intent to violently steal her money and goods. Shaw had met with Miss. Pearse who was walking along a road just outside of the town. He grabbed hold of her and violently threw her into a ditch. Placing his hand over her mouth he managed to stifle her screams and then demanded that she handed over the money she was carrying in her purse. Hearing a carriage approaching he took fright and made off empty handed. Miss. Pearse who was terribly shaken from the experience was able to extricate herself from the ditch and call for help from the passing cab. The Judge characterised Shaw's conduct as most cowardly and brutal and sentenced him to two years' imprisonment with hard labour.

Poor little Billy Delafield.

The same Assizes saw numerous other cases, some of which were of a very serious nature, including that of the charge of murder against a twelve-year-old girl called Mary Griffin. [This story is covered in more detail in 'Grim and Gruesome Plymouth 1860-1959.] Mary was charged with the murder of William Alfred Delafield, who fell from the rampart of Plymouth Citadel in June 1888. William, who was unknown to Mary Griffin, was last seen by his father playing outside of his shoemaker's shop on Frankfort Street, at around ten o'clock that morning. It appears that in his innocence, Billy had gone with Mary when she had asked him to accompany her on a walk. They were then seen entering the Citadel by a soldier on sentry duty. About ten minutes later the soldier heard a child's scream and saw the boy fall through one of the embrasures in the ramparts and onto a heap of stones in the trench below. The soldier ran to the boy's assistance and whilst conveying him into the Citadel in his arms for medical attention he saw the girl who had accompanied him running away. William, he noted, had been stripped of all his clothes with the exception of his shirt, jacket, and collar.

Suspicion soon fell upon Mary Griffin aged twelve, who lived with her mother in Well Street, which was not far from where the boy resided. She denied the accusations but two months later confessed to the crime. She told Detective Mutton of Plymouth Police; "I pushed the little boy Delafield over the Citadel. I saw the soldier pick him up and take him inside. I ran away and went down the Quay." She said she became frightened when she realised what she had done and ran away, leaving the boy's missing garments which were subsequently recovered and returned to his parents. This confession came after she had been sent to a children's home and from where she had absconded and later returned. She confided in a female superintendent that she had tried to kill herself, and afterwards when being examined by a doctor she again made the statement that it was she was who took the boy the Citadel, removed his clothes and pushed him over in order to kill him. She repeated this statement to the police. Mr. H. E. Duke, solicitor, who spoke on behalf of Mary Griffin, asked the jury to consider her mental capabilities and suggested that the boy likely fell out the embrasure by accident. The jury acquitted Mary and the Judge observed that they were a very merciful panel.

Neglect at Octagon Cottages.

Susan Warren of 38. Octagon Cottages, Plymouth, was on trial for the manslaughter of her illegitimate son; Stanley Martin Warren in August 1888. Stanley had died in the Workhouse shortly after being admitted in a state of starvation. Prior to his death, Susan Warren had been charged with neglect.

Mr. E. Dyke, the master of the Workhouse said that on the Friday previous to the child's death at about four o'clock in the afternoon the boy was admitted in a very emaciated and starved condition. Although the mother had said he was sixteen months old Mr. Dyke said he believed him to be much older. Elizabeth Frost a neighbour and wife of a labourer living at 24. Rendle Cottages stated that the mother of the deceased though a married woman lived with man named Martin. She said that when Stanley had been born on April the 12th of the previous year, he had been a perfectly healthy baby. For six months his mother had attended very well to the boy and during that time he was a very robust and plump child. Then through neglect he declined in strength until he became unable to move. She said that the mother was in the habit of leaving him without anyone to look after him often for hours at a time. She would return home drunk and, in the weeks leading up to his death her drunkenness and neglect had grown worse. She would leave the house early in the morning and was often seen to be drunk by breakfast time. She would not return until after the public houses had closed.

Little Stanley in this time had become fearfully emaciated through having scarcely any care or attention. On several occasions Elizabeth had herself bought milk for the child and fed him. Two weeks prior to the boy's death she had taken it upon herself to take him to a dispensary and the doctor there told her that he was dying. When she told Susan Warren what the doctor had said she was verbally abused for having taken the child to the dispensary and Susan Warren said she wished that the boy was dead. On the Friday before his passing, she and Mr. Mayell the relieving officer had removed the child to the Workhouse.

Mr Charles Mayell said that when he saw the child it looked like a living skeleton and appeared to be dying. Mrs. Warren was spoken to, but she was so much under the influence of drink that she did not appear to realise the state of things. When he told her that the child was dying, she expressed no regret. She had apparently given the child brandy and behaved towards it in a manner which showed the most wretched and degraded self-indulgence.

The doctor who had seen little Stanley at the dispensary said that the child when brought to him showed no signs of disease; the cause of death being starvation. He also said that when he weighed the child, he was only nine pounds four ounces. A healthy robust child of the deceased child's age should have weighed around eighteen to twenty pounds.

Susan Warren was found guilty of the manslaughter of her son on the 4th of December 1888 and was sent to prison for two hundred and eighty-four days.

Desperation and starvation.

In early August 1888 at the 'King's Head Inn' Topsham, the Deputy District Coroner (Mr. H. W. Gould) held an inquiry into the death of Eliza Mary Oke aged six months, the daughter of a fisherman. Dr. Bothwell who carried out the post-mortem said that appearances pointed to death from starvation. All of her organs were more or less emaciated, the gall bladder full of bile and there were ulcerations on the cornea - two significant indications of death from starvation. P.C. Leyman, of Topsham, said that when he visited the house, he saw the deceased child lying on the table. Mrs Emma Oke, the mother of the child said that it had vomited and then died. She told him that after suckling the child she had fed it bread and milk. She added that it was a very hearty child but that she had no other food to give it.

Mary Ley the midwife who attended to the mother during and after her confinement, said that she was certain that Mrs. Oke had said that her milk had dried up a month after the birth of the infant and that she could not afford to keep the child unless she could give it nourishment from the bosom. She went on to say that she knew Mr. Oke didn't give his wife very much money and that the family had often been dependent on food given to them by other people. Once a day Mrs. Oke's father brought her a half-quartern loaf. Mrs. Oke she said had never made any complaint as to her husband's treatment. She was very poor and she [Mrs. Ley] had always attended to her during her confinements for no reward. She went on to say that Mr. Oke gathered seaweed and sometimes fished, while Mrs. Oke herself often begged at houses in Topsham for bread. She never saw the husband bring home any money. He was absent from home every day in his boat, but was home at night. She had advised the mother to take the child to see a doctor. Mrs. Oke had said that she would "see about it." Mrs. Ley reminded her that the child was very ill and if she didn't see a doctor then she as well as her husband would probably "get in the wrong box and be sent to prison." She told Mrs. Oke that by calling in the doctor the child would then likely be maintained at the expense of the parish. She went on to say that she did not consider Mr. Oke able-bodied as he suffered from a bleeding nose and faintness.

Rose Bradley the wife of a sailor said that hearing from neighbours that Mrs. Oke was starving she had taken a basin of gruel to the Oke's house, the interior of which presented a miserable appearance. She continued her visits with gruel for several days. Some weeks later she saw the child and was surprised to see how it had altered, it had become much thinner. She said to Mrs Oke; "This is never the child that I saw the other day?" and Mrs. Oke replied that it was and that it ate heartily. Since then, she had frequently seen the mother going out without the child. When she questioned Mrs. Oke where the child was, she was told that it was 'at home asleep.'

William Charles Oke a fisherman and brother of Mr. George Oke, said that for six years he had lived in his brother's house. He had the front room and the attic. The boat belonged to him, but they worked it together and divided the earnings equally. He said his own share was enough to maintain him as he had been a teetotaller for many years. He then produced a book in which were entered the daily earnings of the boat through to May of that year and these had averaged between two shillings and three shillings and sixpence a day. These amounts had to be divided with his brother. In July they gathered seaweed by which they earned from four to six shillings a day. William Oke said he paid sometimes one shilling and sometimes nine and a half pence per week and part of the taxes for his share of the house. He paid the rent direct to the landlord. He went on to say that he had never seen the deceased child ill-treat and when his brother and wife quarrelled, he generally left the house. He had never seen Emma Oke struck by her husband nor had he ever seen her with a black eye. He had heard her complain of "sinking" in consequence of want of food, but he had also heard his brother utter a similar complaint. He frequently shared his bread with them. His brother as well as himself had been short of food when the weather prevented their earning their living. Other neighbours stated that Mrs. Oke and the children often appeared starving and that Mr. Oke would eat the food taken home by the children.

Unknown artist.

After a very long hearing and with many witnesses with often conflicting stories, the jury decided that the parents should be tried for manslaughter at the next Assize. At their trial in December, it was said the George Oke aged thirty-six and Emma Oke aged thirty-three had seven children, and that the deceased child was said to have been killed by them: through not being given proper nourishment. Mr. Kekewich the counsel for the prosecution said that after having gone through the case most carefully he could not see how a charge of manslaughter could be sustained and he did not therefore propose to offer any evidence. The learned Judge said "I am glad you have taken that course; a course which I would expect from a gentleman in your position. I had hoped that the grand jury would have seen their way to throw out the bill. It will be your [the jury's] duty to follow the cause which Mr. Kekewich has properly and humanely taken, suggesting that he should offer no evidence. It will therefore be your legal duty to say that the prisoners are not guilty of the charges brought against them." He then pointed out how the family had a hard life and on top of that Mrs. Oke had struggled to suckle the child. The husband had done his best to support his family and appeared to have worked very hard. There was evidence to prove that he was a sober man and did what he could to support the child. Their only downfall had been in not going to the relieving officer sooner and having asked for help, though it would be very hard to make a man criminally responsible became he had earned his feeling of independence and his reluctance to ask for charity. He went on to say to the jury; "I don't think you twelve gentlemen who are in good and comfortable circumstances will want to condemn a miserable man for having done too much to avoid bringing publicly before the world that he was a person who had completely failed the struggle of life and was unable support himself. It is a matter on which we must feel some commiseration for him. It is not our part to throw stones at this man. I am bound to say that he and his wife have been in prison apparently ever since the 10th August last. We are now at the 4th of December. They have been in prison nearly four months. Under these circumstances' gentlemen you are relieved at all events from any responsibility whatsoever. It will be your duty to find the prisoners not guilty, both on the indictment and on the Coroner's inquisition."

The jury having found the verdict as directed, the learned Judge, addressing the prisoners, said; "I have to deeply sympathise with you for what you have undergone, and although I think there may be something to blame in your conduct, I shall not be the first to throw stones at you."

The would-be jockey.

William James Bunker a twenty-six-year-old labourer, was indicted for stealing a horse valued at eight pounds, the property of John Wills of Plymouth, on the 6th of November 1888. Bunker pleaded guilty and admitted that he had been convicted of a similar offence in June three years earlier. In answer to a question from the Judge he said that he did not mean to steal the horse but was only guilty of taking it. His Lordship thereupon directed him to plead not guilty.
Mr. Moore, who acted on behalf of the prosecution stated that on the morning of the 6th of November, Mr. Wills left his cob in a stable and on his return in the evening the horse was gone. He was later informed that Willie Bunker had been seen in the stable that morning with the horse saddled and bridled. Bunker had taken the horse to the 'Crabtree Inn' where the landlord subsequently handed the animal over to a police constable. Evidence in support of this was given by John Wills the prosecutor, Samuel Ball, John White, and P.C. James. Mr. Moore then cited that Bunker had previously been in a lunatic asylum, evidence in support of which was given by James Mayell the relieving officer who said that the prisoner suffered delusions that he was a jockey and that whenever he saw a horse and cart unoccupied, he would drive it off. He was also subject to fits and was paralysed on one side. This evidence was backed up by a statement from a doctor.

The jury found the Willie Bunker guilty of the charge but were of opinion that he was not responsible for his actions and was ordered to be detained during her Majesty's pleasure at Exeter gaol.

Unknown artist.

Shocking decapitation at Dunkeswell mill.

A shocking and most dreadful accident occurred on the 20th of November 1888 at Dunkeswell, near Honiton. Thirty-six-year-old Eli Hooper the occupier of the mills there, opened the trap-door which accessed the large iron water wheel with the intention of greasing the gudgeon. Adjoined to this wheel was another known as the pit wheel. To enable him to reach the gudgeon of the water wheel it was necessary for him to reach between the spokes of the pit wheel. Whilst in this position it was assumed that by either a rush of water or some other unexplained cause, the wheel was set motion and the poor man being unable to extricate himself was caught by the spokes of the pit wheel and his head cut clean off. His horrified wife Mary Ann made the gruesome discovery. She found his body lying close to the trap door and his head lying in the pit beneath. The inquest into his death returned a verdict of 'accidental death' and great sympathy offered towards his widow in her sad bereavement.
Eli Hooper is buried in St Nicholas churchyard, Dunkeswell.

Fatal bathing incident of two brothers.

A terribly sad bathing fatality occurred on the 1st of August 1889. Artists Ernest Wilson aged twenty-four, and his brother Harold aged eighteen, had been staying in the village of Dittisham for the past three months lodging with a Mrs. Fox. That morning they had taken a boat belonging to William Anniss of the' Passage House Inn' and rowed across the river to Sandridge Point for the purpose of bathing.

They hauled the boat up on to the beach, and after undressing they plunged in the water. All went well until they noticed that the boat had cast its moorings and was drifting down the river with the ebb tide. They both went after it but getting into deep water and neither of them able to swim, they began to shout for help. Their cries were heard by a fisherman named Hutchings who was about a hundred yards away. He began rowing towards them with all possible speed but was unable to reach them in time to save them. He saw the men sink under the water and not rise again. He shouted for assistance and after about two hours of dredging the body of Ernest was brought up in a salmon net. Harold Wilson's body was found a short time later on a mud bank which the receding tide had left dry. The bodies were at once conveyed to the Passage House Inn, Dittisham, and the police informed.

The family of the brothers, who hailed from Wanstead, Essex, were at once telegraphed to inform them of the dreadful news. The message received by the devastated parents read; 'Come at once, both your sons have drowned.' At the inquest into their deaths, the brothers' bereaved father implored that all parents teach their children to swim. Ernest, he said, was a regular exhibitor at the Royal Academy and as an illustrator of books he had achieved a wide reputation. Harold, under the guidance of his older brother had also shown great promise as an artist.

The Peter Tavy love tragedy.

Peter Tavy village and church. Unknown artist.

At the Devon Assizes on the 9th of March 1893, William Williams aged nineteen, the son of a miller at Peter Tavy near Tavistock, was sentenced to death for the murder of seventeen-year-old Emma Holmes Doidge and William Rowe aged twenty-one.

William Williams had purchased a revolver in Tavistock and taken it to church with him on the evening of Sunday the 13th of November 1892. After the service, some cross words took place between himself and Emma. In consequence of what was said he shot dead both her and Frederick Rowe who was walking her home. He afterwards shot himself and then attempted to drown. Whilst in hospital, Williams, known as 'Blutcher' to his friends and fellow villagers, confessed to his father in the presence of P.C. Callard, his reasons for the shooting.

On the 3rd of December, having sufficiently recovered from the wounds he had inflicted upon himself he was brought before the Magistrates at Tavistock charged with the capital offence. Williams a mere youth, appeared in the dock wearing an eye-patch hiding the disfigurement of the loss of his right eye due to the self-inflicted wound; the bullet still lodged in his brain.
Mr. Trebane of Plymouth prosecuted on behalf of the Treasury and Mr. Pearce of Plymouth defended. The witnesses and police officials having been assembled; Williams was led into the dock. He was allowed to sit at the request of his counsel. He wore a light grey suit with a silk handkerchief knotted around his neck and had a white chrysanthemum in his button hole. His parents being so overcome with grief at what had happened they didn't attend the trial. Mr. and Mrs. Doidge and Mr. Rowe however were in attendance. When the doors were opened to the public there was a rush to get seats. Women had their bonnets pulled off in the scramble and

men who still insisted on getting inside even when told the room was full got crushed in the doorway. Once order had been established the trial began.

Mr. Trehane speaking on behalf of Williams said that a few months previous to the tragedy, Williams and Emma Doidge of Coxtor Farm near Peter Tavy, had walked out together on a few occasions. Williams had become very fond of the girl and was aware that other men in the village were also paying her attention, with less honourable intentions than himself. With this in mind, on the 7th of November he purchased a revolver in at Mr. Blanchard's shop in Tavistock. After the evening service on the 13th, Williams came across Emma Doidge, Annie Mudge and William Rowe, who were walking towards Lansford Cross. Emma's brother William who had also been to the church service was walking towards them and could see that Williams was having a verbal altercation with his sister. He overheard him say; "If you don't mind, I'll knock your head off." William Doidge went up to Williams and said; "Not while I'm here you won't!" Williams then challenged him to a fight but William Doidge walked away saying Sunday was not the right day for a fight, but he would go down to Williams house the next day and have it out then. [The altercation had allegedly arisen over Emma telling other men that Williams had been sending her letters.] Williams then went off ahead and the foursome of William Doidge, Annie Mudge, Emma Doidge and Willian Rowe walked on together until they reached Creedy Lane Hill where William Doidge and Annie Rowe stopped to talk whilst Emma and William continued on ahead. A few minutes later they heard four shots ring out.

William Williams had shot both Emma Doidge and William Rowe, he then attempted to take his own life by shooting himself in the eye. Having been unsuccessful in his attempt he then tried to drown himself in a stream at Harford Bridge but its lack of depth only made him wet. Eventually at around midnight soaking wet and badly injured he made his way to the cottage of Mr. William George Doidge a builder who lived nearby. The police and a doctor were called and Williams was later removed to Tavistock Cottage hospital. Prior to his removal, he had asked for his father to be brought to the house. He didn't explain what had happened to him but did make some references to his guilt, including telling Mr. Doidge's daughter that he was; "the worst of the lot."

When P.C. Callard arrived at the cottage he arrested William Williams on the charge of the murder of Emma Doidge and the attempted murder of William Rowe. [William Rowe had not then succumbed to his injuries but passed away at his father's house at nine thirty the following morning.] When asked if he understood the charge, William's said he did. He later at the hospital told the constable the full detail of how he had bought the revolver and committed the deed. He said that he had gone ahead in the lane and lay in a hedge. He first shot William Rowe in the neck and then shot Emma Doidge. He also spoke of his agony of mind after had done it and that he had gone to the bridge and thrown himself into the river but found himself unable to succeed in drowning himself and so went to Harford Bridge Cottage to seek help.

A plea of insanity was put up on Williams behalf but Mr Justice Lawrence in passing sentence said a more cruel and deliberate murder he had never heard of. William Williams was sentenced to death for the murders of both Emma Doidge and William Rowe. Petitions in favour of a reprieve were sent to the Home Secretary, Mr. Luttrell M.P. The petitioners included eight members of Parliament and over twelve thousand other names. A telegram in reply to the plea was received; "The Secretary of State having considered the report of the medical men who examined Wm. Williams and having reviewed all the circumstances of the case, regrets that he can find no sufficient grounds to justify him in advising interference with the due course the law."

William Williams spent his last few days in Exeter gaol awaiting his execution. The day beforehand he was allowed a visit from his two sisters and younger brother. Two warders were present throughout. He appeared quite cheerful and asked after the relatives of William Rowe and enquired as to where Emma and William were buried. He spoke of family matters, especially as to the state of health of his mother. Towards the close of the meeting one of the sisters asked him if he was sure he was going to heaven. He replied that he was sure he was. The following morning at eight o'clock, judgment of death was duly executed upon William Williams. The public had begun to congregate soon after seven o'clock and whilst they were few in numbers, they stood about in groups discussing in subdued tones the terrible double murder and the impending execution of the murderer. The crowd began to grow denser as the hands of the clock moved closer to eight o'clock. As the clock chimed the hour of eight, the warder whose duty it was to hoist the flag over the parapet was seen to lift his hat and this was at once accepted as an indication that the mournful procession was approaching the scaffold - and then slowly the black flag was drawn into position. Quietly and orderly the crowd dispersed, satisfied that the executioner had done his work and that the unhappy mortal who paid the law's full penalty had been sent to meet his maker with as little suffering and torture as was possible.

* On the 5th of September 1893 it was reported that Mr. Rowe, father of the William Rowe, had died at the Tavistock Cottage Hospital the previous Saturday from an illness brought on by excessive grief. This was said to have been the sixth death arising directly or indirectly out of the sad tragedy at Peter Tavy the previous November.

The great gale of 1893.

A dreadful gale swept through Torquay on the 12th of December 1893 and was said to be the worst the region had experienced in many years. It sprang up during the early hours of the morning and increased in violence until mid-day, by which time it was blowing a hurricane. The bay itself was like a sea of foam. Accompanied by sheets of rain the wind tore across from the south-west in terrific gusts. Like great guns the mighty waves thundered against Haldon pier throwing great clouds of spray from thirty to fifty feet over the structure. So strong was the gale that it was with the utmost difficulty that people were able to walk along the more exposed roads and to keep on their feet. Several fishing vessels drifted from their moorings; one was sunk and others damaged. Many tender boats and pleasure boats were either dashed to pieces or sunk when the waves rushed over them. In the inner harbour the sight of wreckage was pitiable. Bits of boats, barrels, nets and all sorts of items were tossed about in indescribable confusion. The hooker 'Ada' belonging to a fisherman named Claddings, which had been anchored in the outer harbour was carried over into the corner of the new harbour. Unsuccessful efforts were made to save her, and three men named Skinner, Taylor and Lear, all tried to get round the end of the fish quay in a small boat with the object of towing her into the inner harbour, but eventually they had to give up. Other attempts were made to get hold of the vessel but she tossed about like a feather and gradually drifted away filled with water and sank, leaving only her masts visible. All the fishing gear on board was thrown out and lost. The boat owner was a poor man and great sympathy was expressed towards him. There was talk of a subscription list being set up to help make good the loss he had so unfortunately suffered.

The same gale that hit Torquay also struck Dartmouth. When at its height, the large chimney stack on York House belonging to Mr. John Way, fell, crashing through the roof. The inhabitants having a narrow escape. Mr. Way who was sitting in the room immediately underneath the broken roof escaped with severe bruising to his foot. Mrs. Longford Browne who lived on the floor below was so greatly alarmed that she rushed downstairs in her dressing gown, and being in delicate health was taken to the Castle Hotel. Shortly after midnight the second chimney stack of the same house fell with a heavy crash and everyone rushed out terrified.

A large crowd had congregated near the Post Office and could only watch as roof tops fell around them and boats crashed into each other in the water. The schooner 'Mary Canning' broke adrift from her moorings alongside the South Parade and drifted with force in the direction of the Railway Pontoon. Luckily, she just cleared it, but did sweep away one of the lamps on the Parade. Her crew were fortunate in getting a rope ashore and hundreds of willing hands held on to it until the vessel was again safely moored.

Telegraph wires were broken down at Mount Boone by falling trees. Communication was later restored at half-post five that evening by Lineman Steadman and a party of the Royal Engineers. The telephone wires across the river had broken and a large chimney stack in Lower Street fell; causing further alarm when it caught fire. Roofs and glass houses in South Town were stripped.

The main road to Kingsbridge was blocked by fallen trees near Lancombe Street. The river ferry didn't resume until two in the afternoon. The steam launch 'Glenolva' from when near Anchor Stone below Dittisham had to run back under Greenaway Quay for shelter owing to the heavy sea. Dartmouth Football Club's new dressing-room and house only recently having been erected, was blown over and across the road and into another field.

Tragic case of diphtheria in Bideford.

In June 1894 a Bideford lady sent home a servant girl who was suffering from diphtheria. Instead of sending her in a private hire vehicle, she sent her in an open carriage which was being used for public conveyance. The Bideford Local Board was informed and directed that legal proceedings should be taken against the lady for this breach of the law. When the summons came to be served it was found that the lady was dead having succumbed to the disease herself. After sending the girl away in order to get the infection out of the house she herself was stricken with the illness and died soon afterwards.

Poisoned sucking matches.

An Inquest was held at Bere Alston on June 29th 1894 into the death of Claudia Mary Field aged two and a half. Claudia was the daughter of Frederick Field the Station Master there.
Her father stated that she had been put to bed by her nurse the previous Friday afternoon as usual. It appeared that little Claudia had woken up whilst alone in the bedroom and getting hold of a box of matches, sucked some of them. No real notice was taken of the incident as she didn't become ill until the Monday when symptoms developed which caused anxiety. Dr. Rowland Hill was called and when told of match sucking incident he treated her for phosphorous poisoning. She passed away on Thursday the 28th three days later. Dr. Hill said when he carried out a post-mortem examination it confirmed the child had died of phosphorous poisoning. The Jury of whom Mr Sobey was Foreman, returned a verdict that 'the deceased died from phosphorous poisoning caused by sucking matches.'

Policeman injured on George Street.

Philip Payne a constable in the Devonport Borough Police Force, in the early hours of Friday the 1st of February 1895 whilst crossing George Street, caught his heel and fell on the icy pavement sustaining a compound fracture to his right leg. The stricken officer lay there until Sergeant Webber who was also on patrol in the area came along. P.C Payne insisted on being taken home rather than to hospital. Sergeant Webber called for an ambulance and once inside Payne in great pain agreed to be coveyed to the Royal Albert Hospital where he was attended to. The leg was set but two days later because of the extent of the injury and the infection that had set in, he was advised on the Sunday afternoon that he would need to have his leg amputated; to which he consented saying it was better to lose his leg than lose his life. Sadly P.C Payne died of shock soon after the amputation on the 4th of February, he was forty-seven years-old.

Philip Payne's funeral took place on Thursday the 7th. The cortege which consisted of a glass hearse, three mourning coaches and six cabs, left his former residence at 6. Ker Street, Devonport, at half-past two in the afternoon. After the cortege came a muster of thirty constables of the Devonport force who were headed by Superintendent Matters, Inspectors Irish, Mutton and Maddock. ex- Inspector H. Webber (Mayor's officer) and Sergeants Clarke, Willcocks, Pascoe, Lethbridge, Webber, and Detective Sergeant Blewett and Detective Down. The Plymouth force were represented by Chief-Constable Sowerby, Inspectors Warne, Wyatt, and Detective Inspector Dart, Mace-bearers Pill and Codd, and twenty-eight constables. From Stonehouse were Sergeant Stone and a dozen constables as well as a number of the Stonehouse Fire Brigade in uniform. The Metropolitan Police were the largest force represented, having a contingent of almost fifty men, their head being Superintendent Smith, Inspectors W. Moorman, Stoops, and Wood. Several military foot police were also present as were several ex-policemen.

P.C Payne was interred at the Plymouth [Ford Park] Cemetery where the service was conducted by the Rev. F. W. Beaumont (Wesleyan) of Devonport. On the coffin lay a wreath from his former comrades, one from the butchers of Devonport Market and a few others from friends and bereaved relations.

Reaching for chestnuts.

Thirteen-year-old Kate Annette Hook was admitted to Teignmouth Infirmary on the 28th of January 1896, suffering from severe burns. Kate lived at 2. Regent Gardens, Teignmouth, with her five siblings and parents William a fisherman and her mother also called Kate.

That morning her mother left Kate at home to look after baby Violet whilst she went out to do her washing. When she left, her mother reminded her to put the potatoes on the fire at twelve noon as she would be home for dinner at one o'clock. At round mid-day, Jessie Strawbridge a servant at Mrs. Colman's dairy opposite the Hook's house, heard someone screaming and ran outside to see what the commotion was all about. She saw poor Kate in the garden with her clothes on fire. She rushed to find Mrs. Hook and in a distressed state cried; "Mrs Hook, come quick, your Kate is all on fire!" Both women hurried back to the house only for Mrs. Hook to find her daughter lying in the street with her clothes alight. Mr. Albert Polyblank another neighbour had also been alerted by Kate's desperate cries and seeing her in flames had taken off his coat and wrapped it around her to quell the fire. A doctor was called and the poor girl was removed to the infirmary with severe burns to her upper body. Still conscious she was able to explain what had happened. She said that she had hidden some chestnuts under a lamp on the mantelpiece, and in reaching up her clothes caught alight. Her apron caught on fire first and tearing it off she threw it at the grate, but not in time to prevent her other clothing also catching alight.

Kate lingered for six weeks before succumbing to her injuries and exhaustion on the 8th of March. A verdict of 'accidental death' was returned.

Harrowing triple murder and suicide at Teignmouth.

A dreadful triple murder and suicide took place in Teignmouth on the afternoon of the 20th of April 1896. Mr. George Haines aged thirty-nine, a lodging-housekeeper at 1. Spring Gardens; a fashionable part the town which overlooked the sea. Without warning he murdered his three youngest children by cutting their throats with a razor and putting an end to himself by the same means.

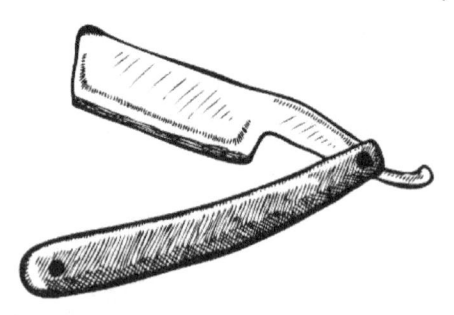

In the house at the time of the tragedy were his wife, an elderly lady lodger called Mrs. Ramsay, a gentleman called Captain Pearson, a servant girl named Bessie Newlands and of course himself and three of his four children. The crime had evidently been premeditated as shortly before lunch that day, George Haines had called in to a barber shop run by Mr. Littlefield and complained that the razor which he had ground a few days earlier had not been done properly and he waited while the barber re-sharpened it. He complained of pains in his head that were coming 'again' and Mr. Littlefield thought he was referring to neuralgic pains from which he had sometimes suffered. George Haines then left and returned home. Nothing unusual seems to have transpired over lunch and it was just before three o'clock in the afternoon while Mrs. Haines was clearing away the table in the dining-room where the lodger had partaken of her midday meal, that her husband seized the opportunity to commit the horrific crime. Bessie, the fourteen-year-old servant along with the children were in a small room in the basement and to the rear of the house adjoining the kitchen. George Haines came in and pushed Bessie out of the room and slammed shut the door. He had only a few minutes earlier sent his eldest boy Harry aged eight, his son from his first marriage, to post two letters. Having shut himself up with the three helpless children, Haines apparently commenced to carry out the massacre. Strangely, nobody in the house heard any screams from the youngsters. It was only on Mrs. Haines coming downstairs that she discovered what had happened. Her screams attracted the attention of Mr. Roberts a gentleman lodging in the adjoining property. On learning what had happened he ran for assistance. Meeting a cab in the street he drove to the Police station. On the way he informed Mr. Groves a photographic operator who was close to the house and also a policeman, of what had occurred. At the station he told Sergeant Richards of the massacre and together they quickly made their way to Spring Gardens. In the meantime, Mrs. Roberts, the lodging house keeper at 2. Spring Gardens, had gone into the house and assisted the almost faint with shock Mrs. Haines to a sofa in the front room.

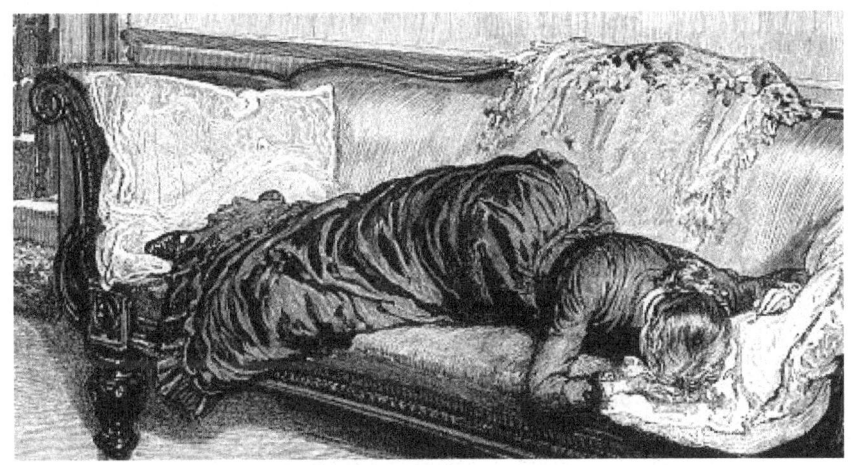

Unknown artist.

Mr. Groves the photographic operator had also entered the premises and was directed by Bessie Newland to the room in which the tragedy had occurred. There he saw the three innocent little children; John Edward George aged four; Daisy May aged three and Fowler Rockett aged 10 months; lying on the floor in pools of blood. They were fully dressed except for the baby who was minus his socks. Two of the children were lying together on the hearth rug and the third was about a yard away lying with his face downwards and one leg slightly drawn up, and with his little fists clenched. Mr. Groves fearing that the murderer might still be at large waiting to despatch of more victims, he sent away the eldest boy Harry who had just returned from posting the letter and who he met in the passageway. Having armed himself with the kitchen poker he commenced to search the house for the culprit. P.C. Martin had now entered the property and joined Mr. Groves in the search. Reaching the servants bedroom at the back of the house, they were horrified to find the body of George Haines with his throat badly cut and with an open razor covered in blood by his side. On the stairs leading to the landing there were traces of blood giving rise to the speculation that the poor man after destroying his children must have cut his own throat before leaving the room. He had then run up the stairs where he dropped down dead through loss of blood.

News of the tragedy spread like wildfire and in very short time a crowd of several hundred persons had assembled in the vicinity of the house. Sometime later Police Superintendent Williams of Bovey Tracey arrived to investigate the affair. The house was taken charge of by the police and nobody except the relatives of the family and the lodgers were allowed to enter. A doctor sought and attending to each of the victims, pronounced life extinct. Mrs. Haines was still lying on the sofa prostrate with absolute inconsolable grief.

The inquest into the deaths of Henry George Haines, Daisy May Haines, John Edward George Haines and Fowler Rockett Haines, was held at Mr Marks's 'Railway Hotel' the following day before Mr. Hacker the Coroner and Mr. Coleridge the Chief Constable of Devon. Superintendent Williams of Bovey Tracey watched the proceedings on behalf of the police. Sergeant Richards of Teignmouth Police was also present during the enquiry. The Coroner advised the jury that the case they were dealing with was one of a very serious nature and unusual for Teignmouth. A case in which the violent deaths of four persons had occurred, three of them being children, the other a man, their father. Their deaths had occurred under circumstances which evidently pointed to a series of crimes having been committed. It was therefore beholden to them to very carefully investigate the case and to determine upon the evidence and the circumstances relating to the deaths as to who was responsible for them. The jury were then taken to 1. Spring Gardens to view the bodies before returning to the Railway Hotel to continue the inquiry.

Annie Haines the grieving mother and widow was the first witness called, she described how her husband Henry George Haines had followed the occupation of an hotel proprietor since the family had moved to Teignmouth three years previously. She had noticed him acting strangely for some time and particularly the day before the murders. He had asked her if she thought he were mad on a number of occasions recently. On the day of the tragedy, George had woken at four a.m. and again asked if she thought him mad; she didn't answer although she did think something was wrong with him. She noticed he had been ill for some time and it had affected his temper, she had even mentioned this to her doctor. George then got up and made them both a cup of tea which was an unusual thing for him to do. He lay down again but soon got back up and was pacing the room saying he was mad. Annie went on to say that her husband had given the children their lunch at one o'clock that day and was about to send the servant girl to post a letter but she suggested that Harry should go instead. Annie then went upstairs to attend to the lodger's lunch and when she came back down a few minutes later she found her children dead.

Henry Littlefield, of 13. King Street, Teignmouth was the next witness called. He said that at about eleven o'clock, George Haines had come to his shop with a razor and waited while it was being sharpened. He'd complained of pains in his head, and referring to the recent Portsmouth tragedy which had been the talk of the town. Haines had said Matthews* ought to be shot without judge or jury.

Bessie Newlands the Haines maid, described how she was working in the kitchen when Mr. Haines came in and going into the pantry he shut the door on her. She said that he must have then murdered the children, though she didn't hear a sound and knew nothing of it until she heard Mrs. Haines screaming. It was then that she went to the pantry and saw the children lying dead.

John Roberts, a visitor from Clifton near Bristol who was staying at the property next door, described how he heard a scream and went to investigate. He found Mrs. Haines sobbing and saying that her husband had murdered her children and killed himself. He didn't take much notice at first thinking she was suffering from hysteria but on entering the pantry he discovered the bodies of the children. Other witness came forward and gave their account of the tragedy including Harry, the son of Mr. Haines from his first marriage.

The funeral of the three children together with their father took place early on the morning of Thursday the 23rd of April. The inquest was put on hold for the day on Wednesday so that arrangements could be made for the internment. The burials took place at the early hour of six forty-five so as not to attract a large gathering. The bodies were each placed in a separate coffin and then onto a single hearse. The few mourners at the graveside at St. Michael's Church East Teignmouth, watched as the coffins were then placed in two separate graves; the children being buried together.

On the recommencement of the inquiry Sergeant Richards said that he had sent a telegram to Mrs. Burgess who resided at 52. Dartmouth Road, London, asking her to forward him any letters she may have recently received from Mr. Haines, her brother. The following day he received in the post a letter addressed to Mrs. Burgess and enclosed with it was a letter to Mrs. Ramsay who lodged with the Haines. These were the letters young Harry had been sent to post. The first letter although sent to Mrs. Burgess was actually written by George Haines to his wife Annie. In it he accused her of 'bad doings' and at times it was rambling and didn't make sense. The letter to Mrs. Ramsay accused his wife of having been in the Captain's room the previous evening. Mrs. Burgess in a letter to the Coroner said that she had last seen her brother four months previously when he had come to visit her in London. She said he appeared very strange and had an irritable temper. The Coroner in summing up, pointed out that the jury must have some reasonable evidence of insanity before they could find the deceased man insane. The letters certainly disclosed that there was something working in his mind, although it appeared that there were no grounds for jealousy. The jury after a short retirement, returned a verdict of 'wilful murder' in the case of each of the three children and of *'felo de se'* in the ease of the father.

* The Portsmouth tragedy refers to the case of Philip Matthews, formerly a coachman from Teignmouth, who murdered his daughter Elsie in April 1896 and left her body in a field at Copnor, just outside of the city.

Little Queenie Baker abandoned in Devonport.

Arthur Palmer who had recently been prominent in the public eye, having been associated with the infamous Reading murders [see next story - Polly Palmer baby farmer] arrived at Devonport on Sunday the 3rd of May 1896, and was brought before the Magistrates the following morning on a charge of abandoning a child in May the previous year. Palmer had only just been dismissed by Reading Magistrates the previous day on the capital charge of being an accessory in the murder of a number of infants. He was immediately re-arrested on the charge which now saw him standing in the dock at Devonport.

Moustachioed Palmer, who was of a smart and fashionable appearance, looked somewhat worried as he viewed the densely crowded courtroom. A large number of people had gathered outside unable to gain access. Directly in front of the prisoner and seated at the solicitors table was Mrs. Smale of Salisbury Road, Lipson, Plymouth. Next to her sat a little girl; Queenie Baker, who she had adopted a few weeks after the child having been found abandoned on the streets of Devonport. Queenie, a pretty little thing who looked the picture of health continually looked up at the man in the dock who only a few days previously had referred to as her 'other Dada' when shown a picture of him. Palmer though appeared oblivious of her presence. Arthur Ernest Palmer was described on the charge-sheet as living at 76. Mayo Road, Willesden, London, and employed as a commission agent. He was charged with the abandonment of a child aged about four years old in May of the previous year, in a manner likely to cause unnecessary suffering. Palmer pleaded guilty to the charge. Superintendent J. Matters was first called to give details concerning the case. He stated that on the 17th of May 1895, the prisoner and his wife were living at 2. Gloucester Cottages, Morice Town, and had with them a little girl who was then about four years of age. On the same day the child was found wandering about the streets. She was taken to 66. Princes Street and had been in the charge of a custodian since that day. On being informed that Mr. Palmer was in the custody of Reading Police on Saturday the 2nd of May 1896, he made his way there with a warrant which was read to Palmer by the Chief Constable of Reading Police, Mr. Tewsey, in connection with the charge. Palmer replied that he knew nothing about it and had never been to Devonport.

Jessie Skinner residing at 12. Yorke Street and formerly of 66. Princes Street, took to the stand. She said that on the 11th of May 1895, just before nine o'clock in the evening she saw the little girl [Queenie Baker] wandering about in Princes Street all by herself. She spoke to the child and established her name and that she was from Bristol. The girl also told her that she had been wandering the streets all afternoon and evening. Not finding anyone who claimed the child as being theirs, Jessie Skinner took her to the Town Hall where the police officer on duty asked her to take the child home for the time being, which she did. She said the little girl was cold and hungry and that she ended up looking after her for five weeks.

Mrs. Barber of 2. Gloucester Cottages, Morice Town, said she knew the prisoner. On Thursday the 9th of May she had apartments to let and the gentleman standing in the dock applied and said that he required a furnished room and that he only wanted it for a week. The gentleman then took possession of the room the following day. He was accompanied by a woman who she believed to be his wife. She went on to say that he enquired at what time he could get the daily papers, and during their stay the postman brought parcels and letters for him by almost every post. The prisoner and his wife would leave the child for hours at a time in bed. They would put the child to bed at about five o'clock in the afternoon, and on many occasions, she had taken the liberty to unlock the door to see if the child was all right. On one occasion when her husband was pasting some wallpaper, Palmer came out into the street and asked him if he had a spare brush, adding that it was a long time since he had done any of that kind of work. Whilst they were in conversation, Mr. Barber witnessed the prisoner's wife through the parlour window grab hold of the child by her hair. Incensed he went in and had words with her and Mrs. Palmer gave the excuse that Queenie had been misbehaving herself and that she could not do anything with her. The Palmer's handed back the key to their room on the 17th of May, giving it to the Barber's young son. Mrs. Barber being out having gone to a family funeral. The boy watched as the Palmer's walked towards the nearby park steps with the young girl walking behind them. They met with the postman who said; "I have a parcel for you." The boy heard Mrs. Palmer say; "Give it to me now," but the postman refused saying he had to deliver it to her lodgings. Mrs. Palmer then returned to 2. Gloucester Street and the parcel was handed over. Whilst there she changed her dress and the trio left again shortly afterwards. The following day Queenie was brought to the house by Mrs. Skinner and Detective Blewett. Mrs. Barber said she identified the girl as being the child who had been at her house with Mr. and Mrs. Palmer.
William Barber, son of Mrs. Barber, reiterated the evidence of his mother as being what he had witnessed.

Mr. Foster J. Bone (the magistrate's clerk) stated under the Act for the Prevention of Cruelty to Children, the prisoner was liable to a fine of twenty-five pounds or in default a period of imprisonment not exceeding six months. The Magistrates then retired and during the course of their consultation conferred with the Chief Constable. After about a quarter of an hour's absence they returned. The Chairman Mr. May, addressing the prisoner said; "You are charged with an offence to which you have pleaded guilty. A great offence in the eye of the law and your punishment will be three months imprisonment with hard labour." The sentence was received with slight applause which was immediately suppressed by the Chief Constable. The prisoner was then removed from the dock and placed in a cell awaiting removal to Plymouth Prison.

*Unfortunately, this court hearing does not appear to cover WHY Mr. and Mrs. Palmer had the little girl Queenie Baker staying with them, neither why they chose to abandon her. Queenie told the lady who found her wandering the streets that she was from Bristol. Maybe things will become a little clearer in the next story.

Polly Palmer the baby farmer….. and her mother, the serial killer.

This is a tale most terrible – women who took advantage of unfortunate mother's and took from them their child and their money; both handed over on the promise of giving the youngster a better life.

On Monday, the 12th of August 1898, a young woman calling herself Mrs. Stewart who described herself as a farmer's wife, went to Devonport to receive a baby, the three-week-old child of a widowed sailor's wife called Jane Hill. Mrs. Hill had seen an advertisement in a newspaper offering to adopt a child and she being desirous to part with her illegitimate offspring wrote to the woman who had placed the advert who agreed to take the baby for twelve pounds. That evening at North Road Station, Mrs. Hill handed over her daughter to Mrs. Stewart, as well as the twelve pounds and an extra two pounds to cover travelling expenses.

Reaching Newton Abbot on the mail train at nine thirty that evening, Mrs. Stewart along with the other passengers were asked to change trains. On the platform she enquired of a wheel greaser if she could get to Oxford that night. As he didn't know he in turn enquired with a guard who informed her she could get no further than Didcot and on account of the difficulty in getting lodgings he advised her to stay in Bath, which she did.

Early the next morning a workman named Mills, an employee of the Great Western Railway Company was cleaning out several carriages which had formed part of the mail train from Plymouth the previous evening. Under a seat in the ladies' compartment, he found a healthy female child about three weeks to a month old, wrapped up in a brown paper parcel. In another parcel were some towels and under-linen. In the same carriage he also found a quart bottle containing nearly a pint of milk. It was evident that the child had been in the carriage all night. There were no marks on the clothing that gave any clue as to the identification of the child

106

which was subsequently removed to the Newton Abbot Workhouse by P.C. Fayter. Enquiries were then made and suspicion fell on the woman who got out of the mail train the night before and enquired about getting to Oxford. She was later traced to Bampton Station, and from there to Brize Norton where she and her husband had been living for the past few months. The couple were arrested the following morning and conveyed to Witney Police station near Oxford, and from there to Newton Abbot. The arrested couple were Mary Ann Palmer and her husband Arthur.

On Thursday the 15th of August, Mrs. Hill having been informed of the arrest [possibly through a newspaper appeal for the mother to come forward] she made her way to Newton Abbot from Devonport and identified the child as hers. The utmost praise was given to the wheel greaser who had taken such careful notice of Mrs. Palmer, that he was able to give the police a perfectly accurate description of her, thus enabling a swift arrest.

In September 1898, Mary Ann (Polly) Palmer and Arthur Palmer were brought before Mr J. F. Robinson and Dr. J. W. Ley at Newton Abbot Police Court. Mary Ann was charged with abandoning the child of Mrs. Hill, by leaving it in a railway carriage at Newton Abbot Station, and the latter with aiding and abetting her in the act. Police Sergeant Coles stated that from information he'd received on the Wednesday, he proceeded to Witney in Oxfordshire where he found the prisoners in the custody of the local police. He was informed that they had been arrested at Brize Norton, a village about five miles from Witney. After a statement was given by Arthur Palmer to Superintendent Cooke of Witney. Coles said he heard the officer say to Mr. Palmer; "Do I understand you to say that you knew your wife had gone to Plymouth after a child?" Mr. Palmer then replied; "Yes." The Superintendent then said; "You were present when your wife returned without the child?" Again Mr. Palmer replied to the affirmative. At this point Police Sergeant Coles read the warrant of arrest to both prisoners and told them he was to take them to Newton Abbot. They both said they understood the implication of the warrant.

P.C. Fayter described how at around seven thirty on the Tuesday morning he received the information that a baby had been found at the railway station at Newton Abbot and he immediately made his way there. He found the infant in the care of one of the porters, named Thomas John Wills. The child was very cold and shaking and the clothing it was wearing was very wet. The child was also wrapped up in brown paper. He took the child from Mr. Wills care and removed it along with the bottle of milk found in the compartment to the Police Station, and from there to the Workhouse. On this evidence Police Sergeant Coles asked for the couple to be remanded until the following Tuesday, which was granted.

Mr. Palmer then requested that some of the money which had been found on his person at the time of his arrest might be handed over for the purpose of obtaining legal aid in the defence of his wife. Police Sergeant Coles responded by saying that the police had every reason to believe that the money was part of the proceeds of the abandonment of the child at Newton Abbot. Mr J.F. Robinson said that under those circumstances the court could not hand over any of the money. Mr. Palmer declared that the money which was found on him when he was arrested was that which he had earned during the summer hay-making, harvesting, and from the sale of a hundred head of poultry. The Bench considered the fact of the money being found on the prisoner and felt there was enough evidence to support the fact that it could have been the money given by Mrs. Hill to the female prisoner.

Ann Hill, a widow who resided at 56. Chapel Street, Devonport, was next to take to the stand. She said that the female prisoner had advertised in the 'Western Evening Herald' offering under the heading of 'Adoption' to take the child and give it a good home in the countryside of Oxfordshire. After having exchanged correspondence, she met with the woman who called herself Mrs. Stewart at North Road Station, and paid her twelve pounds to take the child. She also gave her two pounds to cover her railway expenses. They then went to the registrar of births, marriages and deaths in Devonport where the child was registered in the name of 'Mary Ann Florence Stewart,' which was of course a false name.

Dr. Ley; "Did you willingly allow this to be done?"

Mrs. Hill; "Yes, I didn't know that I was doing wrong, and I don't believe the prisoner thought so either. She was very anxious to have the child registered in her name which she had given me as Mrs. Stewart and had signed herself 'Mrs. Stewart' in her letters."

In reply to Sergeant Coles, Mrs. Hill said that she had no idea that there was anything suspicious in any of the prisoner's actions. During a conversation she had with her on the Monday afternoon, Mary Ann Palmer had made the remark; "Don't think this is another case of Mrs. Dyer* because it's not." Mrs. Hill had then replied; "No, I would see her hanged and her daughter too." [She had no idea at the time that she was actually talking to the daughter of Mrs. Dyer, the infamous baby farmer and murderer.] Mrs. Hill then added that she saw the female prisoner and her baby daughter off from Millbay Station on the mail train that evening. Sergeant Coles asked Mrs. Hill if the female prisoner was the woman to whom she had paid fourteen pounds and into whose care she had handed her child? Mrs. Hill said she was, but she was now wearing her hair tied back. When she had last seen her, she had been wearing a fringe. She was though wearing the same bodice. Dr. Ley asked Mrs. Hill if she had made any inquiries with reference to the character of the woman to whom she was handing over her child to. Mrs. Hill said that from the manners of the woman and the letters she had received, she had imagined her to be 'all right.' She then asked the court for permission to take the child back with her to Devonport, but the Bench declined the request saying the child was better off at the Newton Abbot Workhouse than with her.

The Palmers were charged and sent to trail at the next quarter sessions which were to be held at Exeter the following month. On the 20th of October Arthur Palmer aged twenty-eight and Mary Ann Palmer aged twenty-four, were indicted for unlawfully abandoning a three-week-old female child in a railway carriage at Newton Abbot on September 12th, thereby endangering the child's life. Here Mary Ann Palmer gave a slightly different account of what had occurred by way of a signed statement; "When I got to Newton Abbot on Monday September the 12th the woman [Mrs. Bryant] I gave the baby to was of middle height, dark eyes and hair. She was dressed in a black bonnet, a black cape and grey dress. I have never seen the woman in my life before, but she asked if I had been to Plymouth and said; "You have a young baby there," and I said "Yes, I've just taken it from its mother." She asked me if I had far to go and I said "I have to go to Oxford." She said; "I don't suppose you want anyone to adopt that baby?" I said "No, but I am going to advertise for someone to take it to nurse." She then said, "Well, I have been advertising for one to adopt myself. If you wanted anyone to adopt that one, I would do so for twenty pounds." I replied "I don't want anyone to adopt it, I have adopted it myself for less than that. I only want to put it out for a while." Then she said; "Well, if you will pay me ten pounds, I will take it for twelve months for you." I asked her where she lived and she gave me her address. I gave her the money and she promised me she would write to me the next day and I have not heard any more of her. The address the woman here referred to was according to Mrs. Palmer, 'Ivy Cottage, Exeter Road, Exeter,' but, said counsel, there was no such address in Exeter and the accused's statement had been proved by the telegrams since found, to be false. Mrs. Palmer sent two telegrams from Bath the morning after the abandonment, one to her husband saying: "Bath, all well; meet eleven train. Flo." This was sent in accordance with the prisoner's plans and 'all well' meant that Mrs. Palmer was at Bath without the child and with the money. The other telegram to which the Bench's attention was drawn to was sent to Mrs. Hill, from Bath saying; "Got to Bath all right; baby very good: only cried once; will write to-morrow. Stewart." It was clear to the Bench that Mr. Palmer was aware of his wife's activities. Both prisoners were found guilty and the jury were then told of the previous case of child abandonment against Mr. Palmer in Devonport. The Chairman said the prisoners had been found guilty of a very serious offence. He could hardly find words to express on behalf of the court, the gravity of the offence. They had been guilty of a cruel and unfeeling act towards an infant child. They had taken it from its mother professing to take care of it and treat it as their own, when the female prisoner had barely received the child into her custody before apparently making arrangements for deserting it. She tied it up into a parcel and put it under the seat of the railway carriage, certainly indifferent as to what would happen to it. The natural result of what she did might possibly have killed the child. Mary Ann and Arthur Palmer were both sentenced to two years imprisonment with hard labour.

*Amelia [Annie] Dyer was Britain's most prolific infant serial killer. She was sentenced to death and was hung on the 10th June 1896 at Newgate gaol in London. She was thought to have killed between

two and four hundred innocent babies that she had taken into her 'care' in over a thirty-year period. Amelia, or Annie as she was known, had for many years engaged in the wholesale traffic of babies and infants whom she undertook to adopt on a payment of fees ranging from ten to fifty pounds and upwards. Having obtained as much money as possible from the parents of the children she then strangled the poor things and threw their bodies into the Thames. The chief witness against Annie Dyer at her trial in 1896 was her daughter; Mary Ann [Polly] Palmer, who it was thought was an accessory in many cases. Arthur Palmer was also thought to be an accessory in the murders but without enough evidence the charges against him were dropped. He was then re-arrested [see previous story] and charged with the child abandonment of four-year-old Queenie Baker in Devonport in 1895, to which he admitted his guilt and was sentenced to three months imprisonment with hard labour. Mary Ann however was cleared by a confession from her mother admonishing her of any knowledge of the murder.

Amelia Dyer – unknown photographer.

Annie Dyer's nefarious crimes were discovered after a barmaid called Evelina Marmon gave birth to an illegitimate daughter called Doris in a boarding house in Cheltenham. She sought adoption for her child and placed an advertisement in the 'Bristol Times & Mirror' newspaper.

In the same newspaper she saw an advertisement that looked like the answer to her prayers, it read: 'Married couple with no family would adopt healthy child, nice country home. Terms ten pounds.' Evelina contacted the person who placed the ad and a few days later received a reply from a Mrs. Harding. Mrs. Harding said how much she would like a sweet little girl to call her own and that she wasn't after a child for money, but for company and how much she and her husband adored children although they didn't have any of their own. A week later, Evelina handed over her precious child and the ten pounds. She was surprised by Mrs. Harding's advanced age, but the woman appeared affectionate towards the baby. She accompanied Mrs. Harding and her daughter to the railway station where she bade them a tearful goodbye. A few days later she received a letter from Mrs. Harding saying all was well. Evelina wrote back enquiring about her daughter but got no reply. Mrs Harding was actually Amelia Dyer and had not travelled to Reading as she had told Evelina; instead, she went to Willesden, London, where Mary Ann and Arthur were living. There she found some white edging tape used in dressmaking and winding it twice around baby Doris's neck, she then tied it with a knot and left the poor child to die a slow choking death. It was alleged that Mary Ann helped her to wrap the body in a napkin ready for disposal. The following day Wednesday the 1st of April, a baby boy named Harry Simmons was brought to the house. With no more edging tape available, Amelia Dyer cut the length from around Doris's corpse and used it to strangle the little boy. The following day both bodies were put into a carpet bag along with some house bricks for added weight. Heading towards Reading, Dyer, at a secluded spot near a weir at Caversham Lock, forced the bag through railings and into the River Thames.

A few days earlier a package had been retrieved from the Thames at Reading by a bargeman. It contained the remains of a baby girl, later identified as Helena Fry. Police were able to make out a microscopic name and address written on the paper the child had been wrapped in. The name on the packaging was 'Mrs. Thomas.' This information led the police to the door of Amelia Dyer. With not enough evidence to arrest Dyer, the police put her under surveillance and when a prospective client came calling, Amelia Dyer answered the door to not a young woman in need of a carer for her child, but the police. Inside the property the detectives were overcome by the stench of human decomposition, although no remains were found. There was however plenty of other evidence including the white edging tape, telegrams regarding adoption arrangements, letters from mothers inquiring about the well-being of their children, and other related paraphernalia. The information gleaned from this search of the property gave the police the shocking certainty that at least twenty children had been placed in the care of 'Mrs. Thomas' within the last month.

Picture courtesy of blogspot.com

Helena Fry, the baby found in the Thames on the 30th of March had been handed over to Amelia Dyer at Temple Meads station in Bristol on the 5th of March. That very same evening she had arrived home carrying only a brown paper parcel. She hid the package in the house, but after three weeks the odour of decomposition prompted her to dump the parcel in the river. She was arrested on the 4th of April and charged with murder. The police had the Thames dragged again, and six more children's bodies were discovered including Doris Marmon and Harry Simmons; Amelia Dyer's last victims. She later told police that she could tell which children had been hers by the white tape around their little necks.

Poor Evelina Marmon, eleven days after handing her precious little girl over to the kindly seeming Mrs. Hardy, she was brought by the police to Reading to identify the remains of her daughter.

Amelia had made a lot of money from baby farming. She would always assure the mother's that she was a respectable married woman who only wanted to give a child a loving home. Sadly, soon after the receipt of each child she murdered them. In 1879 a doctor had alerted the authorities to the large number of child deaths he had been called to certify in Dyer's care. Unfortunately, instead of being convicted of murder or manslaughter, Amelia Dyer was sentenced to six months' hard labour for neglect and was therefore able to on release continue the dreadful deeds. After her subsequent arrest in 1896 it was speculated as to how many of the abandoned babies found in ditches, trains and other such places in Plymouth and Devon had been taken by Palmer or her mother for money on the promise of giving the child a loving upbringing. There were very likely many women in South Devon who had given up their child wondering what had become of its fate. In 1896 Mary Ann Palmer was to have gone on trial for aiding and abetting her mother Amelia Dyer, for the murder of Frances Jessie Golding, but the jury threw out the bill after a Coroner's inquest discovered that the body they were holding the inquest on was not that of the missing child. Mary Ann Palmer was said to have walked out of the dock with a jaunty air.

Death by gas poisoning.

In early November 1898 a nineteen-year-old messenger boy called George Lee was found dead at the foot of his bed at the Duke of Cornwall Hotel in Plymouth.

Old postcard of the Duke of Cornwall Hotel – private collection.

A page boy named John Britton, sharing the same room at the top of the hotel was found unconscious and removed to hospital. An escape of gas in the vicinity of the bedroom was noticed a few hours earlier, shortly after midnight by another employee; Edward May a kitchen porter, who called the night porter George Finch and together they found the escape was coming from a pipe on the landing just outside the room in which the men were sleeping. George Finch applied a light to the gas and it produced a jet of about four to five inches long. He put the light out and then plastered the wall near the escape with soap. Testing it again, he found there was no escape visible.

At six o'clock in the morning George Finch knocked on the men's door to rouse them for their daily work. Getting no answer, he pushed it open and found George Lee lying at the foot the bed. John Brittan was lying on the floor - both men were unconscious. He also noticed that a considerable amount of plaster had fallen from the wall dividing the room from the passage. Immediately medical aid was called for and Dr. Parsloe of 5. Buckland Place was soon on the scene and who commenced artificial respiration on George Lee. After twenty minutes he thought he saw him breathe. Injecting him with ether and strychnine he continued for two more hours, but eventually abandoned the case as hopeless. Dr. Bushell was also sent for to attend to John Britton, who had constant attention and eventually regained consciousness at around two o'clock the following morning.

At the inquest into George Lee's death, it was said that a small explosion had occurred in their room shortly after midnight; caused by a gas pipe supplied by the local gas company splitting. The gas was not coal gas but a mixture of coal and water gas which contained more carbon monoxide than coal gas. Unfortunately, the leak had escaped into the room where the men slept, which although spacious and relatively well ventilated was without a chimney. The inquest into George's demise brough a verdict of 'accidental death by gas poisoning.'

Unbelievable aquittal!

In this case I have chosen to only use only the first names of the perpetrator and the victim, for reason you will see as you read on.

William, of Park Place, Heavitree, near Exeter was the [until this occurrence took place] caretaker of Barnfield Hall, which belonged to the Exeter Literary Society. He was charged in December 1892 with having criminally assaulted Emily, a girl under the age of thirteen who was the daughter of a neighbour living only a few doors away. On the 6th of December Emily was on her way to the hospital, her route taking her past Barnfield Hall. When she was on opposite side of the road to the building, near the cab stand at Southernhay, William called out to her and offering her a penny he said to come with him to a room where there was a lovely warm fire burning in the hearth. Emily said she couldn't as she would be late, but he insisted. He led her by the hand into a room which she later described in detail to the police. It was here he committed a dreadful sexual assault, and afterwards gave Emily the penny he had promised. She hurriedly left and instead of going to the hospital went straight to her step-sister Mary's house in King

Street and told her what had happened. Her sister took her home and a doctor was called to carry out an examination. Dr. Andrews examined Emily that evening and found evident injuries relating to a sexual assault. Mr. Bell, another doctor who examined the little girl two days later came to the same conclusion. William was arrested by Detective Sergeant Vickery on the 10th of December. When charged with the offence he replied; "So it's rumoured, but I'm not guilty."

Giving evidence at his trial the following March, Emily said that she had met William who she knew as a neighbour, on her way to the hospital and that he offered her a penny to come with him into the Hall. Once inside he committed the heinous act. Mary, her stepsister, told the court that Emily had come to her house in an excited state and complained to her of the assault, and it was she who alerted the police. Robert, the father of the girl, who bizarrely didn't seem to believe her version of events or even the proof given by Doctor Bell or Andrew's, told the jury that when his daughter had told him what had happened, he had whipped her for telling lies! She had in the past he said been known to tell one or two untruths and had a few days previous to the alleged assault taken refuge in the prisoner's house when there had been an argument in his own.

Doctor's Andrews and Bell both reiterated the evidence they had originally stated at the Magistrates Court; that when they examined Emily, she had evident signs of sexual assault and was in great pain.

William Baker of Heavitree, stated that after the arrest of William, he had overheard the father of the girl express his hopes that the prisoner would be acquitted. When cross-examined, Robert admitted that a few days previously in the 'Windsor Castle Inn' he had said that he'd always been good friends with the prisoner and had nothing against him, but denied saying that he hoped he got off. He said that he had said he 'hoped the case was over.'

Mr Duke, solicitor acting on behalf of the defence, said that William had given a complete and utter denial to the charge. He then called the prisoner to the stand. William told the court that he was a Royal Navy pensioner and had served twenty-three years in the service, retiring as a first-class Petty Officer. Under cross examination he admitted that Emily had passed Barnfield Hall and that she had spoken to him outside, but he did not invite her in and hadn't seen anything more of her until he was brought before the Magistrate. He said there had been a meeting at the hall at three-thirty that afternoon and it lasted until five-fifteen. The rumour of the alleged assault was brought to him the following day when the librarian's wife and a press representative came to see him. He was there and then suspended from his post so he went to the police station to ask if the rumour was true. He was then arrested two days later. Evidence as to his good character was given by his wife who said he had always been a very good husband and father.

James Collings a market gardener, Charles Parr a painter and Ann Rice; all of Heavitree, also gave excellent character references. Mr. Duke gave a very eloquent speech on behalf of the prisoner in which he said it was a gross and unfounded charge. He said that the girl's evidence stood without the least corroboration and the case was a most unsatisfactory one. The jury returned a verdict of 'not guilty' and the prisoner was discharged. The decision was greeted with a round of applause.

* How and why the doctor's evidence was ignored I have no idea – only the judge and jury can answer that. The families continued to live as neighbours. Emily went on to marry and have five children with her husband. She also trained as a midwife.

Alleged child murder at Ottery St Mary

At the Ottery St. Mary Police Court on Friday the 20th of January 1893, Rosina [known as Rose] Elizabeth Richards, a cook who had for the past five years been in the employment of Mr. Thomas Payne of Mount Pleasant, Salcombe Regis, was brought up on the charge of the wilful murder of her new-born female child. Rose was brought to the courthouse in a cab and was allowed to have a seat by the fire. She was neatly attired in a plaid dress and blue cloak, and wore a feather boa and a brown hat. She appeared not to take much interest in the proceedings.

The child she was said to have murdered had been born between six and seven o'clock in the evening of the 30th of December 1892. It was alleged that afternoon Rose had said that she didn't feel well. Later that evening Annie Maria Barratt another of Mr. Payne's servants went to the bedroom and found Rose had given birth. She wrapped the child in a petticoat and placed it at Rose's request in a box that had previously been used for storing hats. The child at this point was alive. When Annie asked what they were to do, Rose told her to go and tell the gardener what had happened. Instead of returning with the gardener, Annie returned to the room with the gardener's wife; Mrs. Annie Collier and Miss. Barker, the grand-daughter of Mr. Payne. Mrs. Collier noticed Rose had been drinking brandy and that there was a blood-stained handkerchief on the child's chest. When she asked what it was doing there, Rose said that she had used it to try and stifle the child but had been unable to do so. She also said; "I thumped it into the box because I thought I should kill it." When a shocked Mrs. Collier replied; "Oh how could you?"

Rose simply replied; "I'm doing it all for your sake." When it was suggested that she and the baby should be seen by a doctor, Rose responded "No, I want it to die." Despite not wanting herself or the child to be seen by a doctor, Dr. Bingley Pullin was called and arrived at the house later that evening. He was led into the kitchen by Mr. Payne and Annie Barratt and shown the child who was lying in a box. On first sight he thought it was dead, but picking it up he found it to still be alive. He used friction on the little girl's chest to get her breathing and then had some hot water brought in a basin which he placed the child in. With a flannel he applied the hot water to her body and then he tied the umbilical cord. Whist bathing her he noticed bruises on her right cheek, side of the head and her right arm. She also had cut on the inside of her right upper lip which had been bleeding. Wrapping her in a flannel garment he placed her by the fire in the care of Annie Barratt and Mrs. Collier.

Returning to the bedroom he found Rose lying in bed partially dressed. He asked her how the little one had come to have a cut lip. She responded by saying she had banged it on the box. (Though later on in court he said he couldn't remember whether she had said 'in' or 'on' the box.) He told her that her daughter was alive and he wanted to have her brought to her. Annie Barratt then brought the baby upstairs and placed the crying infant at her mother's breast. Annie left the room and in Mrs. Collier's presence Dr. Pullin asked Rose to tell him exactly what she had done to the child. She again repeated her earlier statement of "I banged it on the box." On him asking why she had put the child in the box, she said "because I thought it would die." Dr. Pullin then left Rose and the baby in the care of Mrs. Collier. It was during this time that Rose admitted to Mrs. Collier that her husband George was the father of the child.

The following morning, Dr. Pullin was notified by Fanny Smith, the nurse whom he had requested to spend the night with mother and baby that the child had died at around two-thirty a.m. whilst on her lap. He in-turn reported the matter to the Coroner. The following day he along with his father; also Dr. Pullin, carried out a post-mortem examination. As well as the bruises to the child and the cut lip, they also found a fractured skull and fractured jaw. At the inquest he was asked if such injuries could have been caused by the banging of the child's head on the box, he said it could have been. The cut on the inner lip might very well have been caused by the lip meeting with the edge of the box. When asked if he thought that the child had died a natural death or was it brought about by violence, he said most definitely by violence. The fracture to the skull had been the cause of death. Asked if it was possible that in trying to deliver the child by herself, could this have produced the fracture and the bruises? Dr. Pullin said maybe the bruises, but certainly not the fracture.

Annie Barrett when called to give evidence said that she had been in her present situation for two and a half years. She had noticed something the matter in the appearance of Rose about two months previously and had mentioned it to her, but she denied it.

Rose was then asked if she had anything to say in her defence. She said the George Collier had been aware of her condition and that he had told her to keep it quiet from his wife and that he had promised to come and take the baby away at the first chance. The jury decided that Rosina

Elizabeth Richards should appear before the next Devon Assizes to be charged with the wilful murder of her newly born daughter.

On Friday the 10th of March, Rose appeared before the Judge at the Devon Assizes. The Right Hon. Coleridge told the jury that the prisoner was charged with the destruction her new-born child, and when they had heard the facts of the case would have no doubt in the opinion that there could only one of two results, either conviction for murder or acquittal altogether. The evidence was then gone over once again. In regards to the statement made by Rose saying that George Collier would come and fetch the child, the defence said there was no proof of such an arrangement having been made. The doctors had agreed that the injuries except the fractured skull were possibly consistent with self-delivery and would suggest that injury to the skull was probably caused accidentally during birth. They were not prepared to say that the injuries were quite inconsistent with self-delivery, though they would say it unlikely. Rosina Richards was the only person who could say how it happened, and by the rules of English law she was unable to give evidence in the witness box. The Judge summing up said to the jury that after hearing such statements, were they prepared to condemn the woman to death? Not one of the witnesses so far as he remembered could positively say whether the prisoner told them that the child was banged in or on the box. But the medical evidence alone was such that the jury could not reasonably condemn the woman to the utmost penalty of the law. Before they could come to such a conclusion, they had to convince themselves beyond the possibility of doubt that the injuries were inflicted maliciously by the woman. If there was one thing which was stronger than another in the human mind it was maternal love, and the presumption that such love existed in every mother was so strong that unless there was the clearest evidence to the contrary, no jury should find a verdict of wilful murder. The jury after few minute's deliberation returned a verdict of 'not guilty' and Rose Richards was discharged.

Frederick Heard.

This is our first meeting with Frederick Heard, a colourful character who will shall come across on a number of occasions in future pages.

At the Borough Police Court in Totnes on Monday the 20th August 1895 Frederick Charles Heard, the former publican, owner of a refreshment room and well-known cab proprietor of 14. High Street in the town was summoned by his wife Elizabeth, for assaulting and beating her a few days previously. Frederick pleaded not guilty. Mrs. Heard said that her husband had promised to be a different man if the Bench would overlook the offence and she wished to withdraw the summons. It was through drink she was sorry to say and he had promised to become teetotal. Frederick Heard in recent times had become something of a public nuisance, and promising he would leave the town that day as he was looking for another business the Bench spent some time in private considering the case. Returning to the courtroom the Chairman said they had decided under the circumstances to hear the evidence before giving a decision.

Elizabeth said that on the afternoon of the 16th her husband came and knocked at the door of her mother's house in Fore Street where she was now residing and asked for a pawn ticket. She gave it to him but declined to allow him to come into the house. He then placed his foot against the door so that she couldn't close it. She tried to push him out, whereupon he grabbed her by the arms and tried to pull her outside too. In the struggle her bodice was pulled to pieces. He pushed his way into the property and in fear she left to go in search of a policeman and ask for protection. She added that she didn't believe he would have done such a thing hadn't he been under the influence of drink.

In answer to a question from the Mayor and with much unwillingness, Elizabeth said that her husband had struck her across the face leaving a mark. The Magistrate's clerk then said; "You stated when you applied for the summons that you stood in fear of him?" Elizabeth agreed and said when her husband was 'in drink' he was a madman and that she had also applied for a separation order because of his drinking habits though she had not seen him worse for drink since the assault. Frederick Heard replied saying that it was because he had been allowed to see his children and felt more content. He said his wife had let him see his children the day after the assault, having not seen them at all in the previous six weeks.

Florence Stoyles who witnessed the assault gave evidence stating that she had seen Frederick put his hand to his wife's face knocking her in the eye. She said the language he used was not decent, though she didn't hear him making threats. In answer to a question regarding there being a disturbance at the house the previous Saturday night, Mrs. Stoyles said she hadn't been aware of one.

Police Sergeant Brownson said that on the 16th Mrs. Heard came to the Police Station in a very excited state. Her bodice was torn to pieces and she said that she was in bodily fear of her husband and asked him for protection. Frederick Heard had followed her to the station where she turned to him and said; "You blackguard, you struck me a blow in the face and pulled me about and nearly killed me. It's a continual thing!" They then had an argument and Mrs. Heard begged for protection saying her husband would murder her. Sergeant Brownson advised taking a warrant out against the defendant who had been drinking.

Frederick Heard told the court that he was truly grieved. He had been married for twenty-five years and only in the last few months had there been any quarrels. He had gone through the bankruptcy court and sold his home in Paignton. His wife went to Totnes with their three children to stay with her mother and he followed her there the day after the sale of the house, but when he arrived, he was told she wasn't there. He went back to Paignton, and from there to Plymouth and then on to Newton Abbot and finally back to Totnes. He had seen his wife going into her mother's house with one of their children. He went to the house in an attempt to see his wife and children, but was denied admittance whereupon he broke a panel in the door and was sent to prison. Having being released from prison he again went back to the house and that was how he found himself standing before the Magistrates that day. Not being allowed to see his children he said had driven him from bad to worse. He hoped the Bench would give him another chance as he was determined to take the pledge.

The Chairman stated that the Bench had very seriously considered the application made by the defendant's wife that the case might be dismissed, but had now come to the conclusion that they could not entertain it. They had considered whether they should send him to prison. They had however taken a more lenient view and decided to inflict a fine of three pounds plus six pence in costs - or one month's imprisonment. Frederick was also told that he must clearly understand, that if he EVER came before the Bench again, he would be much more severely dealt with. The fine was paid.

Frederick Charles Heard was hauled before the magistrate at Totnes on the 4th of September 1895, two weeks after his last appearance. He pleaded guilty to having been drunk and disorderly. Police Sergeant Brownson said that he had been summoned to the Guildhall steps at around half past one the previous Wednesday afternoon where he found Heard creating a disturbance and very drunk. He was badly cut about the face and was falling about. Mr. Higgs a stonemason, told the court that Frederick Heard was a continual worry as he was in the habit of going to his house [he was the brother-in-law of Elizabeth Heard and at whose house she was now living with her children and mother] and causing a nuisance. He said that on the previous Wednesday, Heard had again turned up at the property and been refused entry. Higgs said that he had pushed him away from the door and Heard who was very drunk, fell down. Another witness, a man called Stobbs, said he had seen

Frederick Heard about an hour before his arrest. He was near to the 'Dartmouth Inn' trying to fight with a wall and talking about his wife. The Mayor (Mr. Mitchelmore) summing up, said there had already been four convictions against Frederick Heard in the past twelve months and he would now be sent prison for a month's hard labour.

*In 1895 Fred had accrued huge debts through the failure of his business as a publican in Exeter. He had sold his coach and horse to try and cover the debt; this in turn also ended his business as a cab proprietor.

Cruelty and misconduct.

A decree nisi was applied for on the 19th of June 1897 by the Royal Courts of Justices in London, to Henry Symons a cider merchant residing in the hamlet of Tuckenhay near Totnes, because of his wife's misconduct with Frederick Charles Heard, a cab proprietor.

In applying for the divorce, Henry Symons stated that he and his wife had married on the 13th of April 1879 in the parish church of Torre near Torquay. The marriage had been a happy one until his wife Gertrude had taken to drink and when under its influence had acted violently towards him. On one occasion throwing a lighted lamp at him which set fire to the bedclothes. In 1891 when he had been ill, she was found dampening the sheets on which he was going to sleep and said that she wished him dead. She later told him that she no longer wished to live with him. He moved out of their marital home and into the property next door (which he owned) with his children. After they separated, Gertrude had thrown stones at him whilst he was riding by in his carriage. Eventually he had to move further away owing to her annoyance. The previous the March, Frederick Charles Heard had moved in with Gertrude having left his wife. Gertrude had property in her own name which brought in about two hundred pounds a year in rent [equivalent to over eighteen thousand pounds in today's money] and she also owned the house in which she lived. An agreement was put in place and signed by Gertrude Symons and Frederick Heard, in which they had agreed to live together as man and wife for the rest of their lives, and Mrs. Symons signing over her house called 'Spring Bank' worth several thousand pounds [In today's money this is well over half a million pounds] to Frederick Heard. A decree nisi with costs was granted, also custody of the children. On the 7th of January 1898, the divorce was made absolute.

1900-1950

It's Fred again.

At Plympton Magistrates Court on Monday the 23rd January 1901, Gertrude Symons and Frederick Charles Heard were sent to prison for one month without the option of a fine. On the 7th June the previous year the couple were discovered by P.C. Richards at Ivybridge, drunk and driving a one-horse trap. Heard was too far gone to be allowed to proceed on his way and Symons was not only drunk but also disorderly. A youth was then procured who drove the trap with the two defendants to Plymouth.

Gertrude Symons had nothing to say in her defence but Heard communicated to the Magistrates a pitiful story and promised to mend his ways. He said that since a big misfortune had befallen him some five years earlier, he had given himself away to drink and it had added trouble to trouble. He said he had recently taken the pledge and intended to begin the New Year afresh and try to get on in life. He would never get drunk again. He said that he believed Mrs. Symons had also become teetotal.

The Bench retired to consider their verdict and whilst they did, Heard made jocular remarks to those seated in the court. When the Magistrates returned, the Chairman (Mr. J. J. MacAndrew) said they had decided to convict both prisoners and could not do anything other than send them both prison for a month.

No sooner had they been released from prison than they picked up their old habits again. In September at Dartmouth Guildhall, Frederick Heard and Gertrude Symons both of Totnes, were charged with being drunk and disorderly. Mrs. Symons being fined two pounds plus costs and Heard ten shillings plus costs. Gertrude or Gertie as she was most likely known as to those familiar with her, was brought before the courts on a number of occasions over the coming months; with and without her partner Fred Heard. In September 1901 she was fined forty shillings or the option of fourteen days imprisonment for being found drunk in Victoria Road, Exmouth. The fine was not paid.

By April 1900 the couple were living in the Lipson area of Plymouth. Gertrude was charged with being drunk and disorderly in Clifton Street on the evening of the 26th of June.

The Chief Constable stated that she had been before the court seven times previously; she had also been fined and imprisoned in other courts across the county. Gertrude was sent to gaol for one month with hard labour. Frederick Charles Heard was charged with being drunk and incapable in Market Avenue the same evening and in such a state as being unable to talk. The Chief Constable said Heard had been nine times before court. He also said that the couple regularly attended court together. Frederick was fined ten shillings plus costs.

At Exmouth Police Court on Tuesday the 28th of October, Gertrude Symons was charged by P.C. Weeks with being drunk in Victoria Road the previous afternoon. She was fined forty shillings and costs, or alternately to spend fourteen days' in prison. The fine was not paid. Days after her release she was again imprisoned for a month with hard labour, this time for being drunk in Northernhay Street in Exeter on the 13th of October. Gertrude was now of no fixed abode. The chairman of the jury expressed sorrow at seeing her in the court, knowing she was of a previous good position.

Dreadful incidents at Sutton Pool, Plymouth Barbican – a week apart.

John Prynn a crewman on board the Fowey fishing lugger 'Kathleen,' on Friday the 27th of October 1900, fell from the quayside at Plymouth Barbican and became wedged between the quay wall and another boat the 'Lodore.' He was eventually rescued but in an extremely exhausted condition.

Just over a week later at quarter-past eleven on the evening of Saturday the 3rd of November, Mr. Ernest Davis a lighterman of 26. New Street, Barbican, noticed the body of a man floating in the water at the bottom of some steps directly under the window of the Customs House. With the help of William Matthews of 36. New Street, he was able to bring the body ashore. P.C. Sloman who was in the area at the time found the body to still be warm and began carrying out artificial respiration. At the same time getting a message relayed to the Central Police station to ask for a doctor to be sent immediately. Dr. Cooke arrived soon after and continued to carry out artificial respiration but to no avail and the gentleman's life was soon after pronounced extinct. In his pockets were found money, a knife, a bottle of medicine, a pipe and two handkerchiefs. The man was said to have been around thirty years of age, of a medium build and with brown hair and moustache. He was wearing a blue serge coat and vest, bowler hat, plaid trousers, a soldier's shirt and knitted socks. The medicine bottle in his pocket offered no information as to his identity. At the inquest into the gentleman's death, him still not having been identified, the jury returned a verdict of 'found drowned.'

Servant gave birth after falling from a stool.

Ethel Pinhey, a twenty-one-year-old domestic servant, gave birth to a male child at the residence of her mistress Mrs. De Legh, at 4. Palace Place, Paignton on Monday the 29th June

1903. She told the nurse who was summoned to help soon after the birth having been discovered that she had fallen off a stool whilst hanging some clothes and that's when the baby had been born. It died soon after. A post-mortem was carried out by Dr. H. Adams and he noticed a number of abrasions and scratches on the child's head. Internally there were two definite fractures of the skull; irregular and somewhat splintered. A blood clot was also found under the rear of the skull. Both lungs were inflated indicating the child had drawn breath. At the inquest into the poor little baby's death, Dr. Adams said that from the post-mortem in his opinion the cause of death was from a direct blow which produced the fracture to the skull. In addition, the child had lost a quantity of blood owing to the cord having been cut. Dr. Cosens who was also present at the post-mortem told the inquest that he felt it was not impossible but highly improbable for the child to have sustained such injuries by falling to the floor at the time of birth. He believed that the child had died from a direct blow from a blunt instrument, although when he attended the property soon after the death had been discovered he saw no such instrument in the room. The blow he said must have been dealt with very considerable force. A juror asked if Dr. Cosens thought that the death of the child could have been caused by a blow or kick from the mother whilst she was unconscious? Dr. Cosens said he did not.

Ethel Pinhey, under oath, said she had no father or mother and had lived at Mrs. De Legh's house as a servant for the previous ten months. On June the 29th she had been in the garden hanging out clothes when she fell from a chair which strained her very much. Soon after that the child had been born. She absolutely denied using violence in any way whatsoever towards the child. The father of the child she said had promised look after her but had failed to do so. The Coroner in summing up said that it was a question for the jury to consider whether the accused to get over her trouble killed the child, or did they believe her statement. The jury retired for half an hour and on their return gave their verdict; 'death caused by accidental injuries during birth.'

Blacklisted.

At Exeter Police Court, Frederick Charles Heard, a cab proprietor of no fixed address and who was well known in Totnes and Plymouth, pleaded guilty to being drunk and incapable in North Street on the 12th of January 1903, having only been released from prison the previous day after serving a two-month sentence. Fred begged to be given another chance as arrangements were being made to get him into a Church Army Home in Bristol. However, having been convicted three times for drunkenness during the past year the Bench said that he was an habitual drunkard under the new Licensing Act and ordered him to be put on the publicans black list. He was also fined ten shillings plus costs or the alternative was to be sent to prison for fourteen days. He opted to go to prison.

In early March Fred was again charged with being disorderly, this time in Old Town Street. He was seen waving an old silk hat and flourishing postcards of Plymouth celebrities. Shouting out that revenge was sweet and that he should get it later on. A crowd of about three hundred people surrounded him and the street became completely blocked. This time he told the Magistrates that he was thinking of leaving Devon and going to London. At this point the case was adjourned for a week to see whether he would keep to his word and leave the town. As you've likely guessed Fred didn't go to London, and on his next appearance before the Magistrate's he was again sent to prison. On his liberation from Exeter gaol at the end of April, he was met by Adjutant Kenyon and members of the Exeter Corps of the Salvation Army. During his incarceration he had been visited by salvationists and having become truly repentant he expressed a wish to be placed in a Salvation Army shelter so as to enable him redeem his past life. He told them how he had been convicted over one hundred times and Exeter gaol had been his home on more than forty occasions. The following evening, he was presented to the congregation at the Salvation Army Temple where he publicly stated that he had repented his past life, and intended with God's help to live a better one in the future. He was then taken to the shelter in Castle Street, Bristol.

*I wonder if by this point in time Fred and Gertie had parted ways, though Fred being placed in a Church Army hostel in Bristol makes me feel they may still have had some sort of connection as Gertie now aged fifty-three, was seen dancing and shouting surrounded by a large group of children on College Green outside of the Cathedral in Bristol in February 1903. She was fined ten shillings by the Magistrates and locked up. Her name was also put on the blacklist and the Magistrates said they would do all that the law allowed to stop her getting drink. Gertie was the first person to be blacklisted in Bristol, not being allowed in any public house. It's highly possible that Gertie took the pledge and was being supported by the Salvation Army at this point as there are no further records of her being arrested and she appears to have gone on to lead a clean life. I do believe they both wanted to break the habit, Gertie's constitution was just stronger that of Fred; who we will meet again.

A spy in Devonport!

In February 1903, a very pleasant and well-spoken young man going by the name of Richards, for several days attempted with plausible excuses to enter Devonport Dockyard. He was stopped by police at the main gate and told he could not enter. He remonstrated for a while but the officers maintained their stance. Finally, he said he would not trouble them anymore as he had learnt all he wanted to know. This remark naturally created curiosity and inquiries were promptly set afoot and as a result it was established that beyond doubt, he was a paid agent from a foreign Naval Intelligence Department. He disappeared soon after and there was therefore no means of ascertaining whether he had been using a false name. Those who came into contact with the man stated that he had not the least hint of a foreign accent.

Witchcraft fraud in Exeter.

At Exeter Police Court on Saturday the 9th of May 1903 William Henry Thomas, described as a gentleman of Bartholomew Street, Exeter, and Mary Brown alias Annie Fairchild, a widow, were charged with having on March 20th obtained from Ben Crook of Stockleigh Pomeroy, the sum of two pounds and two shillings by unlawful means. There were four other charges relating to sums of money being obtained unlawfully; two pounds obtained from George Rudall of Drewsteignton. Three pounds and three shillings from Edward Arthur Gloin of Beaworthy. Five pounds from Jane Stone of Brixham, and one pound and five shillings from another un-named person. Mary Brown who it was stated had been employed as a housekeeper for Mr. Thomas, was immediately discharged.

Mr. J. Beal the prosecuting solicitor said that William Thomas had been carrying on his business for years and had obtained a wide reputation among the 'poor witted' country people. Many were said to have believed that if a man's wife was ill or his cattle died, they had been 'overlooked or bewitched' and Thomas was reputed to have the power of stopping the 'overlooking.' His receipt books showed that he had been making three hundred pounds a year from this business. One example was the occasion when he had given a farmer who had been losing horses and cattle, a special powder; telling him to throw it around the homestead between nine p.m. and midnight and to say the Lord's Prayer at the same time.

Mr. F. Bodilly the barrister who appeared on behalf of the defendant agreed that the practices must be stopped. He said that it was doubtful whether William Thomas, who had been brought up as a herbalist had even realised the heinousness of his offences. The Magistrates imposed a fine of twenty pounds for each offence with the alternative of one month's imprisonment, again for each case. The fines amounted to one hundred pounds. William Thomas was also ordered to pay the courts costs.

The strange disappearance of a young girl from Oreston.

Fifteen-year-old May Elizabeth Allen known as Mable; a bright and very intelligent girl from Oreston, who two years previously been sent to a school in Plymouth. After being there for some months she told her father that she had passed exams which entitled her to transfer to a higher-grade school. More recently she told her parents a similar story, but that this time she was being sent to a school in London. However, in each instance she omitted to tell her family the name or address of the schools. On Wednesday the 13th of July 1904, she informed her parents that she was to be presented with a medal at the Guildhall that evening and that carriages would be sent to fetch them and other residents of the village so they could attend the prize giving. She then went off to school as usual. That evening her parents and a large number of the villagers of Oreston gathered, waiting for the carriages that had been promised. None having arrived they made their own way to Plymouth Guildhall, which they found to be closed. Enquiries were then made and it appeared the girl wasn't a pupil at any of the schools in Plymouth, Devonport, or Stonehouse! Her family began to fear that she had either been kidnapped or induced by some ne'er do well to elope. Two days later Mable's parents received in the post a letter from her written in pencil and postmarked Hatt; a small hamlet near Saltash in Cornwall. In the letter she said that she had slept in a cornfield for two nights and was very hungry and miserable. She asked if her father would come and collect her and take her home.

Her parents at once proceeded to Saltash and informed the police there of what had occurred. A number of constables were sent out to scour the district. Mrs. Bessie Allen the girl's mother, took a motor bus to Callington and the father went on foot in the same direction. Meanwhile, the constables visited refreshment houses in Saltash to make enquiries but could find no clue as to the girl's whereabouts. No one it appeared had seen her. Mrs. Allen in the meantime, shortly before reaching Hatt, noticed her daughter walking along the road heading back towards Saltash. She asked the driver to stop and she dismounting the bus and rushed towards her daughter who fell into her arms in tears. They then proceeded to walk back towards Saltash where they were met with on the road by Mr. Allen who had been walking towards them. The family then returned to Plymouth and mother and daughter spent a few days staying with friends away from the prying eyes of neighbours. The father returning to their home in Oreston to face the questions from well-meaning neighbours and journalists who had been closely following the story. He told them he was just thankful to have his daughter back and admitted that for the previous few months his daughter had continually been telling them falsehoods culminating in the Guildhall presentation story, and it was because of her deceit that she had run away from home. She was now heartbroken at the level of her dishonesty and constantly broke down in tears when questioned. It appeared that she had been unhappy at Mount Street School which she had left, telling her parents that she had been sent to the higher-grade school. She had in-fact not been going to school at all, but had spent her days walking on the Hoe and other such places. When the crisis came to a head, she decided that there was nothing she could do other than to tell the truth or run away. He said she was a very sensitive girl and he thought it best not to bring her back to Oreston, but to move far away. The villagers however said that 'Mable' as they called her was such a lovely girl and refused to entertain any detriment to her character. And said that she would receive a warm welcome should she choose to return to the village.

Anonymous letter leads to the death of two lovers.

Walter James Copp (known as Charlie) a young man employed as the head boots at the Westminster Hotel, Plymouth, and Fanny Williams (known as Fan) a cook, disappeared from Plymouth on the evening of the 2nd of September 1904. The couple had hired a rowing boat at West Hoe and proceeded out into the Sound. Two hours later the boat without its occupants was seen floating past the pier. Hauled ashore it was found to contain a woman's straw hat and a man's cap. There was also a piece of paper tied to one of the seats on which were written the names of hotels in Exeter, Swansea, and number of other towns. A memorandum book was also left behind with a note addressed to Mr. Williams [Fan's father] in Bodmin. The note said; 'Good-bye to all. We have agreed to die together to save ourselves from the slurs of other people. If we float ashore let us be buried together. Fan wants some flowers on her grave.' Realising the couple had either attempted or had committed suicide, James Farrell the pier-master at West Hoe, alerted the police.

Unknown artist.

Charlie Copp a native of Tiverton, and Fanny Williams a native of Bodmin, had been courting for nearly two years and had got engaged the previous November. Just over a week after the couple had gone missing, on the 10th of September, Fan's body was found floating in the Hamoaze. At the inquest into her death, it was said that she had been employed as a cook for Mr. Wilson at Thorn Park House, Mannamead. Her sister Catherine who was a domestic servant at 3. Thorn Park Villas, also in Mannamead identified her body by a buckle ring that her sister always wore. Catherine said that she had last seen Fan on the 1st of September, when she appeared as bright and cheerful as ever and all had seemed well in her relationship with Charlie. She had certainly not indicated or acted in a way that led her to believe she would take her own life. Catherine said she had last seen Charlie the same evening when she'd called in at the Westminster Hotel along with her brother Joseph. They had talked about family affairs, but not about her sister. The writing in the memorandum book produced, she recognised as being Charlie's. When asked about the slurs mentioned in the letter, she said she had no idea and had never heard of any accusations made against Fan. Though earlier on the Friday evening, the day of her death, she said Fan had received a telegram though from whom she did not know, possibly from Charlie Copp.

The doctor who carried out the post-mortem remarked that Fan's body had bruising around the back of the neck which appeared to have occurred prior to death, though as her body was so badly decomposed it was hard to tell. The jury returned an open verdict.

Charlie Copp's body was found floating near the Plymouth Breakwater three days later and an inquest was held later the same day. The Coroner said he had taken the opportunity of reading some letters found on the body of the deceased, which he felt may well solve the case of the terrible tragedy. These included letters from Fan to Charlie, in one she admits that some time previously she had given birth to a child and asked for forgiveness. Another letter sent anonymously included a birth certificate showing that on the 14th of April 1900, Fan had given birth to a son in Bodmin. Fan had apparently been trying to live an upright and industrious life since the birth of her illegitimate child and had hidden [with all best intentions] the truth from her fiancé. Another letter from Fan, again admitting to the birth and regretting that she had not felt able to tell him. She asked that she might see him for just five minutes to explain and say 'goodbye.' She further added that she hoped he would find a better girl than her and that he would be happy. The jury returned a verdict of 'suicide during temporary insanity' and heavily censured the writer of the anonymous letter whom they considered morally responsible for the death of the young couple.

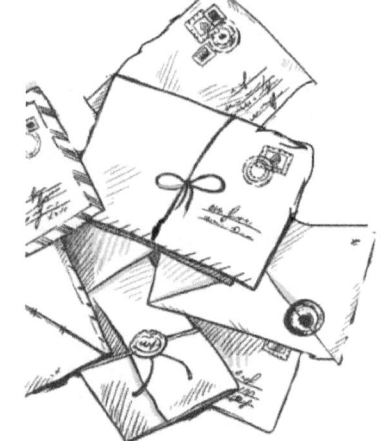

Fan's body was interred on the 14th of September, the day after Charlie's body had been found. Mourners lined the route of the funeral procession and hundreds of women waited at the cemetery gates for the arrival of the hearse. They were greatly disappointed when they realised that the young lovers would not be buried together as requested. This was explained to them that as the inquest into Charlie Copp's death had not yet taken place it was impossible, and that there were also other funerals that needed to take place. The following day Charlie was laid to rest. The route to the cemetery was again lined by hundreds of people. With a view to preventing scenes such had been seen the previous day, several Constables were stationed inside the cemetery. The staff of the Westminster Hotel where Charlie had been employed and those of other hotels in which he had previously worked, raised a subscription amongst themselves and purchased a handsome everlasting wreath in the shape of an anchor set inside a glass frame which was to be placed upon his grave.

The longest detour home!

William Green, a fish and egg merchant based in Plymouth Market disappeared in August 1904, finally returning home in mid-October. Mr. Green's story was a rather remarkable one. With a little over five pounds in his pocket he decided to treat himself to a holiday in Lowestoft, Suffolk. He spent an enjoyable few days' in the seaside town before heading south to London. After seeing the sights, he left the city with the aim of returning home and wrote to his relatives in Plymouth notifying them of his intention. He also sent a telegram to a friend in Bristol asking him meet him at the station there. For whatever reason, William Green changed his mind and instead of proceeding to Plymouth, he headed to Liverpool. There he was taken ill and a doctor suggested that he should take a sea voyage – the fresh sea air being beneficial to his health. William decided to act on this advice and rather than tell his relatives in Plymouth of his plans, or take a boat trip rather than a train journey back to his home port; he booked himself a passage to New York. This was during a period of time when the 'shipping wars' were taking place, so rather than taking a trip direct from Liverpool to New York, William Green for the fare of two pounds, travelled to Grimsby and from there to Hamburg in Germany where be joined a steamer bound for New York. On reaching New York, he along with other immigrants were placed in quarantine on an Island. He was detained here for several weeks. Finally, owing to him having little money and not being in very good health the American authorities refused him admittance to the country and the shipping company took him back to England.

Sympathy and help for Fred please?

A letter was sent to the Editor of the Western Evening News in November 1904 with reference to the gentleman we have got to know fairly well [and I have only covered a few select mentions of his court appearances – Frederick Charles Heard.] It seems that the Salvationists had been unable to redeem Fred and his stay at the Salvation Army Hostel in Bristol was over, he'd gone back to drinking and had returned to Plymouth.

Sir, In your issue of the 17th inst. I see an account of Frederick Charles Heard being again summoned before the Magistrates for disorderly conduct. Again, he is sent to prison. Now, I think it is a disgrace to the Borough to send a man like Heard to prison for what he does not seem able to help. The policeman in his evidence said Heard was 'a fair lunatic.' The Chief Constable said his actions 'were idiotic.' If that be so, why is he not admitted to an asylum? It can serve no useful purpose to send him to prison. It is only an exposure of the prison and an expense to the town. It has been said that Heard is harmless, and therefore cannot be sent to an asylum. But who knows how soon he may become dangerous? I have known Heard for many years, and at one time as remarked by Judge Edge, he was a very useful man. Certainly, he is more to be pitied than blamed.
      SYMPATHY.

A curious case of memory lapse.

Just after seven o'clock on the evening of Tuesday the 10th of January 1905 a cab pulled up outside of Totnes Workhouse and a lady alighted from the box and entered the lodge where the Master (Mr. W. Beer) happened to be at the time. She enquired as to the whereabouts of her girl Jane, who she said she was expecting to meet there at what she thought was a hotel. When Mr. Beer enquired as to her name, she said she didn't know or where she was staying. She knew that she had been born in New Zealand and was very tired after her long Journey.

She remembered that her husband had died twenty years previously and she thought she had children still living in New Zealand. The cabman who had been requested by the lady to wait for her after paying her fare and saying she wouldn't be long was then spoken to. He was unable shed any further light on her identity, saying he had picked her up at the cab stand in Paignton and she asked him to drive her to the Totnes Union. He said she had got inside the carriage, but quickly got out saying she was afraid and insisted on riding outside with the himself.

The lady who was said to be middle-aged was well dressed in black, her jacket was trimmed with fur and on her fingers, she wore valuable rings. In her purse she had sufficient money for ordinary use. Mr. Beer invited her inside and gave her a room for the night in the hospital wing. Whilst she rested her handbag was gone through to see if there was anything in it which might lead to her identity. This resulted in the discovery of black bordered envelope addressed to 'Emily Eard, Maori Street. Christchurch, New Zealand.'

The following morning, she had made quite a recovery and realising she was in hospital had no idea how she had got there. Looking out of the window she saw the weather vane and said that it bore her initials 'E.W.' and that her name was West. Paignton Police were contacted and they said that a woman called Elizabeth West had been reported missing. Glad to have been found, Elizabeth still though couldn't account for ever having lived in Paignton, never mind having travelled to the Workhouse from there the previous evening. Later that day her daughter arrived and after seeing her mother said she thought it best she remained in the institution for the present time as she had been suffering from regular bouts of memory loss though had never gone off on her own before. Elizabeth had for twelve years been a matron at Winchester college in Hampshire.

Fred in trouble again.

In 1905 we again see our old friend Frederick Charles Heard getting himself into trouble. Fred now aged sixty-one, had been staying at Gibb's Lodging House on St. Andrew's Street, Plymouth since his release from prison. On the 3rd of January he was in court charged with being a 'lunatic wandering at large' when on the previous day he had been seen in Treville Street and Old Town Street by P.C. Allen who had been closely observing him throughout the day. At two o'clock in the morning he had seen him carrying a sheep's head under one arm and a basket of rabbit skins on the other. He was shouting; "Rabbit skins, four for a shilling." At three in the afternoon P.C. Allen saw him flourishing a Christmas card in one hand and a newspaper in the other, again offering them for sale. At five-thirty he was in Old Town Street with three empty basins and a pepper dredger shouting and damning like an idiot. At this point he was arrested. Asked if he had anything to say, Heard replied; "Didn't you hear me when I was carrying the sheep's head, say that I was Doctor Heard, a specialist in curing depression of the brain?" (laughter from the court room.) Dr. Wolferstan said that he had examined the defendant and found him to be of unsound mind. Fred was then told he was to be detained in the Workhouse for fourteen days. His response was; 'it's a very good place to be.'

In August 1805, Fred who had a week earlier been remanded to Plympton Workhouse for medical observation, escaped and was at large for six hours. When found he was taken to a Police Station where he remained until the following morning when he was brought before the Plympton Police Court. Fred said that he had been attacked by three women near the 'Lyneham Inn,' and robbed of one thousand pounds. Fred Heard was certified insane by Dr. Prance and taken to Exminster Asylum in Exeter.

The illegal abortionists.

Charlotte Maria Williams aged forty-seven, the wife of James Williams a Plymouth chemist, was found not guilty of participating in the performing of an illegal operation at the Devon Assizes held in Exeter in November 1906. The offence having taken place in September upon a woman called Elizabeth Stark.

James Williams had for some years been carrying out his business as a chemist at 60. Cecil Street, Stonehouse. His wife was being charged as an 'accessory before the act' in the initial stages of the offence which her husband then committed. It was said that she had counselled, procured and abetted her husband in the commission of the offence. She was charged under Section 1 of the Accessories, Aiding, and Abettors' Act. 1861. (Abortion was illegal in the UK until April 1968. The Abortion Act having been passed the previous year.)

It was said that Mrs. Williams had received a letter from Mrs. Stark the wife of a labourer living in Gunnislake, Cornwall. In return she sent a bottle of medicine through the post. On the 19th of September Mrs. Stark came to the shop and said that the medicine hadn't worked and could she have some more. Mrs. Williams told her that if one bottle hadn't worked then even another twenty wouldn't do any good. Mentioning to Mrs. Stark that her husband had some acid that would sort out her problem she showed her an instrument which she said he would use to carry out the job. Reassuring Mrs. Stark that she had nothing to fear she said; "You needn't worry, you'll be alright. It's nothing like the *Essery case." Mrs. Stark still under some apprehension as to the effects of the medicine she had taken asked Mrs. Williams if it had done [the baby] any harm. Mrs. Williams said that unfortunately it had and she would need to undergo an operation. She led Mrs. Stark upstairs to a bedroom where Mr. Williams carried out the procedure.

Once recovered, Mrs. Stark left the shop and caught a train back to her home in Gunnislake. Three days later she began to develop a high fever and quickly became quite ill, culminating in her giving birth prematurely. A doctor was called and in consequence of what she told him he informed the police which then led to the arrest of Mr. Williams and to the discovery of instruments in his shop which could be used to bring about an abortion. Mrs. Williams was also arrested on the account of the statement given by Mrs. Stark which was read out to her. She told the police that she most certainly hadn't sent Mrs. Stark any medicine. On this response the officer advised her not to say anything more until she had seen a solicitor and very wisely, she heeded his advice.

At her trial the jury were asked whether Mrs. Williams when sending Mrs. Stark up to the bedroom, was she aware that her husband was going to attempt to carry out an illegal abortion? If so, then she was guilty. Standing in the dock Mrs. Williams stated that she had never met Mrs. Stark before as far as she was aware and had certainly not sent her any medicine; though she knew her husband made up medicine's in his shop. She also refuted having received a letter from Mrs. Stark and said she didn't recognise the handwriting on the letter [shown to her.] When asked if she knew that her husband was not a qualified chemist, she said she was aware, but that he usually had a 'man' with him in the shop though he had left a few months previously. She also denied having shown Mrs. Stark a medical instrument; the device when shown to her she denied ever having seen before. She said that her job was simply to help serve in the shop when her husband asked her to and to deal with his correspondence – adding that customers never wrote asking for medicines. When asked if she could recall her husband ever taking a woman upstairs. Mrs. Williams said that she thought at one time he had maybe taken a woman up to treat her for cancer.

Mrs. Stark was then called to take the witness stand. She told the courtroom that she had paid Mr. Williams ten shillings to carry out the operation. She said that she hadn't been overly anxious to get rid of the child until Mrs. Williams told her that having taken the medicine it would already have made the baby very weak. She admitted that she knew what she was doing was wrong and unlawful. The question now was as to whether it was Mrs. Williams or Mrs. Stark who was telling the truth. Why would Mrs. Stark invent such a lie? Was it a case of forgetfulness on the part of Mrs. Williams? It was very unlikely that Mrs. Stark would invent such a story and if only partly true, Mrs. Williams would have known what her husband was taking the woman upstairs for. Mr. Lawrence acting on behalf of Mrs. Williams asked the jury not to judge the woman for her husband's misdeeds, especially bearing in mind the fact that according the prosecutions own showing not only did she not use the instrument but did not take any part in the operation. Mrs. Stark had been the one who was more conspicuous for forgetfulness; her account of the conversation with Mrs. Williams having developed in detail over time, and it was on her evidence alone that they were asked to convict her. Knowing that the 'Essery' case which was notorious in Plymouth at the time, wasn't it more likely that Mrs. Williams would not have drawn herself into such a conversation with Mrs. Stark knowing that she would just be digging a hole for herself? The Judge reminded the jury that to find someone guilty their guilt had to be proved beyond all reasonable doubt. After a few minutes' deliberation the foreman of the jury said that they had returned a verdict of 'not guilty.' Mrs. Williams, who had been composed throughout the trial burst into tears burying her face in her hands.

Fifty-five-year-old James Williams an unqualified chemist, had already been found guilty of the crime of carrying out an illegal operation. He was now brought up from the cells to receive his sentence. Standing in the dock facing the Judge he was asked if he had anything to say before sentencing was carried out. He responded with; "I have never been in court before. I have a wife and a baby solely dependent upon me. I hope you will show me some mercy, the same as our heavenly father would show mercy to us. In my own conscience I am not guilty with intention. I am satisfied before Almighty God that I am not guilty of that sir. If God were to call me away to that blessed heavenly home, I would not have that on my mind. I grant that the trial has gone against me. It might be a curse that Almighty God has put upon for I know not what."

The Judge reminded Mr. Williams that it was clear that he <u>was</u> guilty of the crime and that Mrs. Stark had come to him on recommendation and therefore he [the Judge] wondered how many other illegal operations had he carried out? It was also evident that Mr. Williams was not a qualified chemist nor did he have a qualified assistant working with him. The Judge was also keen to point out the dangers Williams had put the woman under by working with unclean hands and unwashed instruments. Imposing a sentence of five years penal servitude upon James Williams, Mr. Williams asked if he could see his wife. "Certainly," said the Judge "subject of course to the regulations of the prison."

*The Essery case referred to, was in regards to Alice Essery of 13. Egerton Crescent, Plymouth, also the wife of a chemist, who coincidentally at the same Assizes as Mr. and Mrs. Williams, was indicted with twenty-four charges of performing illegal operations. She was also sentenced her to five years' penal servitude.

Ghosts of past preachers?

In April 1907 it was reported that numerous people had been hearing voices and curious sounds coming from various parts of the building at St. James's Church in Exeter. These sounds were usually heard just before the start of morning and evening services. The sounds were said to resemble that of psalms being chanted. Sadly, St James' Church which was built in 1836, was hit by a bomb in May 1942 and the damage being so great that it was later demolished.

Old postcard of St James' Church and Schools – private collection.

Opera singer's attempted suicide.

In September 1907 a number of newspapers reported that Rose Braun, a talented soprano vocalist who was well known in musical world as Mme. Rose Ettinger and wife of Mr. Francis Braun, was found suffering a bullet wound to the face.

Mr. and Mrs. Braun had been staying at a lodging house at South Molton near Kingsbridge, where they were in the habit of spending a portion of summer holiday. Alice May Ettinger – her real name, had been born in Oregon, Ogle County, Illinois in 1877. She had travelled to Europe at an early age where she had performed extensively. Whilst in England she met and married Francis Braun a baritone vocalist from Liverpool in 1899.

In May 1907 the Braun's had participated in a concert arranged in aid of a fund for providing a new organ for the parish of nearby Thurlestone. It was noticed by many in the audience that Mme. Ettinger did not appear to be in good health and it was rumoured that she had been suffering from acute indigestion and that Dr. Pettinger of Kingsbridge had been attending to her for gastritis for some time. On the evening of the 2nd of September, Mrs. Susan Johns who lived in the neighbouring property to that occupied by the Braun's heard the report of a firearm coming from the Braun's cottage. She at once raised the alarm and Mr. Kennedy who was visiting a neighbouring property, proceeded with her to the cottage where they found Rose Braun lying on the bed with a revolver lying on the floor at her side. It was loaded in all five chambers with one having been recently discharged. Medical aid was promptly summoned and Dr. Pettinger who had attended to Mrs. Braun only hours earlier was soon in attendance. Rose Braun was conscious when he arrived and appeared to understand what was taking place. She was taken hospital and efforts were made to extract the bullet, but the doctors who operated on her were unable to locate it even x-rays proved unsuccessful and it was assumed that the cartridge that she'd fired had had the bullet extracted because had the cartridge contained a bullet and been fully charged; there was little doubt that on it being fired at such a short range it would have gone right through her head. There was also of course the possibility that the bullet had been swallowed or embedded itself in the bone at the back of her mouth and near to the spinal column and therefore would have been undetected by the x-rays on account of the density of the shadow thrown by the bone.

Having made a recovery, on the 20th of September, Rose Braun was charged at Kingsbridge Town Hall with having attempted suicide at South Molton.

Susan Johns of 2. Clarence Place, South Molton who was the first person on the scene after hearing the gunshot described hearing the gun and then finding Rose Braun in the bedroom which was full of smoke and seeing the revolver. Sarah Miller a widow who lived at 1. Clarence Place, South Molton, said that Mrs. Johns had knocked on her door and asked if she and her visitor Mr. Kennedy would accompany her into Mrs. Braun's house. When they discovered Mrs. Braun and asked her what had happened, she responded by saying she had shot herself. Mrs. Miller described how Rose's lips and nostrils were blackened, apparently from the gun-powder and she told her tearfully that she wanted to die.

Other witnesses were then called; Dr. James Wilson said that under anaesthetic he had examined the wound but failed to discover any bullet or the appearance of one. The following afternoon along with Dr. Lucey at Plymouth, he made another examination and a found a wound in the hard palate extending upwards and backwards for about two and a half inches. It was circular in shape and there was a good deal of damage to the nasal bones, but he still failed to find any traces of the bullet. The next morning, he had a skigram taken along with x-rays, they also failed to reveal any traces of the bullet. Dr. Pettinger, Rose's personal doctor, spoke of how Mrs. Braun had been ill and for the previous two or three nights to the shooting and had been unable to sleep. He had given her sleeping draughts which had sadly not produced the desired effect. She was in a state of very low spirits and depression, and in his opinion, she would not have been in the right state of mind to have been accountable for her actions. He also spoke of the gastric issues which had made her life a misery and left her in low spirits for a number of months previously.

In summarising the case, instead of giving Mrs. Braun the trouble, anxiety, and worry of being sent for trial to the Sessions or Assize at Exeter. The Judge decided that the prosecution had proved that Mrs. Braun was not at the time of the attempted suicide in such a sane state of mind as to be capable in law of committing the offence with which she was charged. He asked the jury to discharge her on the evidence of her doctor and that she would now be taken care of by her friends. She was in much better in health and it was very unlikely anything similar would occur again. After a brief retirement for consultation the jury returned to the courtroom and said that on the strength of the medical evidence, they found that it was a case of the lady having been temporarily insane, and they handed her over the custody her husband.

Rose Braun Ettinger passed away at her home in London on the 13th of May 1909. Her death was said to have been caused by heart failure, she was just thirty-two.

Theft of pretty roses.

Frederick Charles Heard, now pretty much always described as being a 'well-known character,' pleaded guilty in June 1909 to a charge of stealing a rose tree and some roses from the garden of 'Tregenna' on Decoy Road, Newton Abbot, the previous Monday morning. Mrs. Maud Elliott who lived at Tregenna, said there were a great many roses growing in her garden, but on the Monday morning she missed a number of them along with a small rose tree.

Muriel Williams a domestic servant at Mr. Patey's house close by, told the Bench that at about six o'clock on the Monday morning she saw Heard go into the garden and knock at the door. When no-one answered she saw him then pull up a rose tree, pick some roses and then walk away.

Fred in his defence said that he had been driven to it. He had recently come out of gaol and had no money and 'had taken the flowers rather than go thieving.' He said how he had previously held a good position but had come down through misfortune. He was sentenced to fourteen days imprisonment and the Chairman remarked that he had a host of previous convictions against him.

Gas explosion on Wilton Street.

On the 27th of October 1907 Mrs. Badcock of 117. Wilton Street, in the Stoke area of Devonport, decided to clean the glass surround on the gas light in her front room. After having replaced it and wiped down the gas lamp, her husband noticing the smell of gas opened the windows and doors to let it escape. Soon after when he thought it had likely all dispersed, he lit a match – there was an almighty explosion and Mr. Badcock was badly burned about that hands and face. The curtains and window blind in the room were also completely destroyed.

Oh Reverend!

In October 1907 the Reverend Arthur Robinson, pastor of George Street Baptist Chapel in Plymouth, was dramatically arrested shortly before he was due to conduct a morning service. The congregation who by this time were already seated, were informed that the service was being abandoned as the pastor was unable to attend.

The reason for the Reverend's arrest was due to an incident that had taken place in the back lane of Embankment Road in the Prince Rock area of the town a few days earlier. Mrs. Florrie Pearce had been looking out of one of the back windows of her house, which looked onto the rear of the properties in Wentworth Place, when she saw a man acting peculiarly in the lane. He continued with his activity for about fifteen minutes. In the meantime, Florrie had called her neighbour Mrs. Harding who lived in the flat below to come and have a look. Mrs. Harding enraged at what was taking place ran out into the lane and said to Reverend Robinson; "You're a dirty nuisance. If there were a policeman near, I would give you a charge!" At this the Reverend ran away and Mrs. Harding gave chase, following him down the lane and into Grenville Road where she lost sight of him. She did though come across a policeman and informed him of what had occurred. Whilst they were in conversation another woman came forward and said she too had seen the man acting questionably in the lane.

On the day of his arrest, Detective Sergeant Martin and Detective Morrish, along with the three female witnesses took up different position in Guildhall Square. The women were told to give a signal if they saw the man they had witnessed in the back lane and on this signal the police would make an arrest. At a quarter to eleven Arthur Robinson was seen crossing the square. On receiving the signal, Detective Morrish followed Robinson who was dressed in a frock coat and silk hat. Overtaking him, he stopped him as they passed through an archway leading to Westwell Street. He was just about to make the arrest when Robinson was briefly stopped by two women with whom he exchanged greetings. Still unaware of who Robinson was, he moments later made his move and arrested him. The two of them then made their way back to the Guildhall Square where the women all confirmed that he was the same man they had seen in the back lane. Robinson indignantly exclaimed that it was a case of mistaken identity, but despite his protestations he was led away to the Police Station where he told officers that he was the Revered Arthur Robinson and that he was on his way to conduct a service at the Baptist Chapel. Meanwhile back at the church his non-arrival had caused much consternation, especially anxious was his wife who was sitting in the front row. The police then arrived and informed the church deacons of the arrest and the sensitivity of the charge. The service that evening went ahead with a larger congregation than usual owing to the wildfire like spreading of the news of the charge against Reverend Robinson.

On the 31st of October Arthur Robinson stood in the dock to hear the charge of 'wilful and indecent conduct in the highway, in and between Cathcart Avenue and Wentworth Place, with intent to insult Florence Pearce on October 22nd 1907' put to him. Sergeant Philip Pill said he identified the defendant as the man who ran by him on the waste land behind Grenville Road at about 4 p.m. on the 22nd of October. He then made a report in consequence of what he was told by three women. Mr. Robinson he said was arrested in a dramatic way the previous Sunday morning as he was making his way to the chapel on George Street. Strange evidence was then given by five witnesses to show that on several occasions, another man or other men, had been mistaken for Mr. Robinson. Arthur Robinson was then sworn in. In the course of being cross examined he was asked; "Are you beginning to believe as suggested that you have a double? I think it must be so. You swear positively that you were not near that place on the day in question?" Arthur Robinson said that due to an illness he had suffered in March of that year it had left him in a position of not being able to run. He also said that his movements and attire on the day in question meant that it could not have been him who the women say they saw.

Splendid testimonies to the character of Robinson were then given by Rev. David Barron of Portsmouth, Rev. G. B. Berry the vicar of Emmanuel church Plymouth. Also, from Rev. W. K. Burford the pastor of Sherwell Congregational church, and Rev. Bell Johnston the pastor of Mutley Baptist church Plymouth.

Witnesses for the prosecution were then called to give evidence. Mrs. Florence Pearse who lived on Embankment Road said that on the Tuesday afternoon while attending to her child in the bedroom she noticed a man walking up and down the lane at the back of Embankment Road and Wentworth Place, which run at right angles to each other. After a time, he disarranged his clothing and faced the wall looking up at the windows. He afterwards stood at the opposite side of the lane and repeated his former conduct. She said that along with two other women she had gone in pursuit of the man who ran away. Mrs. Pearse said she was sure the defendant was the same man she had seen from the window. Cross-examined she said that he had been wearing a bowler hat and a dark suit. On Sunday while waiting to identify him, one of the detectives suggested to her that the man wanted might be wearing a silk hat and a frock coat. Subsequently there was a conversation about how the man was dressed.

Mrs. Jane Harding also gave evidence and expressed her conviction that the defendant was definitely the same man. His actions she said had shocked her modesty. Under cross-examination she was forced to admit that since her widowhood she had given birth to three children by one man and one by another.

Mr. Pearce in his speech on behalf of the defence, denounced the police for the way they had gone to work and said they had acted absolutely illegally. The court then adjourned to consider their decision. After a twenty-minute private consultation, the Magistrates returned and the Mayor speaking with emotion said; "Arthur Robinson, the justices are satisfied that the prosecution has entirely failed to bring home the offence you are accused of and dismiss the summons. I may say the Bench wish to associate themselves with me in an expression of the utmost sympathy with you in the terrible ordeal through which you have passed and you leave this court without a stain upon your character." (Prolonged cheers). Many swarmed around Mr. Robinson and shook hands with him and in the excitement, he was nearly swept off his feet. A few tried to sing the Doxology, but their voices were drowned out in the cheers which were taken and renewed again and again by the multitude in the square outside. A number of the principal witnesses for the prosecution were subjected to hostile treatment as they left and were jeered at. During the hearing of the charge the members of George Street Baptist Church held an all-day prayer meeting from eleven a.m. until the result of jury became known.

Serious farm accident.

Herbert Fairweather was a thirty-seven-year-old market gardener. In November 1907 he was helping out on his brother-in-law John Tully's farm near Brixham when he met with a most terrible accident. He was attempting to put a belt around a revolving wheel on a piece of machinery that he had been working on when a section of his coat became entangled. Before the engine could be stopped, the unfortunate man was whirled around at a terrific pace. His clothes were completely torn off, with the exception of his collar and boots. A doctor was sent for and he was removed to the Cottage Hospital.

Fred's fiftieth court appearance.

Here we meet up with Fred again, the newspapers now describing him as 'a notorious character' known across Devonport, Stonehouse and Plymouth, and who was formerly known in Totnes, Exeter and Paignton. Fred had pleaded guilty at Plymouth Police Court in May 1908 to stealing three scrubbing brushes, a pair of men's socks and two pairs of lady's stockings; the property of Arthur Welland.

P.C. Albert Wilce said that at twenty past three the previous Tuesday morning, he came across Frederick Heard in Russell Street carrying a parcel. When asked what was in the parcel, Heard replied; "I've cleared out from my lodgings and taken my property with me." Asked to open the package, Fred declined and was taken to the Police Station. There the parcel was opened by the inspector who detained the property and allowed Heard to go. He was arrested the following evening when the owner of the property was found. Admitting his guilt, Fred was sentenced to three months imprisonment with hard labour. He protested at the length and severity of the sentence saying he was being sent to a 'dog's kennel.' The Chief Constable reminded him that this was his fiftieth conviction at that court in less than four years.

It seems that no sooner is Fred out of prison then he's being sent back. At the Totnes Borough Police Court before Messrs. B. W. Hayman and F. T. Tucker, Fred made another of his regular appearances in early October. This time on the charge of the theft of a razor. Thomas Oliver a hairdresser on Totnes High Street, identified the razor produced in court as his property. He said that Fred Heard had been in his shop the previous day to have a shave. After Fred had left the shop, he noticed that his razor was missing and informed the police. P.C. Cooper who investigated the case said he made enquiries and as a result Frederick Heard was arrested in Torquay with the razor still in his possession. In answer to the charge Fred said, "Well, I suppose

I must've took it, but I had no intention of stealing it. I shaved myself and while talking I suppose I must have put it in my pocket and didn't know it was there." The Bench sentenced him to twenty-eight days with hard labour.

The Mount Boone Spectre.

For many years there was rumoured to be a ghost who made periodic late-night visitations to Mount Boone, Dartmouth, though there were no tangible evidence to the origin of the rumours. For some time, nothing had been seen or heard of the unwelcome visitor other than from the imagination of a few superstitious individuals who swore that the ghost had pursued terrified members of the fairer sex. This gossip reached fever pitch in early December 1908 when a story began to circulate around the town that a tall figure had been seen to spring from the hedges, and when the poor victims attempted to make their escape, he would pursue them at close quarters. Some people even went as far to say that the ghost wore a mask and that none of his features were recognisable.

Bands of men and youths, the majority armed with sticks, began to nightly patrol the neighbourhood. The searches however were not without their amusing moments. One evening a group of men were startled by the appearance of a stalwart figure who suddenly leaped from a hedge into their midst. The ghost was certainly not of the type which they had mentally created, he was clad in dark blue and wearing the helmet of the Devon Constabulary; P.C. Causley, who had been sent to Mount Boone owing to complaints received in consequence of the noise caused by the ghost hunters, scattered the group with even more alarm than probably the much sought-after ghost would have done! The crowning incident of the whole show came later that evening when at half-past ten, a breathless youth came in search of P.C. Causley telling him that the ghost had been found. He said that it had been caught near the cemetery and was surrounded. He also volunteered the startling information that the apparition was 'spring-heeled' and had jumped over a hedge. He was also wearing a false beard and whiskers. Having received this valuable information, two policemen then made their way to Mount Boone. When they arrived at the spot indicated by the youth, they discovered a shivering half-scared traveller of the road surrounded by a crowd of youths. The terror of the poor wretch was increased four-fold by the appearance of the two police officers. The poor man pleaded to be allowed to continue his tramp to his next place of residence - the Workhouse at Totnes. The crowd of heroic ghosthunters however wanted to satisfy themselves as to the truth of his story and so a match was struck and the boots of the unfortunate man were then examined in order to prove that they were not 'spring-heeled.' His hair was also inspected to make sure that it was not false. The wanderer was then allowed to continue his weary tramp, the crowd dispersed and the night's farce came to an end.

Fatal fire at Dawlish.

Three lives were lost in a tragic fire which occurred at Dawlish in the early hours of Tuesday the 22nd of December 1908. The outbreak took place at 2. Sea Lawn Terrace, a three-storey property which was situated only twenty yards from the sea and near to the railway line. The property was occupied by Mrs. Gladys Howe, a widow, who had recently come England from South Africa along with her children; Gladys, Reggie and Madeline. Also living at the property was Sarah Cunningham, an elderly lady who acted as nursemaid to the children. They also had living with them a little girl called Josephine Chamberlain, whose parents at the time were on an expedition in South Africa.

Mrs. Howe raised the alarm at quarter to two in the morning, by calling out from her bedroom window. George Moon who lived at number 4. Sea Lawn Terrace heard her cries and those of her children, and seeing plumes of smoke coming from the upper two windows at the front of the property he raced to the fire alarm call point on the Strand, calling in at the coastguard station on the way. The fire brigade and coastguard were soon on the scene; the coastguard arrived first, the station being only five hundred yards away. The men raised a long ladder with which they rescued Mrs. Howe, Gladys and Reggie. Mrs. Howe had slight burns to her neck, but suffered terribly from shock and smoke inhalation and had to be taken to hospital. Gladys and Reggie who were unharmed were taken in by neighbours.

Due to the flames and acrid smoke, it was impossible to reach the rooms in which slept Miss. Cunningham who was in her seventies, Madeline aged five and Josephine aged two and half. The fire brigade arrived about ten minutes after the coastguard, but their work was hindered by the build-up of silt around the nearby hydrant which meant that the hose couldn't be attached. This necessitated them going to another hydrant further from the scene, and the line being attached it was found there was not sufficient hose for them to reach the building. More hosepipe had to be sent for causing a further delay of about twenty-five minutes before water could be used to extinguish the fire. In the meantime, the fire had spread to the adjoining property, number 1. Sea Lawn Terrace; both properties were destroyed and number 3 suffered damage to the roof. The firemen worked hard to save the rest of the terrace from being consumed by the flames. When the blaze was finally extinguished, the bodies of Miss. Cunningham, Madeline Howe and Josephine Chamberlain were found badly charred on the ground floor of the property.

At the inquest into the fire, Mr. Hirzel, a solicitor who lived at number 1. Sea Lawn Terrace, said that he had offered to knock a hole from his property to Mrs. Howe's through the wall in the kitchen in an attempt to reach those still trapped in the house but Mrs. Howe had said that her kitchen chimney hadn't been swept for nine months and it would likely cause the fire to spread. He said he felt that his property could have been saved if there had been a partition wall in the roof space.

The seat of the fire was thought to have been in the kitchen itself. It was also stated that when the fire was detected, Mrs. Howe had placed Madeline and Josephine at the front of the property by the bedroom window, but when she left the room to try and rescue the other children the girls had become frightened and ran back to their own bedroom where they had become overcome by smoke and had then perished in the flames. The fire was said to have started accidentally.

A North Devon ghost story.

In February 1909, Charles Walburton was cycling along a North Devon road at around eight thirty in the evening when he passed a woman dressed in white night attire. Her blonde hair was down and flowing freely, she was also wearing slippers. A little further along his route he saw two abandoned bicycles, the riders he assumed having seen the woman dressed all in white, supposing her to be a ghost, had thrown their bicycles aside and bolted into the fields. Mr Walburton said the woman was evidently walking in her sleep…. [or was she?]

Gagging sensation at West Hoe.

Frederick Lodge aged twenty-two, a former 'boy sailor' onboard H.M.S. GOSHAWK in Plymouth but now residing at Kensington Gardens in Notting Hill, London, on the 16th of March 1909 had been to visit Captain Harcombe with the hope of getting a recommendation from him for a prospective situation in the town. Shortly after midnight he was found lying unconscious in a back lane at West Hoe. Residents nearby heard strange sounds but thought they were coming from cattle in a nearby enclosure. Two ladies however became convinced something was wrong and one of them a nurse, opened her bedroom window and called out; "Who's there, anyone in difficulties?" But only low moans could be heard. She hurried to the spot where the sounds appeared to be coming from and found a young man bound and gagged with two white handkerchiefs forced into his mouth and a scarf tied tightly around his eyes and mouth and fastened in a reef knot under his chin. His hands and feet had also been bound with wire, giving him the appearance of a trussed fowl. He was barely conscious and kept calling out 'take him away!' Doctor Parsloe who was called to the scene gave restoratives and then had the young man taken to hospital.

The following day Frederick told police that he was staying at the Commercial Hotel in Saltash and that he had left Captain Harcombe's residence at nine thirty-five the previous evening so as to catch the ten past ten train to Saltash. He missed the train and whilst waiting on the platform a stranger approached him and asked him to change a five-shilling piece. He took the change from his pocket and handed it to the stranger who then said; "hold on a minute," and went to speak to another man who was on the same platform. After a few minutes both men then left the station and separated. He then gave chase to the man who had his money. When he reached the lane where he was later found, he said the other man (likely wearing rubber shoes) must have come after him as he was seized from behind and something thrown over his head which he thought must have been drugged as he fell into unconsciousness. He said that as well as the five shillings, he was now missing another eighteen shillings and a return rail ticket to London. The police unable to find any trace of the alleged assailants along with doctor's who had Frederick under their observation at the hospital, all thought it rather suspicious. A number of other doctors in the town took a keen interest in the case and many paid a visit to the hospital. A London journalist contacted one of the doctors asking him if he thought Lodge was a 'romancer,' in how he accounted for the extraordinary way in which he was bound and gagged and had seemingly been unconsciousness for such a long time. The doctor smiled, shrugged his shoulders and said; "Well, Lodge has been both a sailor and an actor. That might explain some things." It was true that after serving on the training ship where he had shown himself to be an able musician, Frederick Lodge had gone on to tour with a number of theatrical companies and had recently returned from Canada, in search of work. The reporter then paid Frederick's mother Mrs. Lodge a visit. She and her husband both worked as caretakers at a large house in Oxford Gardens, Kensington. She told him that the week previously three men had come to her door asking for Frederick as they wanted to give him a good hiding. (At least they were honest in their intention!) Fred, she said, had told her he was afraid of the men and the next day left for Plymouth. It appeared to be some dispute over a girl.

A week later when Frederick was discharged from hospital, police questioned him some more, here he finally admitted that the whole thing had been a set up between himself and two acquaintances to create a sensation. He had gone to Millbay station, but instead of meeting a stranger, he met with two men that he knew from his time in the navy and between them they came up with the story. They then went to West Hoe where the scenario was carried out.

The Police said that charges were likely to be forthcoming, but I can't find any record of this taking place. Fred was probably issued with a caution and told to leave the town. He returned to London and in 1911 was working as a rocking horse and mechanical toy maker.

More reports of witchcraft.

It was reported in 1909 that particularly in the West Country, there was still a strong belief in the power of witchcraft. A recent case had been reported in Totnes of a girl whose arm a doctor said needed to be amputated. She was taken to the 'wise man of Newton' and her arm healed.

Devon execution list.

In 1909 The Western Times printed a list of the all the executions that had taken place in Exeter between 1800 and 1893.

1800 April 6, James Pooley, John Trick, William Thorn and Henry Pinsent; sheep stealing. John Dease; highway robbery. Richard Fisher; bullock stealing. J. Belson; stealing from the Dockyard.

April 21, Robert Boast, William Blades, Samuel Hughes and Thomas Hoist; using forged notes. W. Smith; highway robbery. John Allen; forgery.
August 27, Matthias Jewell, William Hockaday; housebreaking. J. Pollard; forging a seaman's will.
1804 April 7, Henry Hunt; horse stealing.
1805 April 5, Simon Coiner; forgery.
August 12, Betsy Heely; murder.
August 23, John Hayes; rape.
1806 August 4, Vincent Lopez; murder of a Spanish prisoner.
August 13, J. D. Rendall; forgery.
1807 August 5, Cogesto Cunado; murder.
1808 April 6, Benjamin Payne; murder.
August 16, George Godbear, murder.
1811 August 12, Jane Cox; murder.
1812 April 3, J. Williams; highway robbery.
1813 March 28, Thomas Luscombe; murder.
1814 August 6, William Vincent; murder.
1815 March 27, Samuel Norton; murder.
April 7, S. Summers; administering poison.
August 4, J. J. Chisholm; forgery.
1817 March 24, Robert Finsom; wife murder.
1818 March 23, John Green; murder.
April 3, J. Prinn; unnatural crime.
 November 13, Samuel Holnyard; forgery.
1819 March 21, Mary Woodman; murder.
April 2, John Atkins; unnatural crime. John Northcote; bullock stealing. Samuel Hellings; administering poison.
1820 April 3, Thomas Musgrove; sheep stealing.
August 18, John Cribble, forgery.
1821 April 26, John Bagwill; highway robbery. Jas. Bowden and William Bowden; housebreaking.
August 26 Phillip Chappie; murder.
1822 April 2, John Perry; arson.
1823 April 4, John Bolt; shooting at Jane Joslin.

June 23, J. Radford; alias Bright; murder of Sarah Down.
1827 April 2, Thomas Friend, murder of Edward and Sarah Glass on Wooland Down.
April 16, John Orchard; forging a will.
August 24, John James and George Campion; burglary at Tiverton.
1829 April 3, Thomas Helson and William Trethew; robbery and wounding.
August 17, Keziah Wescombe; murder of husband. Richard Quamtame; accessory to the fact.
1830 March 25, George Cudmore; murder.
August 20, William Bissett Cornish; unnatural crime.
1832 March 26, Mary Rallaway; child murder.
1836 August 12, Thomas Oliver, alias 'Buckingham Joe'; murder.
1849 April 6, James Landick; murder of Grace Holman.
1853 April 1, George Sparkes; for the murder William Blackmore.
1854 August 4, Llewellyn G. T. Hervey; the murder of Mary Richards at Torrington.
1861 March 30, Robert Hacked; murder Sergeant. Jones at Plymouth.
1866 March 28, Mary Ashford; poisoning her husband at Honiton Clyst.
August 18, John Grant; murder of a boy at Plymouth.
1869 October 11, William Taylor; murder at Devonport.
August 10, Thomas Macdonald, murder of Bridget Welsh at East Stonehouse.
1877 November 19, William Hussell; wife murder at Barnstaple.
1879 Annie Tooke, child murder.
1893 March 28, William Williams; Peter Tavy, for the murder of Emma Doidge and William Rowe.

Drunk and disorderly in Paignton.

In May 1909 Fred Heard our well-known friend was once again charged with being drunk and disorderly, this time in the Preston area of Paignton. He had been seen brandishing a walking stick with which he was threatening to 'brain' passers-by. He then accosted a Salvation Army man on Hollacombe Road who he was said to have grossly assaulted. On being arrested Fred swore at the police officer before spending the rest of the night in cells shouting obscenities at the top of his voice. In his defence, Heard made a rambling statement as to how far he had fallen in life. He was sentenced to fourteen days imprisonment with no option of a fine.

Drunk and disorderly in Exeter.

Fred was once again making one of his regular appearances in court – and the newspapers, this time at Exeter in July of the same year, where he pleaded guilty to being drunk and disorderly in the High Street, and to having stolen a waistcoat from the shop of Charles Gilpin at 48. Teign Street, Teignmouth.

Fred should have appeared a few days previously at the same court to answer a charge of being in possession of a dog's collar of which he could not give a satisfactory explanation; not having a dog, but had sent word saying that he was unable to get to the city in time for his appearance. Something you have to give Fred credit for is that he always turned up on time for court appearances and warrants for his arrest were never [as far as I know] issued. He expressed his sorrow at the predicament he found himself in and said he was glad to be getting locked up as the police always looked after him, fed him well, and gave him a new pair of trousers. Inspector Lewis said there were over one hundred previous convictions against Heard and having some sympathy for our friend's plight, he said he was prepared to withdraw the dog collar case. The Bench sentenced Fred to four months' imprisonment.

Fall from the sea wall.

In September 1909, John Saunders a fifty-year-old hairdresser living at Knighton Road, Plymouth, was taking an afternoon stroll along Madeira Road near to the Citadel when he saw a man fall from the wall that ran along the sea edge of the footpath, onto the rocks below. Unable to reach the man from where he was, he ran to the Royal Corinthian Yacht Club steps and along with two young men in a rowing boat who happened to be nearby, they made their way to where the man had fallen. They carefully moved him onto rocks higher up and then summoned Police assistance. A large plank of wood was procured and the injured man was placed upon it and taken to the Barbican from where he was removed to hospital. The gentleman died of his injuries four hours after admission. He had sustained a fracture the skull and broken leg. The man remained unidentified, though it was suspected he may have been a merchant seaman named Andrews.

A welcome return.

In early September 1909 the ketch 'Thomas Gray' of London, owned by Mr. Farrant of Rosebery Avenue, Plymouth, and commanded by Captain Frank Walker of 13. Cromwell Road, St. Jude's, in the same town was reported missing. The families of Captain Walker as well as those of the mate Snowden and seaman Fordly were all distraught and had given up all hope of the men coming home ever again.

On the evening of the 23rd the 'Thomas Gray' was seen entering the Cattewater and the three men onboard were safe and well. A message was immediately relayed to London to let the families of Snowden and Fordly know the good news, and Captain Walker as soon as the vessel was made safe, went home to have an emotional reunion with his wife and five children. Mrs. Walker had given up all hope ever seeing her husband again, nothing having been heard of him for such a long period and as it was rumoured in shipping circles that the 'Thomas Gray' had likely been run down by a passing steamer in the night.

Captain Walker relayed the following tale: On the 8th of September his vessel was in Portsmouth when orders were given to proceed to Roscoff in France, where he was to take a cargo of potatoes. The harbour at Portsmouth was crowded with warships and so he asked a tug to take them out to sea. The weather was fine and the 'Thomas Gray' successfully passed the Needles and St. Albans Head and from here shaped his course for Roscoff. Early the next morning at daylight when they had the sails fully set, he noticed the main sail had given way at the first reef point. The second reef was then taken in but the canvas split again. As they didn't have a spare mainsail on board, they had to continue using the head sail and mizzen mast. With reduced canvas the vessel was unable to continue on her course and she drifted about for a number of days, the winds being light. A few days later they spotted another vessel, a German four masted barque. The barque's Captain told Walker their position; seventy miles south of Queenstown in Ireland. The following day another vessel was spotted and the men got into their small boat and sailed towards it, it was the 'Minosia' a steamer from London. They called out but getting no reply they returned to the 'Thomas Gray.' The following day they made their best effort to head back to Plymouth and to get a new main sail, but the north-north-east winds worked against them and the bobbed about in all directions for the next five days not sighting another ship nor land. On the fifth day they spotted a trawler who informed them they were now twenty miles south of Gatley Head on the North West coast of Ireland. The 'Thomas Gray' then again floated aimlessly for four more days without seeing another vessel. They finally came across a Norwegian vessel whose crew gave them the good news that were just off the Lizard in Cornwall and supplied them with some much-needed bread. With their best means available the men steered the boat towards Rame Head in Cornwall and finally into the Cattewater, arriving at eight-thirty in the evening of the 23rd of September. Captain Walker said that they had plenty of supplies of food and water, the only thing they did run short of was bread, which the Norwegian vessel had kindly re-stocked them with.

Terrible fatality near Tiverton.

An Inquest was held at Tiverton on the 9th of January 1910 into the death of Frances Coom, a cook employed by Mr. Edward Wrey of The Cottage, Washfield. Gertrude Snell, a nurse and fellow servant said that on the evening of Tuesday the 4th whilst she was in Mrs Wrey's bedroom she smelt burning and looking out of the window she saw smoke and flames coming from the courtyard. Thinking the house was on fire she raised the alarm and then rushed to the home of her mother who lived at the Post Office close by and asked her to call for help. They both then ran back to the cottage with the intention of dressing the children and getting them out of the house. As they were entering the cottage, Mrs. Snell heard someone faintly calling out "Gertie," the voice was coming from the blaze in the yard. Realizing that the fire was actually consuming Frances the cook, a blanket was hurriedly fetched and dampened and then wrapped around her to extinguished the flames. The poor woman was almost naked, her clothing having been burnt off. P.C. John Crang arrived soon after and when he asked Mrs. Coom what had happened, she said she was about to take down an oil lamp from a high mantelpiece, when it slipped and landed on her head. The lamp caught on fire and so did she. She told him she was born in Brighton, and was fifty-nine-year-old. She repeatedly cried for water and through the intense pain became raging and tried to tear off the dressings he was applying to her wounds. Dr C. E. Liesching who attended to Mrs. Coom when she reached hospital, said she was terribly burned. She told him she had no relatives and handed him her insurance book and a purse containing one pound and seventeen shillings. She died ten minutes after admission to the Infirmary. A verdict of 'accidental death' was recorded.

Battered to death with a broom handle.

The body of Priscilla Small, a travelling gypsy, was found in a field at Kiln Lane near Ashburton, on Sunday the 16th of January 1910. The deceased had been camping with her husband Noah at Ramshorn Down, about four miles from the town on the Chudleigh road. At the inquest into her death Noah, a hawker, stated that his wife was forty-five years of age and until the previous Saturday they had been camping at Ramshorn Down, and on the Saturday, they had gone into Ashburton hawking. They went to the 'Victory Inn' and the 'Engineers' Arms' where they had drinks. They left at just after mid-day and he saw his wife go off down the street with her basket of brushes. He then went to the 'Rose and Crown.' At half-past four he was asked to go to a Mrs Thorn's in Kingsbridge Lane and remove his wife who was the worse for drink; which he did. Later that evening, probably between six and seven o'clock he met with his wife again and they began to walk back to Ramshorn Down. His wife was carrying a basket of brushes and brooms and he was carrying some groceries. His wife being the worse for drink kept falling down. On the third occasion whilst he was helping her to her feet, she told him to walk on ahead as she couldn't walk as fast as he could. After a time, he looked back and not seeing his wife anywhere he began to retrace his steps. He returned to the 'Bay Horse Inn' from which he had not long left and stayed there until closing time. He then made his way back to Ramshorn Down. Enquiring as to his wife's whereabouts, their daughter Betsy said she had still not returned. It being late and him having had rather a lot to drink, he went to bed. The next morning, he got up early and went with his daughter to Caton Cross to see if his wife was at the gypsy camp there – she was not. He left Betsy at the camp and went off to look for his wife with his brother Robert whose caravan was at the camp. They made their way towards Ashburton. On their way they met a boy who said he hadn't seen a woman, but had noticed a basket in a gateway some distance further down the lane. They went to the place indicated and found the basket, and looking over the gate saw Priscilla's body lying next to a hedge. It was bitterly cold and she was wearing only an undergarment, stockings and boots. Noah jumped back remarking; "My missus is in there stripped naked!" His brother in shock, ran back to his caravan. Noah made his way to Ashburton and informed the police. When asked, he admitted that neither of them had bothered to check to see if Priscilla was still alive.

Dr W. Fitzpatrick told the inquest that he went to the field at the request of Police Sergeant Boughton. The deceased was lying as though she had been placed in a comfortable position against the hedge. She was wearing only an under garment, socks and boots. He estimated she had been dead quite some time. There were marks and wounds on her head and breast, but there was no evidence of choking, nor did it appear as if anything had been put into her mouth. At the Mortuary he held a post-mortem examination and discovered an external wound on the left side of her head just above the temple. It was not an open wound but there was a swelling, and it appeared to have been caused by a blow. The wound on the left breast looked as though it had been caused by a kick. He assumed it had occurred before her dress had been taken off, because it would have been more distinct if it had not been done through clothing. There were several bruises on her limbs, but they were old ones. No marks of violence were to be seen around the neck or on the face itself. The skull was not fractured, but on opening it he found a blood clot involving the whole of the left side of the skull next to the brain. This had come from an artery that had broken just under the centre of the wound. Asked if the wound appeared to have been caused by a fall, he said it did not. It was rather high up and to have received such a wound a person would have had to turn a somersault. The deceased could not have got her clothes off and lain down after having received such a blow. It was rather a serious question to settle by himself and he would like another doctor to view the body. The Coroner agreed that another member of the profession should be called to make an examination and the case was adjourned till the following Monday. In the meantime, police arrested Noah Small on suspicion of the murder of his wife.

At the re-opening of the inquest, the Coroner read through Noah's evidence and asked if he had anything to add – he said he didn't. The medical evidence provided by Dr. Fitzpatrick was then read out as well as the second doctor's evidence; Dr E. Wilcox of Ashburton. He concurred with Dr. Fitzpatrick that there was no doubt as to the immediate cause of death. It was due to cerebral haemorrhage caused by the pressure resulting from the blow she had received.

Bessie Elford, landlady of the 'Bay Horse Inn' on North Street, Ashburton, stated that on Saturday January 15th, the couple came into the inn at between five and six o'clock. They had two or three halfpenny-worth's of beer each and Mrs. Small asked for a clay pipe, which was provided for her. They left just after six, and at ten o'clock Mr. Small returned and stayed till closing time. He was alone, and entering the taproom he ordered a beer for everyone there. He didn't enquire about his wife. As far as she could see he was sober when he left and he took with him a pint of beer in a bottle as well as some matches. On the Monday (the day of the first inquest) Mr. Small had paid another visit to the inn and asked whether he was in the bar from seven until eleven on the Saturday. She said he was not and he responded saying that he thought he was there all that time.

Alfred Northway, a farm labourer, said that he saw Small and his wife at the 'Bay Horse Inn' at half-past five on the Saturday evening, the wife being then neither drunk nor sober. Noah Small he said did not return until ten p.m. and definitely did not enquire about his wife.

Ethel Gill of Pitt near Ashburton, said that she met with the Small's in North Street at around six on the Saturday evening. Mr. Small was walking a short distance ahead of his wife who was carrying something that looked like brooms. They stopped near the steps leading to Terrace Walk and Mrs. Small seemed very obstinate and would not go on. Mr. Small was saying, "Come on," and then she saw Mrs. Small fall in the mud on the road. She picked herself up and made her way to some nearby steps where she made a noise like the cry of a baby. Wilfred Routley a general labourer of North Street, Ashburton, also spoke of seeing Mrs. Small lying on the steps at about a quarter to six. Her husband was fifteen to twenty yards further up the road. He was carrying a basket of brooms or brushes and was calling to his wife to come along. When she didn't respond, Mr. Small came back and helped her to her feet. She stood still in the road whilst he went on ahead. After he had gone a short distance, he again called to his wife to follow. She again did not move and again Mr. Small went back. This time he appeared to be coaxing his wife. The woman appeared drunk and eventually followed her husband.

A number of other witness saw the couple including Robert Hewings, a labourer, also of North Street. He said he saw them as he was riding by on his horse. Mr. Small called out; "Nice horse there mister, careful or I will knock you off with a brush," at the same time taking a broom and pretending to use it as a poke. Small then called out "good night."

William Endacott, a baker's assistant met the couple in the road near Rew, just after six o'clock. Mr. Small gave the greeting 'good night' and as he passed then he heard him say to his wife; "The next time you go to prison, you will have to take your children with you."

William John Hamblyn a farm labourer in Bickington, stated that he left his house at half six to go in the direction of Ashburton. It was a very dark night. On reaching Rew Park Cross at eight o'clock, about a mile or a mile and a quarter from Ashburton, he saw something in a gateway and not knowing if was a person or not called out 'good-night' anyway. Receiving no answer, he continued on, only to find a short distance ahead Mrs. Small lying on her back across the road and Noah Small on one knee beside her holding a broom in his right hand. Noah Small asked him to lend a hand in moving his wife, but as he approached, Noah decided he could manage alone. When William Hamblyn said that as he was there, he may as well help, Noah rose from the ground and with a broom in his hand and exclaimed; "If you're not gone, I'll knock you down with this broomstick!" Hamblyn went on ahead but watched for about ten minutes from a distance during which time Mrs. Small did not move nor make a sound. Mr. Small made no attempt to help his wife to her feet but just stood beside her. Returning by the same road an hour and a half later he saw no one.

Betsy Small, the eighteen-year-old daughter of Mr. and Mrs. Small said she was accustomed to going from place to place with her parents in their caravan. Recently they had been camping at Ramshorn Down, and on Saturday morning her father and mother left the camp to go to Ashburton, saying they would be back by half-past four. At half midnight her father returned home alone. He woke her up and asked whether her mother had returned and she replied 'no.' He made no further comment and went to bed. The following morning, she and her father went in search of her mother. They went first to Caton Cross where her uncle Robert Small was encamped and there she was left whilst her father and uncle set out to look for her mother. When her father returned, he told her that her mother had been found dead. She knew her mother was in the habit of getting drunk and had recently been fined at Newton Abbot for drunkenness. About a fortnight previously her mother was going about with black eye, given by her father. Her parents she said often had words about her mother getting drunk and her father frequently beat and punched her when she was in that state. Her mother would often stay out all night when she'd been drinking, because she was too afraid to come home.

Samuel Frank Willis, a butcher of North Street, said that on Saturday evening at about quarter-past seven, he found a jacket (produced) between Longstone Cross and Cuddeford Bridge. His horse shied at the coat and that was what attracted his attention. When told the next morning that a woman had been found without any clothing on, he took the jacket to the police. Abraham Knott an ex-police sergeant said he found a woman's hat near Cuddeford Bridge on the Sunday. Having heard that a woman had been found dead, he assumed the hat must have belonged to her. Examining the surroundings, he came to the conclusion that there had been something of a disturbance there. There were traces of considerable tramping on the ground by the side of the road as though something had been falling about.

P.S. Boughton stated that at ten fifteen on the Sunday morning, Noah Small came to him in a very excited state saying; "I have found my wife; she's dead. My wife, my poor wife, what shall I do? She's dead. She's as dead as a hammer." When asked if he was sure she was dead, Small said that he hadn't checked as he was too frightened to. Sergeant Boughton along with P.C. Champion went to the field. They found Priscilla by the hedge in a reclining position. She was partially dressed, a few feet away they found a skirt and a bodice.

On the 27th of January Noah Small was charged with the manslaughter of his wife, and was sentenced to five years penal servitude. It was said that in a drunken frenzy he had beaten his wife to death with a broom handle.

The mysterious death of William Hunt.

At six-thirty in the morning of the 16th of May 1910, Samuel Clatworthy of Citadel Road, Plymouth, discovered a body in the water under the Hoe. He went to investigate and dragging the body from the water, noticed that some of the gentleman's clothing was burnt. P.C. Wyatt was summoned and the body was removed to the mortuary by the constable and a passer-by; Ernest Gregory, a labourer of Alma Street. From items in the gentleman's pockets, he was identified as being William John Hunt, a forty-seven-year-old watchmaker who for the past five years had lodged in a room on Beaumont Avenue in the Greenbank area of the town. The previous evening, he had left his home at seven-thirty to take a watch to his sister-in-law who lived in St. Budeaux. After spending a pleasant evening in her company, he set off with the intention of walking back to Beaumont Avenue; his route not taking him anywhere near the Hoe. As he had a latch key he was not noticed missing by the other tenants until the following day.

Dr. Williams who carried out the post mortem said that the gentleman's beard, moustache and hair were completely burnt off. His hands were badly burned and there was a slight burn to his right thigh. His coat and trousers also had burn marks on them, although there was no smell of oil on his clothing. He said it would have had to have been a very considerable fire to have caused the damage it did. William Hunt was described as being a very quiet and uncommunicative man and little was known about his affairs, even by his family. The jury returned a verdict of 'found drowned.'

Heard's History.

Well-known character of many of the South-West towns, Frederick Charles Heard made yet another court appearance, this time at Newton Abbot Police Court in May 1910. He was charged with sleeping rough and appeared in the dock carrying a bundle of manuscripts.

P.C. Mortimore told the Magistrates that he had come across Heard early that morning sleeping in a doorway near to the railway station. When asked if he had anything to say, Fred informed the officials that he had been turned out of a common lodging-house because he declined to mix with the others to drink and play cards. He was now engaged he said, in writing the history of his life including his experiences in prison, and he wanted his manuscript to be read. Mr. Murrin, one of the Magistrates, declined to undertake the task of reading the document and dismissed Fred Heard on his promising to leave the town within the hour.

* I think after what we have read of Fred's life so far, we would all gladly have accepted the opportunity to have read his manuscript; sadly, it is most likely that over time it was probably thrown away or destroyed. Maybe, just maybe, it's stored away in an archive somewhere waiting to be discovered.

Fred Heard now back in Totnes.

The 5th of April 1911 saw Frederick Charles Heard, against whom there had already been nearly fifty convictions at Totnes Magistrate's Court alone, was once again standing in front of the panel, this time with a charge of stealing from the till of the Dart Hotel. Mrs. Emily Bow wife of the landlord, said Heard went behind the bar and stole six shillings in sixpences. Heard at first pleaded not guilty but after questioning he admitted the offence. He was sent to gaol for three months with hard labour.

*The 1911 census taken on the night of the 2nd of April shows Frederick then said to be aged sixty-two, an inmate at the Totnes Workhouse. I wonder what happened to the property that Gertrude Symons owned in Totnes and which she signed over to Fred when they said they would spend their life together as man and wife? I think she possibly reneged on her decision and instead of signing it over to Fred, allowed him to 'live off the income' for as long as they were together. Possibly she had now sold the house and was living off the sale? I found her on the 1911 census living in the St. James area of Bristol in a lodging house, but with her own private means of income.

Secret birth at the vicarage.

In March 1912, twenty-seven-year- old Gertrude Elliott a domestic servant for Reverend Henry Jones at Christ Church Vicarage, Paignton, was charged with attempting to kill her male child through suffocation on the 22nd February.

At a special sitting of the Paignton Justices, Bertha Rogers also a domestic servant at Christ Church Vicarage, stated that on the morning of the 22nd she had gone in Gertrude's room and noticed marks on the floor. She then heard the feeble cry of a baby which appeared to come from a tin-box some distance away from the bed. Without making any search she immediately went downstairs and informed Mrs. Jones of what she had witnessed.

Reverend Henry Jones said that he had seen Gertrude Elliott in the kitchen soon after Mrs. Jones had been informed of what had taken place. She admitted to having given birth after he pressed her on the matter saying that she thought the child had been born dead. He said to her; "You know you cannot stay here?" and Gertrude replied; "I know sir; I intended to give notice this morning." Adding that she had planned on going to the Union Workhouse for help. She told him that she didn't expect to give birth for another month and that's why she had intended giving her notice that day. Bertha Rogers added that when the Reverend was talking to Gertrude prior to her returning to her bedroom to await the arrival of the doctor, she heard her say; "I didn't intend to destroy my baby!" Reverend Jones said he wanted the Magistrates to know that Gertrude and her child had stayed with him and his family at the vicarage until the beginning of March, when she moved to the 'Door of Hope Home for friendless girls' on St Marychurch Road, Torquay.

Dr. Adams who had been called to attend to mother and child said that he had gone to the vicarage accompanied by the police. There he found a male child wrapped in various articles of clothing. One layer was wrapped very tightly around the infant who was very blue which was a sign of partial suffocation, otherwise the child was in a good condition. He doubted it could have lived for another two hours under such circumstances. Gertrude told him the baby had been born at about noon, he saw it at two o'clock.

Superintendent Roberts who accompanied Dr. Adams to the vicarage said that rather than wrapped up as it should be the baby was tied up in a bundle.

Police Sergeant Mairs and Police Constable Clarke who were also present said that it was they who informed Miss. Elliott that her child was still alive.

The Bench considered the evidence and felt there was sufficient indications to commit Gertrude Elliott for trial at the next Assize. In June 1912 she appeared before the Devon Assizes at Exeter, where she pleaded not guilty attempting to kill and murder her un-named child. The jury returned a verdict of 'not guilty' and she was discharged. There is a happy ending to this tale and mother and son were looked after and able to stay together.

Believed he was being blackmailed for a murder he hadn't committed.

William George Budd, the thirty-four-year-old son of Dr. Budd of Chagford and said to have been well-known in and around Dawlish and Exeter, was reported missing from his lodgings at Moretonhampstead on the 15th of March 1912. A description was circulated and a reward offered for information leading to his discovery. No definite sightings of him were reported but there were rumours that he has been seen in the vicinity of Two Bridges on Dartmoor. Relatives, police and well-wishers conducted searches, but all were fruitless. Some weeks later on the 24th of April, Arthur Wotton a rabbit trapper of Moretonhampstead, was engaged in burning back gorse at Howton Brake; half a mile from the home of William Budd, when he came across a body. Although much decomposed Budd was easily recognised by his clothes and a stick. The body was beside a hedge and partially under a projecting rock, with a footpath just a few yards away. His body was removed to the Moreton Cottage Hospital and an inquest into his death held the following day.

The body of William Budd was identified by his brother Arthur, a doctor with a practice in Launceston. Arthur said his brother had been a professional violinist, but in May of the previous year had suffered a complete nervous breakdown and ordered absolute rest.
Miss Daisy Middleton, companion to Miss. Budd, the sister of the deceased, said the last she had seen of William was on the 15th of March when he went out for a walk. She remembered thinking he didn't appear as cheerful as he had the previous evening.

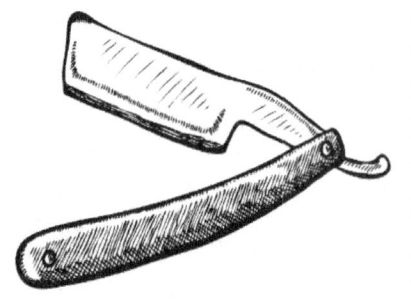

Police Sergeant Osmond told the inquest that on the 15th of March the deceased was reported missing and a description was circulated, the district searched and inquiries made. William Budd was not wanted by the police and neither did he answer the description of any person who was wanted. It was he who was the first to attend the scene on being told that a body had been discovered. He found William Budd lying in a dyke on his back. On his left-hand side lay a bloodstained razor. William had taken off his collar and tie and placed them in his pocket. Lying on the ground were torn-up letters.

Here the Deputy-Coroner (Mr. P. C. Cornish) read out a letter which William Budd had in his pocket and was addressed to: 'Dr. Budd and others, Dartmoor View.' *"Please forgive me for doing this. I have been driven off my head with the worry of the blackmail and persecutions of the last two or three years; blackmail for a murder I have not done."* In the letter he went on to say that he had been hounded and blackmailed by the police for nothing. It was a perfect scandal, and innocent persons were going to be in danger of their lives. Did anyone think he would commit such a terrible murder? After stating that Mr. Ford would explain and detailing how his belongings were to be distributed, the letter concluded: *"I do hope you will bear up in this terrible business and that you will forgive me. Give my love to all. From your heart-broken and loving son, Willie. Friday, March 15th 1912."*

Alex Ford of Cable House, Weston-Super-Mare said that he had known William Budd for a number of years and they had last met at Dawlish in January. Mr. Budd had the delusion that he was being followed by detectives and police officers. Mr. Ford had even taken him up to a police officer in Dawlish and got the officer to confirm that he was not a wanted man, and that seemed to reassure him for a time. He said he didn't know what had brought on these delusions unless it had been the breakdown. He knew nothing about what was in the letter beyond what he had just explained. He recalled an occasion when William Budd had casually mentioned that he was tired of life.

Dr. Alfred Coleridge who carried out the post-mortem said the body was badly decomposed and there was a large and deep wound in the throat; such as could have been inflicted with a razor. A verdict of 'suicide during temporary insanity' was returned, and a resolution of condolence was passed with the relatives. The jury, through the foreman, expressed the opinion that they ought not to be expected view bodies that were in the state of this one. The Deputy-Coroner concurred. William was buried in St. Andrew's Churchyard, Moretonhampstead.

Nonagenarian drowned at the Barbican.

Whilst walking along the Barbican Quay, Plymouth, shortly after midnight one evening in June 1912, a young fisherman named Frederick Witts heard a sudden loud splash, similar to that made by a large object falling into the water. He immediately called out to some other fishermen close by and when they went to the spot where he thought the sound came from, they saw the body of a man floating in the water. Albert Brown who was out in his rowing boat was hailed and made his way to the scene with great haste and was able to help the fishermen lift the body ashore. In the meantime, Police Sergeant Broad along with Constables Carnell and Roach had arrived at the Quay and had started artificial respiration. They maintained their efforts for about forty minutes until Dr. Cooke arrived and certified the man to be dead. The deceased proved to be Harry Lyons who was ninety-two-years of age and a former boatman. His advancing years had prevented him working for quite some time. Harry had no fixed abode and as far as could be ascertained, the last house in which he had slept was the Plymouth Workhouse and that had been some months previously. Several nights earlier he had been seen sleeping on the quay, which apparently was one of his favourite haunts. He had been seen by several men shortly before midnight, including P.C. Roach who suggested he go home. Albert replied saying that was what he was going to do. When pulled from the water he had his old age pension book in his pocket.

* On the 1911 census Harry was recorded as being a widowed 'watchman,' lodging at 37/38 St. Andrews Street, Plymouth.

The mysterious disappearance of William Stenner.

On the wilds of Exmoor, search parties spent days trying to unravel the mystery surrounding the disappearance on the 9th of August 1912 of William Stenner, a labourer at Riscombe Farm, Exford. He had earlier complained to his wife of not feeling well and soon after having had his supper he retired to bed. His wife later entering the bedroom was astonished to find the window wide open and her husband missing. The clothes that he had been wearing that day were on the floor but his nightshirt was nowhere to found. Neighbours were alerted, and marks were found under the bedroom window indicating that he had jumped from the window into the garden and then ran barefoot across it, over a hedge, through an orchard and brambles and thicket to the moors beyond. All through the night a search was kept up by the village constable and several farmers from the surrounding area. The following morning Mr. Morland Greig, master of the Devon and Somerset Staghounds, and Captain Thompson, master the Exmoor Foxhounds joined in the search and although many miles of moorland were covered, Stenner could not be found. Grappling irons were used at a disused limekiln now called Newland's pond which was around thirty feet at its deepest point. The search continued into the next day without any success and the police came to the conclusion that William Stenner had somehow become deranged and had perished from exposure.

In November, after a subscription had been raised to cover the cost of having Newland's pond drained, the work was carried out and the pool was drained to within a few feet of the bottom from where the mud lining and shelving banks were searched, but still no trace of Stenner could be found. It was said that practically every foot of the moor had been investigated and yet there was no sign of the missing man anywhere. Was it possible William Stenner was still alive? In early December the Dulverton Guardians met; for the previous two months they had been giving Mrs. Bessie Stenner and her six children, seven shillings and six pence a week in relief. One of the board members asked whether the Guardians intended on taking any steps to find Stenner as there were rumours that he was still alive. He suggested that the board apply for a warrant for Stenner's arrest. It was also said that Mrs. Stenner and her children had moved to South Molton to be nearer family and where the guardians there were paying her twelve shillings and sixpence a week (this included the Dulverton Guardians money). Another of the board suggested that a summons for deserting his wife should have been issued soon after his disappearance. A fellow member said that it was rumoured Stenner's body was possibly in Pinkworthy pond, but the Chairman dismissed the suggestion. It was finally agreed that an ordinary summons should be applied for. On the 20th of December the Board of Guardians offered a reward of five pounds leading to the arrest of William Stenner.

At the insistence of those who still believed William Stenner to be dead, the draining of Pinkworthy [also known as Pinkery] pond began on the 28th of December. The work was all to no avail as no body was found. It was around this time that the Dulverton Guardians decided to stop paying Mrs. Stenner and the children poor-relief as they believed William to still be alive. On the 25th of February 1913, a farm hand in the employment of Mr. Heal of Riscombe Farm, William's former employer, made the discovery of a body. The tragic discovery was made after he had noticed that the cows were not drinking the water from a stone drain which ran through a meadow not half a mile from the Stenner's former home. Going to the spot he commenced pushing away green slime and duckweed near to the drain. Suddenly, he caught sight of a naked foot a few inches from the drain and on closer examination saw another foot. Greatly frightened he ran back to the farm and communicated his gruesome find to the police. P.C. Padfield of Exford who was on duty some distance away said he was not able visit the spot until the early hours of the next morning when it was light enough to see properly. When he arrived, prepared for what he was about to discover, he brought with him a rope and lying down on his right-hand side he was just able to reach far enough to attach the rope to the dead man's foot and then dragged the body from the drain. The body with the exception of the nightshirt was naked and in a good state of preservation. The features of the man were recognised by those who were present as being William Stenner. His body was taken to the 'Crown Hotel' Exford and the inquest arranged to be held the following day.

Bessie Stenner said that her husband was a very quiet man and there was absolutely no reason for him to leave home. "Did he speak to you before he disappeared?" asked the Coroner. Mrs. Stenner at this question burst into tears and remarked that he went without saying a word to her. She said that for some time before his disappearance he had been having sleepless nights and this made him very low spirited. He had been attended to by Dr. Maloney and actually seemed a little better on the night of his disappearance. The Coroner then asked; "Had he ever said or done anything that would make you think that he would want to take his life?"
"No, nothing whatsoever," replied Mrs. Stenner. Asked if he had ever wandered off before, she again replied; "never." Asked if they had quarrelled, Mrs. Stenner said they had never quarrelled about anything.

Other witnesses included Charles Needs who had spoken Stenner the day before his disappearance said that he had seemed completely normal and they had discussed farm matters. Reginald Hoskins, the farm hand who discovered the body said that the drain was an old mine shaft in which there was five feet of water. The shaft was used for dipping animals and he thought that William Stenners would have had to have crawled into it.

Dr. Maloney who had been attending to Stenners said that a while previously when he heard that one of William's close relatives had committed suicide, he warned Mrs. Stenner to look after her husband.

The Coroner's jury decided that William Stenner's death was 'due to drowning' and showing no marks of violence, a verdict was returned to that effect and that the deceased had committed suicide whilst of unsound mind. The Coroner excused the jury from viewing the body.

Decomposing body found in a disused store.

On the afternoon of the 26th of November 1912 two men, James Turner and his nephew Robert, went to an empty fish store at the Palace Vaults in New Street, Barbican, Plymouth, with the intention of removing some padlocks. Moving the half open door, James Turner was horrified to find behind it the badly decomposed body of William Moreton aged sixty, a familiar face to the fishermen on the Barbican for many years and who was known to Turner. He had been missing for several weeks. Moreton who had no fixed abode was by trade a cooper and had also worked as a fish packer. Due to his drunken habits in recent months, he had been unable to find work and it appeared that he had regularly sought out the empty store as a place to rest at night and without the knowledge of anyone, had died there.

Double tragedy at Buckland Monachorum.

The inhabitants of the pretty little village of Buckland Monachorum lying snugly in a valley about six miles from Tavistock, were horrified when a double tragedy occurred in Milton Combe on Saturday the 26th of July 1913. William John Coombes a labourer, borrowed a double-barrelled gun and shot dead without warning his half-sister Beatrice (Beatie) Greep.

Earlier in the day he had borrowed the gun from a neighbouring farmer Arthur Rodgers at Didham, saying he was going out to shoot rabbits. He was then supplied with five cartridges from another neighbour Mrs. Beer a butcher's wife, who later said he was cheerfully whistling as he walked away. Coombes had planned the killing. He had gone into the kitchen and pulled down the window blind. He then called to Beatie to come downstairs and as she entered the kitchen, he shot her at point blank range. The bullet hitting her in the neck; taking away half her face. He then called to another of his half-sister's Emily, asking her to also come to the kitchen. Having heard the gunshot she called out; "Oh Will, what have you done?" and in reply Coombes excitedly replied with; "Come and see for yourself!" Then putting the barrel of the gun to his mouth, he fired again. Hearing the second shot Emily ran to a neighbour Joseph Curno, calling out that her sister had been shot. She fell in a faint into his arms and it was later feared she would contract a serious illness and die as she lay unconscious through shock for a number of days.

The sound of gunshots quickly brought a large crowd to the scene and within a few minutes P.C. Kingdon stationed at Crapstone, alongside Joseph Curno, entered the property where the tragedy had occurred and found Beatie Greep to be quite dead, whilst Coombes who presented a ghastly sight was breathing his last. The clothes of both the murderer and his victim were splattered with blood which was trickling from their wounds in large quantities.

Although no motive could be given for the tragedy, rumours amongst the neighbourhood began to spread and it was alleged that Will had fallen in love with his step-sister who had rebuked his advances. Will Coombes was described by many as a morose and lazy man. Apparently, he had been in a bad mood at lunch time that day and had refused to join the family in a meal.

The widowed mother of the two victims was not at home at the time of the incident, she was in the South Devon and East Cornwall Hospital in Plymouth suffering from an internal complaint.

Mrs. Collecott aged eighty, who lived in the next-door cottage told the police that on hearing the sound of the gunshot she went outside and looking through the window she saw Beatrice fall slowly to the ground with her hands held up towards her head. She then saw Coombes raise the gun to his face and put his foot up near the trigger. [it's unlikely she could have got outside quickly enough to have seen Beatie fall as this would have been almost instantaneous after being hit by the bullet.]

William Coombes was buried the following Tuesday at the Baptist Chapel in Milton Combe and Beatrice later the same day. Their mother was still in hospital and too poorly to attend their funerals. Her condition no doubt having been made so much worse by the terrible tragedy that had befallen her family. William Coombes had not long left the Navy and had recently moved in with his mother, step brother and five step-sisters.

The chapel at Milton Combe. (Picture courtesy of bucklandmonachorum.org.uk)

A double century.

Frederick Charles Heard of no fixed abode, was brought up before Plymouth Magistrates in August 1913 accused of being drunk and disorderly and using obscene language. The Magistrates were told how Fred had been up before the same court fifty-seven times and had been in prison in various parts of the county on two hundred occasions. On this, his two hundred and first sentencing he was punished with fourteen days imprisonment. It was also noted that being so well-known in Plymouth he was frequently made the butt of jokes by many of the boys.

*This is the last mention that I can verify of Fred. If only the story of his unfortunate life which he wanted to be read had been published.
No more is heard of our friend after this date. What became of him, what was his fate? I've tried to find out what happened after 1913, but it appears he is no longer getting himself into trouble, or at least not being brought before the Magistrates. A Frederick C. Heard died in St. Thomas, Exeter in 1921 aged sixty-five. I would assume this was at the St Thomas Workhouse just to the

west of Exeter at Redhills. Our friends date of birth varies between 1849 and 1856 on the census. There were two Frederick Charles Heard's born in Devon around this time, one in 1854 and one in 1858. One of them passed away in 1907 – definitely not our Fred. Going by the earlier census I'm sure he was born in 1854, making him sixty-seven when he died.

Curious epitaph on a headstone.

In 1915, a Mr. J.W. Tickel of 51. Fentiman Road, South West London, wrote to the Pall Mall Gazette in reference to a curious headstone he had come across in Stoke Damerel Churchyard, it read: EPOP NHOJ Died 3rd of March 1837. He lived 31,775 days.
John Pope was therefore eight-six/seven years old when he died. It seems as though he certainly had a sense of humour!

Mystery of the swimmer who just disappeared.

Whilst playing under Plymouth Hoe on the afternoon of Saturday the 26th of January 1918 two boys; Charles Richards aged eleven and Ernest Day age ten, saw a man go into the bathing area and after undressing he entered the water. The boys watched with interest as he swam (it being such a cold day) but they then saw him disappear under the water. They waited and watched silently for him to reappear, but there was still no sign of him after what felt like a long wait but was probably only about two or three minutes. Becoming anxious, they ran to the Hoe Police Station and informed P.C. Body who was on duty of what had occurred. He came back with them to the bathing shed where he found a pile of clothing, and like the boys had said, there was no sign of the man. A sea search was carried out, but no signs of the man nor a body was found. The clothing was taken to the Central Police station, where they were identified as belonging to William Pleace, a cab driver of Chester Place, Mutley Plain, who had left home at around noon that day.

*William was in his late 50's. Strangely I can find no record of his death – possibly his body was never recovered and his wife believing him to still be alive, never recorded the death. She passed away in 1929 – never having known the final resting place of her husband.

Seven missing sailors.

On the 28th of November 1919, seven naval stokers left their ships without permission; H.M.S, Swindon and H.M.S Silvio which were moored near the Royal Albert Bridge (Tamar Bridge) to row ashore in a dinghy. They were rumoured to have landed as a group of sailors were seen in a street singing and enjoying themselves and were again later seen at Saltash beach. The men were reported missing the following morning and the boat was later found near the 'Mount' training ship, half full of water and the oars missing. Two naval caps bearing the names of two of the missing men were also found.

A strong southerly had blown up late the previous evening and it was thought the men had likely tried to row along the shoreline to their ships and the boat had capsized; although there was no explanation of how it had then righted itself again. On the 4th of December the bodies of all seven missing men were found lying in the mud at Warren Point where they had evidently been cast by the tide. They were fully dressed except for their caps. The men were from the Silvo: Stoker Petty Officer W. T. Bray, Stokers L. H. Galliford, D. K. Davies, A. C. Cotton, and C. E. Thorpe. From the Swindon: Stokers A. Gordon and C. Cronin.

Gripped by invisible hands.

What is behind the mystery behind the unseen hairy hands on the Post Bridge/Two Bridges road on Dartmoor? On this one stretch of this road, three curious accidents occurred between March and November 1921 in which the vehicle unaccountably swerved to the side of the road. The first occasion of this strange 'swerving' resulted in the death of a doctor who was on a motor cycle. The second incident involved a motor coach in which several passengers were thrown out. On the third occasion an army officer was riding his bicycle when he felt two large muscular hairy hands close over his own and force him onto the side of the road in spite of his resistance. As a result of this apparently enforced turning, the young man was hurt and his bicycle damaged. The doctor in the first occurrence was Dr E. H. Helby, the medical officer of Princetown Prison. Were his hands similarly turned against his will by the large unseen hands which so nearly killed the young officer? Who knows the answer but the fact that he shouted to his two children who were passengers in the sidecar immediately before the accident, telling them to jump as there was something wrong, shows he was aware of some sort of danger?

Jumped overboard in the Cattewater.

On the 28th of December 1921, a crew member of the American steamer 'Elkhorn' disappeared under mysterious circumstances during the vessel's stay in the Cattewater, Plymouth, where she had been ballasting prior to setting out for Galveston, Texas. The missing man was Robert Stanley Pyles an ordinary seaman aged twenty-two, and had only recently joined the ship in Antwerp. In the early morning of the 28th he was seen writing postcards, but at breakfast time he was found to be missing. The ship was searched and on the upper deck were found the clothes that he had been wearing earlier. His shoes and socks were in his locker and in the fo'csle his other effects were found intact. It was believed he could only have left the ship in his underwear.

On the 13th of January, the body of a badly decomposed man clad only in vest and pants was found by three watermen floating in the water at Sparrow's Quay, Cattewater. The body had nothing on it which would lead to identification but it was believed to be that of the missing young man.

Chambercombe Manor Farm.

An Ilfracombe based correspondent for the 'South Wales Daily News' in 1922 recounted the following tale, a relic of bygone smuggling days.

Old Postcard – Chambercombe Manor Farm.

"Chambercombe Manor was and still is a most intriguing property. Steeped in legend and history it was mentioned in the Domesday book. Parts of the house are said to be over a thousand years old and carvings in wood and stone have been found long covered over. The manor was owned by the Champernon family. The earliest positive record of it is from 1162 when it was in the possession of Henry De Champernowne, who was then lord of the manor of Ilfracombe. It is most likely that the property came to the family soon after the Norman Conquests. In the early 16th century, it became the property of Henry Duke of Suffolk, father of the ill-fated Lady Jane Grey.

Chambercombe Manor Farm lies in a valley a few miles from Combe Martin and close to the little hamlet of Hele. It is here the ghost has again been seen, but it causes no alarm. A guest at the farm occupying a bedroom once used by Lady Jane Grey, was the one to see her (for it is a woman ghost) but the apparition did no harm and caused no particular excitement. To tell the story of the ghost one has to go a long way back in history. Hele, quite a holiday haunt now, was then the home of bold bad men whose least crime was smuggling. One night a ship was driven or lured ashore, the crew were drowned or murdered and a beautiful Spanish noblewoman on board was made a prisoner. She was taken by the smugglers through an underground passage which then connected Chambercombe Manor with Hele Beach to the house. There she was placed in a secret room and starved to death. It was as recently 1865 that the tragedy was discovered according to rumour. Entry into the room was made during the progress of alterations to the house and the skeleton of a woman was found lying on a bed surrounded and partly covered by mildew and decayed tapestry hanging. This is the ghost which is now reported to 'walk' occasionally but who never harms anyone. I've never seen the ghost, but I was told by the man who conducts visitors to the haunted room that one of the guests says she saw 'her' standing on the stairs a few nights ago

The haunted room stands as it did when the skeleton and furniture were removed in 1865. The roof of the Manor Farm forms the ceiling. A small hatchway in a wooden wall affords a view of the interior. In the courtyard of the farm there are traces of the old subterranean passage. A short distance has been cleared and at the foot of the cliffs at Hele is a small cave, said to be the entry to this tunnel. Unfortunately, it is impossible to force a way through. The roof and the side have fallen in and to discover anything it would be necessary to drive another tunnel from the beach to the valley."

Forde House hauntings.

In August 1923 a number of newspapers printed the tale of a haunting in Newton Abbot, the scene being Forde House which was built during the reign of Queen Elizabeth I.

The legend of a nun being walled up alive has always been associated locally with the house, and a coffin-shaped projection in the wall points out the tragic place where she was entombed. The house was then owned by the Earl of Devon, and was tenanted by his sister Lady Mary Bertie and her husband, Colonel the Hon. Reginald Bertie. During their absence whilst on holiday, Mrs. Saunders who was a prominent local resident and descendent of Sir Richard Reynell who built the house, was staying there with her son. During the night Mrs. Saunders who was sleeping in the room where William of Orange spent his first night in England, was awakened by the sound of heavy footsteps hurrying along the passage way and down the stairs. Thinking her son was ill but wondering why he wore boots; she switched on the light and awaited his return. Dozing off she was again woken by the rushing sound of footsteps coming up the stairs; the unmistakable footsteps of a heavily booted man which made the stairs creak. Loudly calling her son's name and receiving no reply, Mrs. Saunders went into his bedroom which adjoined hers and found him sleeping peacefully and with the door which had been carefully closed the previous evening, now wide open.

The following morning, she asked her son if had slept well. He replied that three times he had woken up to find his bedroom door open and had got up to shut it. Mrs. Saunders then trying the door found it quite impossible to do it without turning the handle. One of the maids asked her if she or her son had been ill as they had heard someone moving about. Mrs. Saunders was now convinced that the legend of the walled-up nun to be true and that the footsteps she'd heard were those of a man pursuing the nun who was gliding along noiselessly.

Some years previous to this event, a maid had apparently gone down to the dining room one night to fetch some brandy for a servant who had taken ill. She was heard to scream and was found in a dead faint. When she was brought to her senses, she said that she had seen someone pass her in the hallway and then disappear.

Around five years previous to Mrs. Saunders encounter [1918] in consequence of footsteps being regularly heard on a certain date each month, the gardener sat up all night in the alleged haunted room, but nothing transpired. The tenants of the house of course denied the story.

* The original Forde House at Newton Abbot was built by John Gaverock in 1545. The structure we see today was built around 1610. Visitors to the property are said to include King Charles I and Oliver Cromwell. It is listed as one of Devon's most haunted locations and ghostly shadows and apparitions have been said it have been seen moving around the building.

Forde House, Newton Abbot. Unknown artist.

A happy ending.

The uncertainty surrounding the sudden disappearance of a Plymouth man named William Henry Boasden of 60. Alexandra Road, Ford, in October 1925, was alleviated following a telegram being received from Falmouth announcing that he had arrived in the port for the purpose of effecting repairs to his small boat. Henry had left home a few days earlier telling his wife he was going fishing in his motor boat. He went to Stonehouse Creek where his boat the 'Milly' was lying, and proceeded down the river. It was not his practice to go outside the Breakwater, but considering the early hour at which he had started it appeared that the fine weather induced him to venture out a little further than his usual comfort zone. An asthma sufferer and having been invalided out of the navy on account of this complaint, he was unable to row very far or to shout.

When Henry returned home from Falmouth from where he had been picked up and towed in, he told the story of how his engine had cut out when he was in the channel beyond the Plymouth breakwater. For four days and three nights he'd drifted helplessly at the mercy of the winds and tide, without food, water or sleep. He couldn't repair the engine and all he had with him was a small sail and a pair of oars that were too heavy to be useful. For two days did not see land. He hoisted two balls as a distress signals and called out to and semaphored the only two ships which passed anywhere near him. His signals went unseen. Fortunately, the weather did not get too rough. Eventually he found himself drifting off the coast near Falmouth where he encountered Surgeon Captain Garde who was out in his sailing boat. Henry was taken onboard, fed and watered and after being towed to Falmouth for repairs, he returned home the following day.

A most horrible case.

A forty-three-year-old 'hammerman' living in of Plymouth, who I shall only refer to by his initials; J.S.H.S. was sentenced to five year's penal servitude on the 2nd of November 1925 after pleading guilty to six out of seven charges made against him for incest and related charges against his own daughter and six other young girls under the age of sixteen. His own daughter being aged under thirteen when the first offence took place and under sixteen when the other offences took place.
J.S.H.S was a widower with four daughters. After his wife died around four years previously, one of his daughter's remained living with him and the other three went to live with relatives. He had over time encouraged his daughter to introduce him to numerous young girls, and in her presence, he committed the sexual offences, some of which he had pleaded guilty to. Three of the girls mentioned in the indictment were as Mr. G.D. Roberts who appeared for the prosecution said to be [in his words] mentally defective. He stated that there were facilities

provided for parents whose children were mentally deficient, and they should have had them put into homes where they could be properly looked after and not exposed to this sort of thing. The offences took place shortly after his wife had passed away, wantonly and with perfect knowledge that what he was doing was wrong. J.S.H.S. was said to have been of previous good character and had no convictions of any kind recorded against him.

Mr. Dunne acting on behalf of the defence for the accused said at first sight it seemed difficult to find anything to put before the court that might tend to excuse what J.S.H.S. had pleaded guilty to, but there were considerations that while they did not excuse him, did to some extent explain what the prisoner had done. J.S.H.S. had served in the navy from 1885 until 1910, and was discharged with his character marked as 'superior' which was understood to mean that his character was better than 'good.' He was called up at the outbreak of war in 1914 and discharged in 1919 as medically unfit. He was suffering at that time from a disease of the throat, and had suffered a very acute attack of scarlet fever along with chronic rheumatism. When he was discharged from the navy, he was unable to find work. Originally, he had lodged in two small attics with very little furniture and effects, and during his wife's illness which lasted about a year after his discharge, he had to sell or pawn practically all the effects he had. His wife suffered terribly from consumption. The appalling series of offences commenced shortly after his wife died. Mr. Dunne said that the court might look upon the case as that of a man whose mind was literally unhinged, the sufferings and hardships and mental agony endured by watching his wife die, and not as a man who had wantonly and with perfect knowledge of what he was doing, chosen to commit such crimes.

His Lordship Judge Rowlatt responded by saying J.S.H.S had acted on good advice in pleading guilty. The public parade of the poor miserable little girls with their horrible stories could only have added to the gravity of the offence. He added that he had been very much shocked at the frequency and the disgusting details of cases of this kind that had come from Plymouth, and it was certainly not a situation that tended to make him err upon the side of excessive leniency. Words failed him to express the horror that everybody in the court felt at such an utter abomination. He made an order for the daughter of the prisoner to be taken out of his guardianship and placed into care.

When a burglar isn't a burglar.

An amusing incident was recorded in Exeter in December 1925. Late one-night, strange sounds - a sort of tapping, were heard coming from an important business establishment on the High Street. The police were summoned and a party of officers steadfastly made their way to the premises to apprehend the burglar or burglars. A cordon was drawn around the building and the proprietor dragged from his cosy bed to bring a key. A thorough search then commenced, with every avenue of escape being guarded. Two men were then spotted on a flat roof, but they turned out to be watchers for the burglars rather than disciples of Bill Sykes. Eventually the mystery was solved; the night was wet, and every time there was heavy rain, water filtered into the building and fell with a loud 'tip, tap' onto the floor from the high ceiling.

The haunted cliff side house.

The following tale comes from the memoirs of Elliott O'Donnell, a well-known psychic investigator and published in the St. Andrews Citizen on the 1st of January 1927. O'Donnell was born in Bristol, but later made Cornwall his home.

'In my opinion, it is a mistake to suppose that only old houses harbour ghosts. New houses can be haunted just much as older ones. The following is an example. Once, when I was living near Plymouth, I took a house on a cliff facing the sea. I had watched it being built and I moved into it some days before the workmen had given it their final touches and departed. It was good-sized, I might even say a large house, and there was no one in it at night other than my housekeeper, a quaint old Cornish woman, and myself. Now, from the very first night I slept there I invariably awoke at about one o'clock in the morning with the echo of some strange noise ringing in my ears, and after I had thus awakened naturally listened, and I constantly heard all kinds of queer sounds which I thought at first were probably caused by the wind and with no suspicion that they might be due anything else occurring to me. One night, I heard in addition to the usual noises, continuous jabbering and muttering and the sound of footsteps pacing up and down the passageway outside of my door. At a loss to account for these noises I asked my housekeeper in the morning if she had heard them and her answer was an unequivocal "yes." She said, "I did hear them. The house is haunted and I'm leaving you today." She was as good her word, and I had to sleep for several nights alone in the house. It was during the regime of my next housekeeper, a regular cockney, that the following incident occurred. I was unexpectedly detained one night in Plymouth where I had gone merely for the day, and on arriving home the following morning I found the house deserted. It was not long however before my housekeeper almost breathless, came staggering in the back door carrying a huge bundle consisting obviously of blankets and sheets rolled up in a mattress. 'Hullo" I exclaimed, looking at her remarkable load with curiosity; "What's the meaning of this?"

"Well," she said, looking daggers at me. "If that isn't adding insult to injury. Can't you see that I slept at a neighbour's? You surely couldn't expect me to stay here all night by myself. Anyway, I wasn't going to - the house is haunted."

"Nonsense!" I said, "you imagine it."

"Oh, that's all very fine," she retorted, "but you can't bluff me. I found it out the first night I came. It's my belief that something beastly comes in from the cliff outside and walks all about the house. I hear it every night, and I'll be bound you do too. But my nerves can't stand it any longer and I shall leave tomorrow." Well, she left and after she had gone, I had the same trouble again. I couldn't keep a housekeeper or servant in the house for more than a week; complaining bitterly of getting no rest at night owing to noises they couldn't explain; everyone I had invariably left in a fit of panic. By this time too, the haunting had developed. At first it only had been strange indefinable noises, footsteps and mutterings, but now there were crashes against doors, and sometimes they opened of their own accord. Indeed, I used to often watch a door handle deliberately turn and the door then slowly open, but whenever I went to look which I did without moment's delay, there was nothing to be seen. I sprinkled the floor and staircases with sand and flour and I tied cotton at varying heights across the passages, but the result was nil. The cotton was never broken, neither sand nor flour showed any impressions, and still the footsteps came. During my brief occupation of the house (fortunately my lease was a short one) a dozen people in all - not one of whom was spiritualist; experienced the phenomena. I am told the visitations still continue. I think without doubt that they originated on the site the house, and whilst I was there had nothing whatever to with any family haunting (although at one time I was inclined to think they had) in connection with myself. I was also led to this conclusion another fact which I ascertained later, namely, that the cliff which the house was built upon had witnessed many a scene of wrecking in olden days. Many a ship I believe had been lured to the rocks beneath and their crews either drowned or were murdered there; to say nothing of other unsavoury happenings in connection with the cliff was more than sufficient to have caused the hauntings in question.

Bravo!

Frank Lakey a lifeguard, at around seven o'clock in the evening of Sunday the 14th of August 1927, jumped into the River Plym fully clothed to rescue a young man called Williams who had fallen overboard whilst sculling near Arnold's Point, Laira. Hearing the cries for help Mr. Lakey, who lived nearby, ran to Blagdon's quay, dived into the water and swam to Williams's assistance. He then swam with him to an empty boat nearby, and having helped him into it, pulled the boat to the quay. This was the thirtieth rescue that Frank had carried out. He was already in possession of a Royal Humane Society's certificate for life-saving in the River Plym.

Whilst outside playing at Arnold's Point, Plymouth, on the 18th of July 1931, four-year-old Ronald Patrick fell into the River Plym and was in imminent danger of drowning, when Leonard Lakey aged ten, the son of Frank Lakey, jumped into the estuary and dragged the unconscious boy ashore, who was soon revived after medical attention. Leonard's father Frank had by this time been responsible for saving over forty lives. Leonard was awarded a bronze bravery medal and a framed certificate by the Port of Plymouth humane Society for his heroic rescue.

Fire at a haunted farmhouse.

Lovehayne Farm situated between the then 'Three Horseshoes Inn' and Wiscombe Park, Southleigh, went up in flames on the night of the 5th of January 1932. Although Seaton Fire Brigade arrived promptly, little could be done, the flames having too firm a hold the building which was topped with very old thatch. In addition to this, the water supply was insufficient to fight the fire.

The farmhouse was occupied by two brothers named Dare; their parents having recently moved out to take on a farm at Dalwood. The brothers planned on joining them when Lovehayne was leased to new tenants on Lady Day [25th March.] For some time, they believed the place to be haunted; peculiar rhythmical sounds like the ticking a clock and muffled footsteps moving about the corridors were said to have been heard on their retiring to bed. On the evening of the outbreak one of the brothers determined not to sleep in the house alone, his brother being away, went to stay at the house of a neighbouring farmer. Just before 8 p.m. he noticed smoke rising from the direction of Lovehayne Farm and raised the alarm. The house was gutted, but the outhouses and ricks were undamaged. The fire brigade remained on the scene until 3 a.m. The cause of the outbreak remained a mystery.

The Western Times on the 15th January printed the following article …… 'Now that fire has destroyed Lovehayne Farm in Southleigh parish, what is to happen to the mysterious ghost which is said to have haunted the place? Will it still go on prowling about the place after dark making noises like a BBC interval signal? Or will the bare walls, which now alone stand, no longer echo to the muffled footsteps passing up and down the corridors when all the rest of Southleigh parish is sound asleep? Perhaps the ghost will follow the example of other phantoms which are supposed to linger about Devon and Cornwall, and trek out into the open country. Perhaps one of these dark nights, two lovers meandering down a lonely lane that way, will hear strange noises in the hedge or yonder clump of trees. It may be only a rabbit scared, a hedgehog, or perhaps somebody's dog in the field; or it may be just the rustic leaves in the wind. Perhaps who knows? They will stop with a startled look remembering the Lovehayne ghost, shudder, and turn back. Such things have happened before and will yet happen. Ghosts thrive on scares, and local superstition generally provides them with the food they need.'

Buckland-Tout-Saints Heartbreak.

A mother and her two of her children were murdered at their farmhouse in Buckland-Tout-Saints, near Kingsbridge in May 1932. Her elder son William having been an hour or so earlier, brutally attacked by his father whilst lying in his hospital bed. He too later died. The victims were Olive Alice Yeoman aged forty-one. Catherine Lucy Yeoman aged eleven. Alfred Charles Yeoman aged fifteen months and William George Jarvis Yeoman aged nine. The father, William Jarvis Yeoman of Lower Sigden Farm, Buckland-Tout-Saints, was charged at Kingsbridge on Monday the 9th of May 1932 with the murder of his son William, and was remanded to Exeter Prison until the following week.

For the two weeks previous to the murders, nine-year-old William had been a patient at the Kingsbridge Cottage Hospital suffering from a poisoned knee, the result of an injury while out playing on his scooter. On the morning of Saturday, the 7th of May he underwent an operation. At two o'clock in the afternoon, the hospital staff were startled to hear shots fired inside the building. Rushing to the male ward, the matron and nurses found the boy bleeding from a terrible gunshot wound to the head. His father was then seen running away. The police were notified and along with a doctor, Sergeant Redwood proceeded to Lower Sigden Farm. There an appalling sight confronted them. In the doorway of the farm, they found the dead body of Mrs. Alice Yeoman. She was lying just inside the doorway in a pool of blood, her face horribly mutilated by gunshot wounds. She had been shot twice, once on either side of the forehead. In an outbuilding known on the farm as the 'bullock shed' which stood in a field some distance away, the second victim of the tragedy was found – Catherine. She was holding in her hand the basket in which were eggs she had been in the process of collecting when shot by her father. Her death had also been caused by gunshot wounds to the head. An empty cartridge case was found nearby. The search continued for the missing fifteen-month-old baby boy.

Mr. Walter Ford who had joined the search, noticed a bundle of litter in a corner between two of the smaller farm buildings. In it was the body of little Alfred. Behind his ear were two deep, sharp wounds, and a knife was found at his side. This little body was taken to the mortuary along with that of his mother and sister. In the mean-time, on the drive outside the Kingsbridge Cottage Hospital, a piece of gun had been found. Telephone messages were sent to all the police stations in the district and from them constables were sent to patrol the roads and to watch all buses, cars and pedestrians. William Yeoman was finally arrested in a field near Malborough, in the South Hams later that evening. William, the nine-year-old son he had shot at Kingsbridge Cottage Hospital, died in the early hours of the Monday morning having never regained consciousness.

The Totnes Coroner (Mr. G. E. Windeatt) formally opened the inquest on the four victims at Kingsbridge on Monday the 9th of May, just hours after the last victim had succumbed to his injuries. William Jarvis Yeoman, husband of the deceased woman and father of the deceased children, was asked whether he wished to attend the inquest - he declined.

Mrs. Eliza Jane Ford of 104. Fore Street, Kingsbridge, identified the bodies. The funeral of the four victims took place on Wednesday the 11th of May at Galmpton. The mourners crowded into the little church, and many more stood outside. They sang 'Safe in the arms of Jesus and Rock of Ages.' In the churchyard where Mr. M. Lane (of the Plymouth Brethren) officiated, they then sang 'There's a Friend for little children.' The coffins of Olive and her baby son Alfred were lowered in to one grave, and in the other were placed the smaller coffins of Catherine and William.

The murder trial was opened on Tuesday the 21st of June at Exeter Assizes. William Jarvis Yeoman aged thirty-seven, a farmer, was charged with the murder of his wife and three children, and with wounding another woman with intent to murder her. Yeoman, a thickset clean-shaven man, stood with his hands behind his back while the indictments were read out to him, and in a clear voice he pleaded 'not guilty' to all the charges. He then broke down in tears burying his face in his hands and sobbing bitterly, several times with a handkerchief he wiped away tears that were rolling down his cheeks. After a few moments he recovered his composure and listened attentively to the counsel. Mr Trapnell appearing for the Crown, described how Yeoman went to Kingsbridge Cottage Hospital to visit his son who was receiving treatment for blood-poisoning, and it was alleged, shot him. A witness Miss. Minnie Higgins, an assistant at the hospital said that William Yeoman greeted his son with the expression, "Hullo, dear." She left him sitting at the boy's bedside. Sometime later when she heard screams and a loud bang, she looked out of the window and saw Yeoman running down the drive away from the hospital. Rushing into the ward she saw the boy lying in bed unconscious with his face covered in blood. On the floor was the butt end of a gun tied up in the mackintosh she saw Yeoman carrying when he entered the hospital. William Yeoman again broke down and sobbed when Nurse Higgins said that until the tragedy, he had been a frequent visitor to the hospital and had always appeared devoted to his son.

Miss Ida Mary Croucher, also a nurse, said that she saw Yeoman sitting at his son's bedside with a coat raised stiffly across his knee. "I told him it was time to leave," she said. "He stood up and pointed his coat towards the boy." I suddenly realised that the coat contained a gun and I took hold of him and said; "You're not going to shoot the boy!" He fired the gun and I saw blood appear on the boy's head."

Nurse Christina Helen Phillips, spoke of hearing an unusual noise like a lot of furniture collapsing, and screaming. In the male ward she saw Yeoman beating the boy furiously. She saw about six blows struck altogether. When she challenged him as to what he was doing, he said; "I'm killing the boy, I am a ruined man." She caught hold of him and tried to prevent the blows. Finally pulling him out of the ward where he ran away down the steps.

Miss Emma Townsend, who was visiting another person in the same ward said she saw Yeoman striking his son with what she thought was a stick. She said he looked 'alarming.' When the Judge questioned her as to what she meant by that, she said he was snarling and crying and making noises. She tried to prevent him hitting the boy and pulled him away several times. He said to her: "I'll give you one!" and struck her on the head causing a wound that bled heavily and caused her to become dazed. She said that Yeoman looked more like an animal than a human being. When asked if she thought him to be demented, she said yes. The Judge's praised Miss Townsend, remarking that she had acted with great courage. Miss. Ida Smurthwaite the matron of the hospital, also said that when she saw Yeoman in the ward holding a stick above his head, he looked quite mad.

Mr Collins acting for the defence, said that it would be necessary to consider Yeoman's mental state at the time the acts were committed. He said he would call a doctor to the stand who would verify that Yeoman had suffered a nervous breakdown nine or ten years previously, and a similar breakdown accompanied by depression in August 1931 which lasted to the beginning of that year. Dr.Twining of Salcombe, who had treat Yeoman for nervous breakdowns on two occasions, said that the previous summer Yeoman was suffering from 'nerve strain' because he was worried about the financial condition of his farm. He described him as being heavily mentally defective, an animal type. The Judge said that if he was mentally defective, why hadn't the doctor taken steps to deal with him? The doctor said because he wasn't 'sufficiently' mentally defective. He wasn't able to read or write; but he could do his farm work and he understood what he was doing. His condition had greatly improved after his father had assisted him out of a financial difficulty.

Frederick John Blee, an agricultural labourer of Old Cross near Ashburton and employed by William Yeoman, said the family were quite happy together when he last saw them on the morning of the 7th of May. Though he did recall an event eighteen months previously when Yeoman had threatened his wife with a gun. He heard her call him a blackguard and a scamp, and believed this was because Yeoman had kicked her when she tried to get the gun away from him. Yeoman told him (Blee) that the trouble arose because his wife was going to have another baby, and he was afraid of what his father would say. Other witnesses said that on the morning of the day the acts were committed, Yeoman appeared on good terms with his wife and family.

Dr. Roy Neville Craig, a neurologist and physician in charge of nervous diseases at Exeter Dispensary, said he could find no trace of insanity in Yeoman, but that his mental age was eight. That was to say he had the normal development of a child of eight. He was incapable of reasoning in an efficient manner. He had tested Yeoman's arithmetical capabilities and found he could not multiply or divide and could only subtract with difficulty. The Judge said that meant nothing in regards to the question of insanity and that a great many people were not very good at dividing or subtracting. Dr. Craig said he found Yeoman defective in reasoning, volition, and foresight.

Dr. Grierson, a medical officer at Brixton prison, said he could find no trace mental disease or disorder in the family. He found Yeoman's general manner to be childish, but his conversation whilst slow was rational. His mental age was between ten and eleven years. There was definite evidence of a mental defect. He said Yeoman suffered from what was known as 'medium grave' mental deficiency. When asked if he thought that Yeoman when committing the murders thought he was doing the best thing? He said he got the impression that Yeoman felt he would be faced with poverty when the child returned home from hospital, as his wife had told him they would starve when the child came home. It had been suggested that the medical evidence showed Yeoman at the time of the murders was so insane as not to appreciate how wrong the crimes were that he was committing. He knew what he was doing, the question was - did he know he was doing wrong?

The Judge in summing up, said the jury should accept the evidence of Dr. Craig and thought that Yeoman was not in a position to distinguish between right and wrong, and that evidence showed him to be a devoted father, yet when he got into difficulties, he thought it the right thing to murder his child. He did not think he had the proper mental faculty to appreciate the difference between right and wrong. The jury who was absent for fifteen minutes returned with a verdict of 'guilty but insane' and was sentenced to be detained during the King's pleasure. Several times when references were made to his son William, Yeoman burst into tears and sobbed audibly.

Plymouth man's fifty first rescue.

Fifty-one rescues off the coasts of Devon and Cornwall was the proud record of Mr. Frank Lakey, bathing attendant for the Plymouth Corporation at Devil's Point, said the Western Morning News on the 8th of July 1932. Frank reached this total the previous Tuesday, after rescuing two St. Austell girls who were in difficulties off the Hoe. Mr. Lakey ran down the steps and plunged fully dressed into the water. This was the third rescue which he had carried out in eight days. In the previous three weeks he had saved the lives of three children and three adults at Devil's Point. His ten-years-old son [Leonard] had the year before been awarded a certificate and medal for lifesaving.

Fatal ending to a summer playtime.

On Monday 11th July 1932, three children; Francis Walke, Harry Smallridge, and another young boy were playing football in the square at Wembury, near to where a bus was parked up waiting to set off for its return trip to Plymouth. Just as the driver started up the engine, Francis said to the other boys that he was going to ride on the bus. He ran to the rear of the bus, and moments later they heard a scream….

At the inquest into the death of the young boy, held at Turnchapel by Mr. A. K. G. Johnstone the district Coroner, the driver of the bus; William Barnes of Prospect Street, Plymouth, said that on the day of the accident he had driven the bus to Wembury and on arrival in the square had turned it around ready to return to Plymouth. Whilst the bus was parked up, he noticed some oil under the vehicle and as complaints had recently been made about leaving oil on the road, he decided to clear it up. He walked around the bus and there was then no one at the rear of the vehicle. He got into his seat and started the engine. Before reversing he looked through the bus and could still see no one behind the vehicle. He reversed the bus about eight to ten feet when he felt a bump and heard a scream. He immediately got out and found a bystander was taking a child from under the bus. He said the boy looked dead, as the rear wheel had passed over his head.

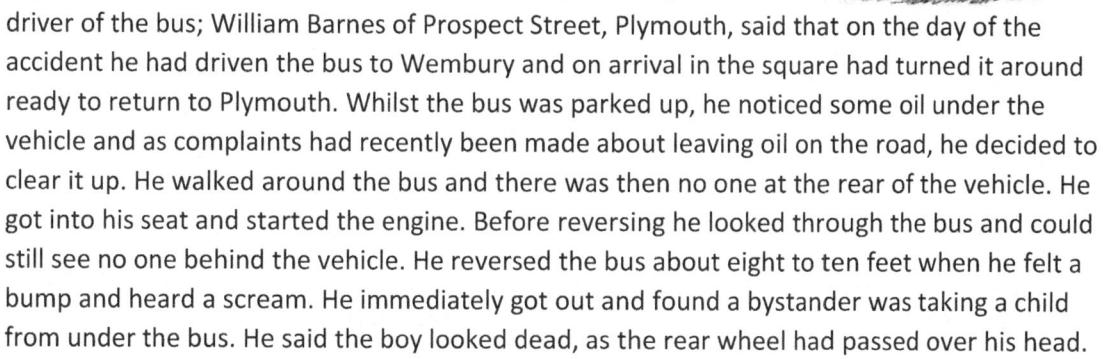

A witness who saw the incident telephoned for a doctor and an ambulance. Mr. Barnes said it was impossible to see the luggage ladder which Francis had grabbed hold of, from any position inside the bus. Kenneth Ferguson of Wingfield Villas, Stoke, the conductor on the bus, said as there were still a few minutes left before they were due to leave and return to Plymouth, he had gone into a shop to buy a glass of lemonade. He was unaware that the driver intended to reverse.

One of the boys Francis had been playing with, Harry Smallridge aged ten of Knighton Village, Wembury, said he was playing in the square with Francis and another boy. Just as the bus started to move backwards, Francis ran across to it shouting to them said, "I'm going to have a ride!" They called to him not to get on the bus but he took notice. Harry said he didn't see Francis mount the luggage ladder.

Constable Martin who was called to the scene, said he had examined the vehicle and discovered a child's hand print in the dust between the second and third rung of the luggage ladder, about five feet from the ground. The Coroner recorded a verdict of 'accidental death,' with no blame attached to the driver or anybody else connected to the accident.

Where have all the ghosts gone?

In December 1932 a newspaper article reported that year by year, fewer and fewer records appeared to come to hand of ghosts being seen and heard in lonely castle keeps and moats. Was the transforming of ancient and one-time stately homes of England into country clubs and hotels discouraging the shadows of those that had at one time inhabited the places to 'give up the ghost' as it were in disgust? There were still a few 'authenticated' ghosts around though who never seemed to tire of century after century of their haunting duty.

Year after year at the 'witching' hour, the local believers would solemnly assemble at Berry Pomeroy Castle, watching and listening. The old castle near Totnes in South Devon, then apparently had two ghost stories attached to it. One of these ghosts when seen, was said to be a warning of death. This ghost was a beautiful lady clothed in rich garments, who walked about wringing her hands as if in distress. The other spectral visitors were three people, though only two of the ghosts were said to be seen. This haunting was said to be of ancient origin and dates back to Norman times. Allegedly, the son of the house of Pomeroy, when walking in the garden one night found his sister talking to a man, who he discovered by eavesdropping on their conversation to be her lover. He knew this man to be an enemy of their family, and so he killed both his sister and her lover - though how or where is not recorded.

* These ghostly visitors to the castle are different to the spirits that are said to haunt it today. Which stories have any truth in them? There certainly is something eerie about Berry Pomeroy.

Sea rescue at Plymouth.

A crowd gathered to watch, as hero Frederick Foster of 14. Castle Street, Plymouth, in May 1933, leapt over a wall and dived into the water to rescue ten-year-old Albert Honey who had fallen into deep water near the Royal Corinthian Yacht Club on the Hoe.

A man sitting on his parked-up motorcycle suddenly called out that he'd just seen a boy fall from the wall. Frederick Foster who was at the time walking along Madeira Road, leaped over the wall to the ground which was twenty feet below. He then made his way across the uneven surface of the rocks to the shore, and discarding his coat jumped into the sea.

The boy was now underwater, but Frederick managed to bring him to the surface and haul him on to the rocks, from where he was pulled to safety by George Sutcliffe, of Hampton Street, who had now joined in the rescue. Foster was unable to climb ashore and was obliged to swim around the rocks to get back on dry land.

Thirty-three-year-old Frederick Foster a docker who was in casual employment, had in 1913, when just a boy himself, rescued another boy from drowning at the Barbican. In 1926 he saved a man from drowning, and in the winter of 1931 saved two boys from drowning off North-East Quay. His grandfather Mr. Thomas Toms, and three of his uncles had similar records of lifesaving to their credit.

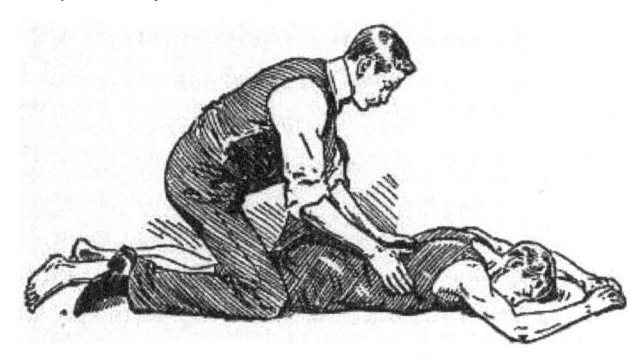

Picture courtesy of wikisource.org

A monster in the water.

A strange monster with a head resembling a horse, was reported as having been seen on the 27th June 1935 by Mr. Norman Aplin and his son Rupert, of Beer in East Devon, while they were out in a motor-boat fishing at four o'clock in the morning. Mr. Albert Ayres another fisherman, stated that he had also seen the monster.

* In 'Grim and Gruesome Plymouth 1860-1959' I wrote a story regarding a lady seeing a sea monster off the coast of Noss Mayo in August 1936. Two weeks previously a mother and daughter on holiday in Brixham reported a similar sighting. It's very likely to have been the same creature. An even earlier sighting was made by officers on board the H.M. Royal Yacht in 1877 off the Isles of Scily.

Haunted house to be demolished.

In the summer of 1935 Radford House, which stood in Radford Park near Plymstock, was signposted for demolition. The house which was reputed to be haunted, had a very colourful past. Sir Francis Drake had allegedly hidden bars of gold and silver from the South Seas in the house. Sir Walter Raleigh had been imprisoned there in 1618 for eight to ten days following his arrest after his ill-fated expedition to the Golden City of Manoa. The house was said to have had tunnels and secret passages concealed behind panelled walls, which by 1935 were only travelled along by rats and mice. It had a reputation for ghosts including those of course of its famous visitors; Drake and Raleigh. It had been the scene of adventures since the days of Queen Elizabeth I, and of battles between Cavaliers and Roundheads. The house, which contained fifty rooms was built in Elizabethan style and had fallen into a state of irreparable dilapidation. Intruders had recently broken in and damaged the walls and mirrors in an attempt to take away some of the more valuable fittings.

The exit from a tunnel through which it was said the residents had fled centuries ago from Puritan attackers was thought to be near Radford Lake. Apparently, there was a small hole in the ground through which a person had to crawl on their hands and knees and then by way of various subterranean caves and passages where it then developed into a stone structure. By 1935 the tunnel had become too dangerous for further exploration, but the great mystery was where did the tunnel end? Did it connect with the house as legend said? Likely there was a hidden doorway in the old mansion or maybe in a fireplace or beneath the floor. It may even have joined with one of the secret passages which were believed to lie behind the panels of the walls. Before the work of demolition was started, all the walls and floors were tapped in an endeavour to find the secret passage, but without success. Many who had explored the old building prior to its demolition said that there were no secret passages or tunnels behind its panelled walls. The reputation of it having ghosts was probably as well founded as most ghost stories attached to old houses. One of the spacious rooms in the house, a banqueting hall, richly panelled in oak and with massive tables built into the wall at one end, was according to local history where Sir Francis Drake dined with his host, and where Sir Walter Raleigh interned in the house when he incurred the displeasure of the Sovereign, took his meals.

Radford House, Plymstock. Picture courtesy of lostheritage.org.uk

The Harris family had been seated at Radford, uninterruptedly for a period of nearly five centuries. In the reign of Elizabeth I, the estate was in the possession of Sir Christopher Harris, who represented Plymouth in Parliament. He was a personal friend of Sir Francis Drake and stored at Radford some of the gold and silver blocks which Drake had brought home with him from the South Seas. At Radford, Sir Christopher Harris entertained Drake and Raleigh, Howard, Hawkins, and the other Captains who fought against the Spanish Armada.

There was allegedly a thrilling encounter between the Roundheads and Cavaliers at Radford, when a silver plate belonging to the house was buried for safety, and lost. A farmer found it nearly two centuries later when ploughing his fields, and it was later sold for over one thousand pounds.

Triple murder at Croft Farm.

Thomas Maye aged seventy-one of Croft Farm, West Charleton, near Kingsbridge, was arrested on the charge of having murdered his wife Mrs. Emily Maye aged sixty-eight, and their two daughters; Miss. Emily Joan Maye aged twenty-eight and Miss. Gwyneth Florence Maye aged twenty-five, on the night of the 11/12th of June 1936. The deaths at Croft Farm created the greatest sensation in the Kingsbridge district for many years.

A lad named Charlie Lockhart, who was employed at the farm, went out at about seven-thirty that evening to go to a dance at Stokenham, four miles away. He came back on a bicycle at around half nine to get his coat. He saw no one in the farmhouse, but heard voices which he thought were those of the girls talking. He left soon after. When he returned to the farm from the dance at around two-forty-five in the morning, he saw blood coming from under a door, and daring not to go in he rode back to the village and summoned the police. Entering the farmhouse, the officers found a hammer on which were discovered hairs belonging to Thomas Maye, his wife, and Emily. There was also evidence that paraffin had been poured over some of the furniture. The Maye's bedroom was full of smoke and a clearly determined attempt had been made to burn Mrs. Maye's body. She was found lying near the bed with a fractured skull. Her body was partly burned, paraffin having been poured over and around it - a deliberate attempt having been made to destroy any evidence. Emily was found on the landing in her nightdress. She had four severe injuries to her head, which had been struck with great violence. Gwyneth was found barely alive at the foot of the stairs. She also had terrible wounds to her head. She died a few hours later having never regained consciousness. When she was found, Gwyneth was lying with her head on a cushion. It looked as though it had been placed there after she had been struck down. Thomas Maye's skull was also fractured, although not so severely as in the case the other three. When found he was able to get up and talk, but this was likely was after a considerable period of unconsciousness according to the doctor who later operated on him.

When the police arrived, Thomas Maye was in bed, his wife being to the side of him on the floor and her part of the bed set on fire. He was wearing his nightshirt which was bloodstained and filthy dirty, as though it had come into direct contact with black and charred material. His sleeves smelt strongly of paraffin and his hands were dirty, encrusted with blood and charred material. It was noted that his feet were also filthy with a caking of black material and blood extending some way up his legs. When the police asked him what had happened, Thomas Maye said he didn't know. He said he had gone to bed and then later on noticed his wife no longer in bed beside him. A further police investigation found that no attempt had been made to ransack or look for items of value, even though there was a great deal of jewellery and a certain amount of money at the farm, none of it had been taken.

At Thomas Maye's trial, Dr. Robinson of Plymouth who attended to him at the hospital, described the three scalp wounds sustained by Maye, and said that they looked as though they had been made whilst Thomas had been lying down in bed. When the judge intervened and said, "Would any of these be sufficient to render him unconscious" Dr. Robinson said; "Straight away my lord," adding that they were serious enough to have killed most people. The Judge then asked if it was conceivable that Thomas Maye could have caused the wounds himself, Dr. Robinson said; "Not in the least bit." He went on to say that the wounds looked as though they had been struck on the left-hand side by someone standing over the bed. He also said that they were consistent with them having been delivered while Thomas Maye's face was covered with the bedclothes. As more evidence was given, it very much came to the Judge's attention that Thomas Maye could not have been the killer. He stopped the trial and directed the jury to return a 'not guilty' verdict, which of course they did. After discharging Thomas Maye, the Judge said; "I feel bound to say that I think that after consideration of the doctor's evidence, this man might have been spared the ordeal."

Thomas Maye appeared to be somewhat dazed on hearing the verdict. When he recovered, he was assisted from the dock and left by a side entrance, where he was met by a couple of friends who offered their congratulations, and by his son Jack, who

quickly led him to a car and drove away unobserved except by a few spectators.
No one was ever charged with the murders at Croft farm.

* It's absolutely tragic that Thomas Maye was incarcerated and put through such an ordeal. Thomas must have had an amazing constitution. After the trial he didn't return to Croft Farm but went to live with his only surviving daughter Mary and her husband Norman. He lived until he was ninety-one, though those last twenty-one years must have been very difficult ones.

Heritage of the West.

On the 19th of February and 1938 a very interesting article appeared in the 'Western Morning News' regarding a book recently published by Ernest W. Martin, called 'Heritage of the West.' The country was then still full of quaint superstitions and customs which still lingered, particularly in parts of Devon and Cornwall. These he recounts, as well as giving us a pen picture of some of the unusual personalities which the Western Counties produced...

In olden days, Good Friday had many strange and interesting customs in the Westcountry. In counties such as Cornwall, so renowned for the excellence of its pies and miscellaneous dishes, and where the hot cross buns were highly spiced and larger than those made in other parts of England. A nineteenth century antiquary described the Cornish bun as 'made of rich currant paste covered with saffron; it is about an eighth of an inch thick and four inches in diameter and is marked with a large cross which divides into four equal portions.' In some farmhouses it was the custom that on Good Friday the bun be allowed to hang suspended from the grimy beams of the kitchen ceiling. The bun was left there, and as per the tradition, the mouldy portions were removed from time to time and mixed with water and made into a paste which was said to be a curative agent for many a complaint or disease. This pseudo-remedy was employed to treat both human beings and cattle. Other people held the superstition that all seeds planted on Good Friday would be certain to grow, while peasants believed it to be the birthday of all ravens. In another chapter he records how even in recent years in Bishopsteignton, on May Day morning, the children paraded in the village calling at each house in the hope of receiving a small donation. The girls carried boxes in which there was a doll surrounded by flowers and the boys held garlands in the form of wreathed poles. This custom the writer said was comparable and identical in origin to a rite in Bohemia [now in the Czech Republic] where the young people wandered from house-to-house chanting; 'We carry death out of the village; We bring summer into the village.'

In his book the writer also refers to the last case of execution for witchcraft in Devon —three Bideford women; Temperance Lloyd, Susanna Edwards, and Mary Trumbles, who were executed at Exeter in 1682. An opponent of conviction for witchcraft in England was Chief Justice Holt, who in 1696 at Exeter prevailed upon the jury to acquit Elizabeth Homer of sorcery. "With this acquittal, an awful chapter in the history of Devon was concluded. So at last, out of the Gethsemane of horror there emerged for aged women in the villages, towns, and cities of our land a peace that descended upon them like heavenly music. England atoned in tears and bitterness for her folly; but the innocent though foolish women who had died left to posterity a tragic heritage that no belated human grief or anguished effort could obliterate or remove."

The following year the 'Western Times' carried another story on the folklore of witchcraft in the South West. Bygone Devon it appears, inspired in its people an awe for the unseen and uncanny scarcely matched in any other part of the country.

Turning over old treasures, a Budleigh Salterton resident who was at the time well known in Exeter; Mr. Alex H. Guest, found a volume published in 1824 entitled 'Mr. Baxter's Certainty of the World of Spirits.' It was a collection of incidents of what Devonians called being 'overlooked.' A term synonymous with being 'ill-wished or bewitched,' and at the time [1939] was still in some parts of the Devonshire countryside to be believed. One of the stories was given in the form of a signed statement by Mr. Anthony Smith, an Exeter surgeon who practised in the late 17th century. "In the house of Mrs. Heron a widow of Honiton, who kept a mercer's shop, there worked a maidservant called Elizabeth Booker, part of whose duties was to sell small wares from a stall before the door. On a certain Saturday (market day) Elizabeth was approached by a woman who asked for a large pin. This the maid refused to give without orders from her mistress, and the woman went away in a rage and threatening that Elizabeth should hear more on the matter. The following day the maid was waiting the table of her mistress when she suddenly gave a great cry, saying that a pin had been thrust into her leg. She remained in agony until the Wednesday when she was removed to Exeter, and there she stoically endured an operation performed by Mr. Smith, who removed the pin with knife.

There was also the tale of the Membury woman who changing herself into a hare and was often hunted by the Cotleigh Harriers. This superstition along with many others, is preserved in the reports of the Devonshire Association Committee, on the folklore of the county. It was seriously claimed that the woman met her end by being carried away by the devil, for her body was found one morning on a branch overhanging a stream near her home, and with her were her three cats. One of the acts of witchcraft alleged against this woman was that of the killing of some horses belonging to a farmer against who she had a grudge. As the man approached with his team returning from ploughing, she drew a circle in the road with two sticks. The horses stepped into the circle and allegedly dropped dead. On another occasion, so the story went, the woman laid a curse on some cows which went blind and died. She then added to her nefarious practices by gazing into a field at a number of lambs, all of who turned head over tail and also died.

The superstition that witches could turn themselves into hares was widely held. It was also believed that a method of shooting them in this guise was to cut a sixpence and put it into the gun. After a hare had been wounded by this means, a North Devon parish tale said that a woman in the village was found to be suffering from a foot injury. Hares were also associated with an ancient belief of another kind, familiar to old residents of Moretonhampstead. There it used to be said that the sight of a hare in the streets was a sure sign that a fire would occur in the town.

Exeter was not without its stories of ghosts and witchcraft. A tale related by the late Sir John Bowring [1792- 1872] concerns an apparition clad in white, which was reputed to come out of a grave opposite the hospital in Southernhay and look over a gate, opening into the narrow Southernhay Lane. People avoided this lane after dark until one night a drunken man seized the ghost's beard and found that it belonged to a goat which had acquired the habit of standing on its hind legs and putting its head over the gate! In a field near Matford Lane, there was once it is said, a ruined house which was haunted, and from which at night came shrieks and the sound of the clanking of chains. Of a less eerie character was beliefs connected with Parker's Well, in the same neighbourhood. Miraculous qualities were attributed to the water of this well and it was not uncommon many years ago to see it crowded in the early morning by people anxious to avail themselves of its healing properties.

Pixies, of whose existence generations of Devonians had no doubt. To be 'pixey-led' was not a rare experience according to county folklore. This tale is told by a Chagford man who many years previously was sent by his employer to Drewsteignton. The man apparently completed the outward journey without mishap, but on his return travelled in the reverse direction to Crockernwell, and then back again to Drewsteignton. There he left the Chagford road and pursued his way to Dunsford. At about two a.m. he was seen by a policeman walking down a narrow road leading to the river Teign, mistaking the gleam of the water for the dusty highway. He had walked at least thirty miles to do a journey that should have only been twelve miles, and the assumption was that he had fallen under the influence of pixies.

The devil also figures in a number of Devon superstitions. The possibility of destructive frosts occurring in May is well known even in modern times. Folklore asserted that this is the outcome of a pact made with the devil by a Devon brewer, who was perturbed by the bad effect on the ale trade by the popularity of cider. It was said that the brewer named Franklin, from Eggesford in mid-Devon, sold his soul to the devil on condition that the apple blossom was to be cut by frost. Hence the frosts of May 19th, 20th and 21st; are known as 'St. Franklin nights' or of three days near that time.

Most colourful of all Devon stories bearing on the unseen is that concerning the ghost of Lady Mary Howard, whose punishment for her crimes is condemned to travel every night in a coach made of bones and drawn by headless horses, from Fitzford House Tavistock, where she lived, to Okehampton Castle. The eerie cavalcade so tradition asserts, is preceded by a black hound with one eye on its forehead, and the purpose of each journey enables the hound to pluck a blade grass from the castle mound and carry it back to the gate of Fitzford House. This penance was said to continue until no grass remained on the mound. Belief of the ghost of Lady Howard, pixies and witchcraft, had long faded in the minds Devon countryfolk by 1939, but other superstitions still remained.

Lady Mary Howard. Unknown artist.

Still going strong in Bristol!

Who should I come across in on the 1939 census but Gertrude Symons, the lady who our friend Fred Heard had numerous adventures and misadventures with! She is now ninety-one years old and living at the same address in the St. James area of Bristol as she was in 1901. Gertie sadly passed away in January 1940 at Stapleton Hill Institution, Bristol; a mental asylum, though her cause of death was likely dementia related. I'm sure her life story would be just as fascinating as Fred's - if only she'd written it down. In an earlier story I mentioned that she was living on her own private means – she was indeed a woman of some wealth and left today's equivalent of over sixty-two thousand pounds in her will to one of her daughter's.

A heartbreaking tale.

February 1941 and nine-year-old Ernest David Lakey, of 4a, Arnold's Point, Embankment, fell and bruised his thigh whilst playing at school. He later died in Swilly Hospital. His father David Francis Lakey told the Coroner; "This is the second son I have lost; my elder boy gave his life for another child."

Assistant pathologist at the Prince Wales's Hospital, Greenbank, Dr. Martin Richard Thomas said he performed a post-mortem examination and found that Ernest had died from poisoning resulting from septic arthritis of the left thigh joint. He could only say it was very likely that the infection was caused by the fall. Returning a verdict in accordance with the medical evidence, the Coroner said poisoning had resulted from an accidental fall in the playground.

* David Francis (Frank) Lakey was the hero who had by 1932 saved over fifty people from drowning. Frank mentions having lost another son who gave his life for another child. I'm unable to find a report on the tragic incident of the young hero, but Leonard Lakey, the then twelve-year-old son of Frank, died in 1933. We must assume whilst carrying out a rescue in the River Plym, near to their home. We came across Leonard in 1931 when he again saved a boy from drowning.

The disappearance of Barry Buller.

On March the 5th 1945 a city-wide search began across Plymouth for eighteen-month-old Barry Buller, who had apparently gone on a day trip to Bovisand with Stella Costello, a friend of his mothers and not returned. Barry was one of three children belonging to Mrs. Buller of 4. South Hill, in the Stoke area of Devonport. Her husband, a naval rating was at that time serving overseas.

Twenty-one-year-old Stella Costello – also known as Hilda Edith Avis Hood and Marysia Naizova, had previously lodged with Mrs. Buller though had since moved out, but as a frequent visitor she had undoubtedly formed quite an attachment to young Barry, to such an extent that it later became known that she has presented him to other people as her own child. The police circulated a description of the missing woman and a number of people came forward saying that a woman fitting the description accompanied by a small child, was seen travelling by train to London. Exhaustive inquiries were then made in London without success and it was thought that Stella was possibly in hiding within the Polish community, as she spoke the language fluently.

We move forward now to 1948, when a woman walked into Cardiff Police Station and stated that she was 'Stella Costello' and was sought in connection with the disappearance in Plymouth in 1945 of Barry Buller, now aged five. The woman said her real name was Hilda Edith Gustek, and she was the wife of Alexander Gustek, a trawlerman of Inkerman Street, Swansea. Plymouth Police sent an inspector and policewoman to escort her back to Plymouth where she was to be charged with the abduction of Barry Buller.

On the 19th of October 1948 'Stella Costello' was charged at Plymouth, with taking eighteen-month-old Barry George Buller by force and with intent to deprive his mother of his possession. Mr W. E. J. Major (prosecuting) said that in early 1945 while Mrs. Buller and her sister Mrs. Blampey, were living at South Hill, Stoke, Costello had knocked at the door and asked if the women could put her up for a while. The sister's agreed and Stella Costello stayed with them for two weeks. She told them that she was a married woman. During her stay she took Barry out with the mother's consent on a number of occasions, and it was afterwards discovered that she spent that time with the child at her mother's house and told her that she was now married and that Barry was her son. She was actually an absentee from the A.T.S. On March 5th 1945, she took Barry out for the day, again with the mother's consent, and said she was going to Bovisand, near Plymstock. Nothing more was heard of the child until five months later when he was discovered living with Mr. and Mrs. Donald Ballard at Rushden in Northamptonshire. They had adopted him after he was found abandoned in a Chinese cafe in the East End of London. Mrs. Buller said that she had been asked to sign the adoption forms but had refused to do so and would continue to refuse. She said that she thought Barry would be happy with his foster parents and supposed it best that he now stays with them, but she had never been asked whether she wanted her child back.

Hilda Edith Avis Gustek, otherwise known as Stella Costello, was found not guilty of taking Barry away by fraud and forcibly detaining him with intent to deprive his mother of his possession. In his address to the jury, Mr Dingle Foot (defending) reminded them that the infant Moses was left in the bullrushes three thousand years ago so that he should be found. "Moses was found by Pharaoh's daughter," he said. "This child was found by the Metropolitan Police." He was referring to the fact that Barry Buller had been left in a Chinese cafe. It was wrong for Costello to leave the child in a cafe he said, but she was a fugitive and could not behave like a normal person. She had left the child where she knew he would be found. Plymouth Police stated that Mrs. Gustek was to await an A.T.S. escort to take her as an alleged deserter to Taunton. Weeping, she was removed from the court.

Sampford Peverell haunted house.

In August 1946 Mr. G. W. Copeland, a member of the Plymouth Field Club, when exhibiting some lantern slides at the Plymouth Athenaeum, told the audience the strange tale of how he visited and photographed the well-known 'haunted house' at Sampford Peverell in mid-Devon whilst on an excursion in 1937 and which he was easily able to identify from sketches he had seen of it in a book. In 1945 he and his wife again visited the area, only to find that the house was no longer there and when they queried this, they were told that it had been destroyed by fire in 1936. Making further enquiries, he found a national newspaper article stating that the house had indeed been destroyed by fire in 1936, the year before he had taken the photograph that the audience were now looking at. Mr Copeland said he wondered if the newspaper which reported its destruction in 1936 had prophesied its fate or whether it was only a 'ghost' of the house which he saw and photographed in 1937.

The haunted house at Sampford Peverell is certainly interesting. The ghostly goings on allegedly began in 1810, when a Mr. Chave and his family were in residence. It was purported that the family were troubled by a poltergeist that resembled a very large rabbit, though it only ever made its presence known when females were in the house. Sally Taylor, an eighteen-year-old servant said that she had caught it twice and that it was very large and heavy and felt like a dog or rabbit. It was so powerful that she could not hold it and that it usually came as soon as the light was put out, but then vanished. She also said that she had been slapped by some invisible means and that she had seen through the sheet, while her head was under the bed-clothes, a man's hand and arm.

The case was debated in the national press and the house gained so much notoriety that in 1811 it was besieged by a mob. Mr. Chave was forced to open fire on the crowd in self-defence, killing a man.

Drawing of the haunted house – unknown artist.

An apprentice boy lodging at the property had been frightened by the apparition of a woman. Persons passing at night had seen strange lights in the windows. The inhabitants were pestered by noises and bangs in every part of the house; stamping on floorboards that would send a vibration through the shoe or boot of others in the room. Bumps and bangs would follow people through the house as they carried out their work. As time went on the poltergeist activity grew worse and the servant girls were violently beaten in their beds during the night, producing bruises and swellings. It was said that onlookers could hear the blows being rained upon them, but when a candle was lit, no person could be seen who could have administered the blows. Bed curtains were knotted and books and candlesticks thrown.

The owner of the property, worried about the depreciation in value of his house, asked Mr. Chave and his family to move out. There was certainly speculation that it was the Chave family and the servants themselves that produced the phenomena. It was also later rumoured that the ghostly activity and noises were made by smugglers behind a false wall. What was the truth?

Death threats in Tiverton.

One evening in early January 1949 several frightened citizens of Tiverton found what looked like bloodstained sheath knives rammed into the wood of their front doors with a note attached saying; 'Beware, death comes to you tonight' The police were informed and carrying out an investigation. They found the blood on the knives to be red ink and put it down to a childish prank.

A Devon Christmas wish.

We'll finish this book with a short abridged story from the closing days of 1949 written in the Devon dialect….

'Tis again soon be time to salute the 'appy morn. People can turn the world upzide down and make strife and cause envy, hatred and malish, and fill up the newspapers with ole murders an' rubbery an ail manner o' wickedness. 'Ave strikes galore an' wretched ole quarr'lin between one country an totner country, or between this party an that party. There's fashism an' communism and vorty other isms, and atom boms and iron curtins. Devalyation and dollar shortage, groun-nuts and dunnaw what-all; but Crissmas comes around all the zame an a gude job too, it do give a body zummat different to think about for a change, instead o' so much ole crisis and problems, wars and romans o' wars. 'Tis nice to zing about paice on airth and gudewill toward men, even if 'tis only for an hour or two. Let's tell about it and zing about it while us have got opportunity. If us was to do a bit more to that instead o' yappin' so much about the bad things, praps us would get a bit more aw't. I shall wish ee all Merry Crissmas. A merry Crissmas to the lot of ee. It do make things a bit more cheerful like and it don't cost ee nort.'

With thanks to the following newspapers from the British Library archives.

Aberdeen Press & Journal
Bath Chronicle & Weekly Gazette
Berkshire Chronicle
Blackburn Standard
Bradford Daily Telegraph
Bristol Mirror
Bristol Times & Mirror
Chard and Ilminster News
Cork Examiner
Cornish & Devon Post
Cornish Telegraph
Coventry Evening Telegraph
Dartmouth & South Hams Chronicle
Derby Mercury
Dundee Courier
Eastern Evening News
East & South Devon Advertiser
Enniskillen Chronicle & Erne Packet
Exeter & Plymouth Gazette
Fife Herald
Globe
Hartlepool Northern Daily Mail
Illustrated Police News
Ipswich Journal
Kentish Mercury
Leeds Mercury
Lincolnshire Chronicle
Ludlow Advertiser
London Daily News
Londonderry Sentinel
Longford Journal
Morning Star
Norfolk Chronicle
North Devon Gazette
North Devon Journal

Northampton Mercury
Pall Mall Gazette
Portsmouth Evening News
Preston Herald
Royal Cornwall Gazette
Salisbury & Winchester Journal
Shepton Mallet Journal
Sherbourne Mercury
St Andrews Citizen
South Wales Daily News
Stamford Mercury
Sunderland Daily Echo & Shipping gazette
Sussex Advertiser
Swindon Advertiser & North Wilts Chronicle
Taunton Courier & Western Advertiser
Tavistock Gazette
Torquay Times & South Devon Advertiser
Totnes Weekly Times
Western Evening Herald
Western Daily Press
Western Morning News
Western Times
Wiltshire Times & Trowbridge Advertiser
Yorkshire Post & Leeds Intelligencer

Made in the USA
Columbia, SC
02 August 2022